PENGUIN BOOKS

FEATURE FILMMAKING AT USED-CAR PRICES

Rick Schmidt has spent over twenty years producing low-budget feature films that have received national and international recognition. He began producing and directing in 1973, with his first feature, *A Man, a Woman, and a Killer*, which was codirected with his roommate, Wayne Wang (*Chan Is Missing, The Joy Luck Club*, etc.). This feature premiered at the Bleecker Street Cinema in New York City and won Directors' Choice at the Ann Arbor Film Festival.

His second and third features, *1988–The Remake* and *Emerald Cities*, completed this trilogy about the American dream.

Schmidt's fourth feature, *Morgan's Cake*, made on a $15,000 budget, was selected by the Sundance Film Festival for its Dramatic Competition (1989), and was also presented at the Berlin Film Festival (Panorama), San Francisco International, AFI/LA, and at New Directors/New Films, where critic Janet Maslin of *The New York Times* called it "a delight."

In 1992 his fifth feature, *American Orpheus*, premiered at the Rotterdam and Seattle International Film Festivals, and won a Gold Award at Houston International for Best Low-Budget Theatrical Feature of the year.

He has recently completed a new feature, *Blues for the Avatar*, produced in collaboration with his Feature Workshops.

FEATURE FILMMAKING AT USED-CAR PRICES

HOW TO WRITE, PRODUCE, DIRECT, FILM, EDIT, AND PROMOTE A FEATURE-LENGTH FILM FOR LESS THAN $10,000

REVISED EDITION

RICK SCHMIDT

PENGUIN BOOKS

PENGUIN BOOKS
Published by the Penguin Group
Penguin Books USA Inc., 375 Hudson Street,
New York, New York 10014, U.S.A.
Penguin Books Ltd, 27 Wrights Lane,
London W8 5TZ, England
Penguin Books Australia Ltd, Ringwood,
Victoria, Australia
Penguin Books Canada Ltd, 10 Alcorn Avenue,
Toronto, Ontario, Canada M4V 3B2
Penguin Books (N.Z.) Ltd, 182–190 Wairau Road,
Auckland 10, New Zealand

Penguin Books Ltd, Registered Offices:
Harmondsworth, Middlesex, England

First published in the United States of America in hardcover
and paperback editions by Viking Penguin Inc. 1988
This revised edition published in Penguin Books 1995

1 3 5 7 9 10 8 6 4 2

Grateful acknowledgment is made for permission to reprint
"The Rules of the Game," an interview with Ray Carney by
Diane Cherkerzian, *Visions* magazine, Summer 1993. By permission of
Ray Carney and Marie-France Alderman. © 1993 Ray Carney.
© 1993 Marie-France Alderman.

ISBN 0 14 02.4560 X
(CIP data available)

Printed in the United States of America
Set in Postscript ITC Century Book
Designed by Ann Gold

For Julie

I read recently that Americans are buying
used cars for an average of $6000
and I thought, Why don't they take the bus
to work and make a feature film instead?
—Rick Schmidt

CONTENTS

Foreword: The Rules of the Game
  (An Interview with Ray Carney)   xv
Preface   xxix
Acknowledgments   xli
Introduction to Low-Budget Feature Filmmaking   1

1. STORY CONCEPT FOR A FEATURE FILM   5
Where Do Ideas Come From?   6
Selecting the Right Concept   9
Eleven Essential Qualities of a No-Budget Concept   10
Writing Your Concept in One Sentence   12
Expanding Your Idea into a One-Page Treatment   13
Improving a Treatment Through Detailed Characterization   17
Registering Your Treatment   23

2. SCRIPTWRITING FOR NO-BUDGET FEATURES   25
Writing Scenes on Index Cards   27
Expanding Cards into Scripted Scenes   29
Scripting by Collaboration   33
Finalizing Your Script   35
The Shooting Script   37

3. BEGINNING   39

Defining Your Production Limitations   40
Profit Sharing   42
Deferred Payment   42
The Contract   44
Contract Checklist   45
Budget   47
Filming Costs   47
Editing Costs   50
Build an Editing Bench   52
Raising Money for Your Feature   58
Grants   62

4. PREPRODUCTION: PREPARING TO SHOOT A FEATURE   64

People   66
Casting the Crew   67
Casting "Real"Actors   68
Casting Nonactors   70
Places   72
Storyboarding   74
Long-Distance Locations   74
Things   75
Camera Equipment   76
Which Lenses?   77
Sound Gear   78
Lighting Kits   82
Examples of Lighting on Rick Schmidt Features   82
Selecting Your Lighting   84
Hollywood Lighting   85
Lighting for Low Budgets   86
Saving Money on Filmstock and Sound Track   89
Support Equipment   90
Equipment Checklist   91
Paperwork/Errands/Lists   93
Preproduction Checklist   94

5. PRODUCTION: FILMING AND DIRECTING   96

Fifteen Rules for No-Budget Feature Filmmaking   97
Picking Up Rental Equipment   99
Morning of the Shoot   100
Loading Equipment, Picking Up Actors and Crew   100
Organization on Location   101
Loading the Camera   103
Focusing the Eyepiece   104
Camera Maintenance   105
Placing the Camera for Your First Shot   105
Tips for Lighting on Location   106
Using a Light Meter   108
What to Shoot? How to Shoot?   109
Supporting Your Story with Images   111
The Long Take   112
"Freeze" Method of Shooting for Cuts   113
Cutaways and Pauses for Transitions   113
Shooting Without Sound   114
High-Budget Effects   116
Directing Actors on Location   116
Directing from Behind the Camera   118
Feeding Cast and Crew on a Budget   120
Continuity   121
Shooting Titles on Location   121
Location Miracles   122
Saving Film on Each Sync Take   123
Benefits of a Tight Shooting Schedule   124
Movie Stills/Video of "Work in Progress"   125
Developing and Work Printing with the Lab   126
Processing Without a Work Print   128
Video versus Film Work Print   129
Money and the Lab   131
Checking Your First Footage   132
Checking Your Recorded Sync Sound   134
Screening Footage for Cast and Crew   136
Completing the Filming   137

6. POSTPRODUCTION: EDITING YOUR FEATURE   139

Making the First Splice   140
Syncing It Up   140
Rick Schmidt's Secrets of Editing   146
Edge Numbering   148
Filing Your "Outs"   150
Viewing Your Footage as a "Movie"   151
Placing Scenes in Order of Your Story   152
Cutting for Structure   153
Testing Your Edit   155
Beginning a "Rough Cut"   156
Discarding Your Favorite Scene   157
Sound Effects and Music   158
The "Breakthrough Cut"   160
The Missing Pieces   160
Adding Narrations   161
Photos as Transitions   163
Shooting Additional Footage   163
Final Tightening and Pacing   164
Finalizing the Structure   166
Preparing Sound Rolls for the Mix   168
The Sound Mix   173
Screening Your Sound Mix   173
Conforming Original for Printing   174
AB Rolling from a Work Print   175
AB Rolling Without a Work Print   182
Cue Sheet for Printing   182
Lab Procedures for Printing   184
Screening Your Answer Print   186
Assembling Your Print   188
Screening Your Print for Cast and Crew   189

7. PROMOTION OF A NO-BUDGET FEATURE   191

Preparing Your Promotional Package   192
Film Festivals   197
The New York Premiere   201

Promotion by Letters and Phone   202
American Showcases   202
Television Premiere   206
The Film Market   208
Distributors   209
Agents   212
Other Forms of Distribution   213
Advertising for Alternative Distribution   215
Setting Prices   216
The Long Haul   216

8. REALITY CHECK   218

9. COLLABORATIVE FEATURES   221

Feature Workshops   222
Ten-Way Collaborative Features   224
Collaborative Budget   226
Ten Short Stories versus Ten Segments   229
Quality Control Agreement   230
Writing/Directing En Masse   232
Auteur Theory Debris   233
Editing by Segments/Cinematic Jazz   234
Consensus (or Not)/Final Cut   235
Promotional Power/Pulling Strings   237

10. SHOOTING IN VIDEO   239

Selecting the Right Video Format   240
Budgeting a High-Quality Video Feature
    (at Used-Car Prices)   241
Lighting for Video   246
Shooting and Directing in Video   247
Saving Costs on Video Editing   247
Promoting and Selling Your Video Feature   248
Video versus Film   249

11. DIGITAL TECHNOLOGY AND THE FUTURE   251

The Digital Sound Mix   252
Digital Music for Films   253
Digital Sync Sound on Location   255
Digital Printing at the Lab   256
Filmlook: Video That Looks Like Film   258
Digital Editing   259
Your Digital Filmmaking Future   265

APPENDICES   267

Appendix A: Collaboration Agreement   269
Appendix B: Sample Contract for Deferred Payment
    and Profit Sharing   271
Appendix C: Deal Memorandum   276
Appendix D: Sample Investment Agreement   278
Appendix E: Release   280
Appendix F: Location Agreement   282
Appendix G: Music Rights Agreement   284
Appendix H: California Limited Partnership Agreement   287
Appendix I: Purchase Offer (Limited Partnership)   327
Appendix J: Collaborative Feature Agreement   338

Index   341

FOREWORD

THE RULES OF THE GAME
AN INTERVIEW WITH RAY CARNEY

BY DIANE CHERKERZIAN

Author's Note: This interview with Ray Carney, a noted professor of Film and American Studies at Boston University, was conducted for the Venice, California-based *Visions Magazine* (Summer 1993 issue) by Diane Cherkerzian, a film critic and free-lance writer living in New York. In her introduction she identified Carney as "a prolific writer" (eight books, including *The Films of John Cassavetes*, Cambridge University Press, 1994, and more than one hundred essays) and as "a teacher who inspires passionate devotion among his students." She related how a young man she met who was sitting outside of Carney's office told her that "One course with him is a college education in itself." I want to thank Diane, along with Marie-France Alderman, editor/publisher of *Visions Magazine*, and Ray Carney for permission to reprint this provocative interview as a foreword to this new edition.

DIANE CHERKERZIAN: **In preparing for this visit, I came across a number of articles you've written about what you call the "disgraceful state of American film reviewing." You are quite hard on all of the major reviewers. In fact, a couple years ago you wrote in *Partisan Review* that the average chess or bridge column in the newspaper, or the reporting on the**

sports page, is more intelligent than the writing on film. Do you still feel that way?

RAY CARNEY: The problem is that most film reviewers don't function as critics. They're consumer ombudsmen, and their so-called criticism consists of the trooping out of the same stock responses the average viewer is limited by. That's in fact how most reviewers define their job. They think of themselves as keeping their fingers on the pulse of the public, when they should be trying to cure the patient or at least be telling him how sick he, his culture, and most of its corporate creations are. Anyway, if a critic is just a surrogate for Joe-six-pack, why not hire George Gallup to do the job? He could poll the first-day audiences and eliminate the middleman.

A critic is not supposed to be Everyman. His job is to question just the sorts of simplistic assumptions that audiences take for granted. I think it was Horace who defined the function of criticism as "breaking the chains of the present." That's what 99 percent of the writers on film—even in our universities—never do. They don't call us out of our cultural prejudices and imaginative shortcomings. They don't buck intellectual fads. The result is that they've missed the boat on virtually every major American filmmaker of the past thirty years.

Who do you mean?

Barbara Loden, Elaine May, John Cassavetes, Robert Kramer, Mark Rappaport, Charles Burnett, Paul Morrissey, and Jon Jost, for starters. They are the great artists of recent American film. They are mapping the emotional geography of our culture, but where is the heated debate about them—pro or con? Meanwhile, what films *were* getting extensive coverage? *Star Wars, Raiders of the Lost Ark, Fatal Attraction, Thelma and Louise, 9½ Weeks, Pretty Woman, Silence of the Lambs,* and hundreds of other pieces of meretricious nonsense. Why, a single review wasn't enough for these films! Look at an index to *The New York Times* if you don't believe me. They were treated two, three, four, five, or more times—in a daily review, a Sunday review, a feature article, an interview with the star, an interview with the director, and then maybe a summary "think-piece" article. And they were taken seriously! No one was jeering at their silliness, laughing them out of the room. Am I the only person in America who thinks there's something wrong with this picture?

But surely there aren't enough art-film releases to fill the review columns, to have enough movies to review every day?

That raises the larger question of why are films written up on a daily or weekly basis anyway. There are no obligatory reviews of the painting-of-the-day or the poem-of-the-week. Why is cinematic garbage reviewed at all? Just to fill column inches and justify the reviewer's paycheck? Wouldn't it be better to wait a week or a month until something important appears? The reviewers have so completely internalized the value system of the studio publicity apparatus that they don't even realize how much they have become an extension of it. They're not critics, but publicists— stoking up interest for up-to-the-minute coverage of the trend-of-the-minute. They treat the whole job as if it were no different from reporting the weather—and obviously take it about as seriously.

But what about the argument that the filmmakers on your list don't deserve extensive journalistic coverage because their work is not popular?

The logic is circular, since the reviews help to create the popularity. And, beyond that, have we actually reached the state of decadence where everything, including criticism of the arts, is only a popularity contest? Is automatic critical coverage guaranteed to anyone who buys his way in? Why does the fact that a movie is released by a major distributor have anything to do with whether it gets reviewed? Has the business ethic really gotten us to the point where if something costs fifty million dollars and opens in 500 theaters, it deserves to be reviewed by Vincent Canby no matter how idiotic it is, but if it costs fifty thousand and plays in a college auditorium, it doesn't deserve to get mentioned, no matter how wonderful?

According to the same sales figure logic, the *Times*'s restaurant reviewer should forget about La Grenouille and Aureole and start covering the local Pizza Hut and McDonald's outlets. The art critic should make sure he writes up the black velvet Elvis paintings. The book review editor better not miss a Tom Clancy or Stephen

xviii   **FOREWORD**

King novel. All kidding aside, shouldn't the film reviewer take his job at least as seriously as the restaurant reviewer? At the very least, shouldn't there be one reviewer at each major publication assigned to covering the *real* works of art in film—no matter how small their budgets or limited their releases? There's *no one* at any major publication I know of doing that now.

Doesn't Pauline Kael's promotion of the early work of Coppola, Lynch, the Coen brothers, Toback, and DePalma disprove that?

(Laughing) You're asking the wrong person about Pauline Kael. [Carney has written a number of articles attacking her work.— DC] Kael wasn't interested in art; she was a connoisseur of kitsch. As far as I'm concerned, she was the single most unfortunate influence on the last thirty years of American film reviewing—stylistically, intellectually, and aesthetically. OK, so she went out front and championed certain filmmakers' work before anyone else did. But doesn't it matter that she was wrong about each and every one of them? Have any of them produced a major work?

Kael was the Michael Milken of film reviewing—she had a genuine flair for rhetorically inflating the value of a worthless stock and creating a stampede on the part of others to buy into it based on the inflated value. Look at how it worked in practice: Kael canonized *The Godfather, Dressed to Kill, Raiders of the Lost Ark, Fingers, Blood Simple,* and *Blue Velvet* as masterworks. Since most critics, like most stock market investors, are more or less sheep, they followed her lead. Once they jumped on the bandwagon, the fiction acquired a life of its own, and she seemed astonishingly prescient. Reputations were made, canonical *oeuvres* were established based on one or two works, careers were avidly tracked, with the critics wagering on each of the successive works. The only problem is that it was all a shell game. A few years went by and the initial offering inevitably went back to zero, since there was no intrinsic value to start with. Subsequent works (not surprisingly) failed to live up to the "promise" of the director's previous work. The six movies I named were eventually perceived to be merely quite ordinary or worse than ordinary. (Most people seem to have realized this about the DePalma, Spielberg, Toback,

Coen, and Lynch movies, though there are those who have invested so heavily in Coppola that they still can't admit that they
are holding worthless promissory notes.)

But it's always said that she was a great writer.
   Doesn't great writing have something to do with being smart,
being perceptive, being critically "right" about a work or a career?
Is it great writing if you're consistently stupid and wrong? Are
we in such an alexandrine age that great writing has become nothing more than jazzy metaphors, panting exclamations, the snap,
crackle, and pop of adverbial self-stimulation? But what's even
worse is that the awfulness lives on in all of the Kael-clones she
spawned over the past twenty years. You come up against her
lamentable legacy every week in the *Village Voice, New York*, and
the *Boston Globe*—both in the schlock sensibility and in the
costume-jewelry glitz of the writing itself.

**How about Vincent Canby's receptiveness to the work of Ol-
iver Stone and Spike Lee in the *Times*? Doesn't that represent a major critic going to bat for serious work?**
   Stone and Lee don't represent serious filmmaking—unless you
mean taking themselves seriously and taking press coverage seriously. They are an invention of the media—which they masterfully
manipulate. They don't make art; they make publicity events—
perfectly ordinary movies dressed up with topical gimmicks and
stylistic tricks. It's a standard Madison Avenue technique to get
attention, and Hollywood did it for decades before they came
along. Stanley Kramer made a career of it—with one bad movie
after another—each of which declared its artistic seriousness and
importance in capital letters. Any so-called daring or controversial
reference will apparently fool most reviewers into thinking they
are dealing with "cutting edge" artistic material.
   Take away the tricks and gimmicks and *Do the Right Thing* is
a routine 1950s studio social problem melodrama with every ster-
eotype and cliché in the book. *Malcolm X* is a live-action Disney
cartoon for adults (although it's not as good as Disney—the death
of Bambi's mother is emotionally much more complex). *JFK* is
just another breathless, brain-dead murder mystery. *The Doors* is

a sappy music video. These films owe their notoriety solely to their ability to work in "issues" that journalists equate with artistic seriousness. They provide something for Susan Stamberg to discuss and Ted Koppel to organize panel discussions around. That has nothing to do with art.

Stone and Lee are not exploring; they're pushing buttons. They are not searching for truth, taking chances, trying to understand complex emotional and intellectual realms. They obviously have their minds made up about what they are going to say before they ever start shooting. It's only the even greater awfulness of most other mainstream films that makes us desperate enough to take them seriously.

But you are assuming that what reviewers say matters. Vincent Canby and Gene Siskel have both argued that the power of reviewers is grossly overrated, and that many movies are completely critic-proof. They will make it or not, independently of what critics say.

That may be true in terms of blockbusters. Arnold Schwarzenegger and Steven Spielberg would probably continue to make money even if their films were critically savaged (though it's quite interesting how rarely they are—the reviewers shrewdly never risk alienating their readers by taking a position too different from the lowest common denominator). But who cares what happens to those movies, anyway? They are just business deals to make a quick profit for venture capitalists. The sad reality is that the movies that most need critical support—the ones the critic can truly help or destroy—are the ones least likely to get it: small-budget independent works. Given the terrifying economics of film production, distribution, and advertising, the only way for a small film to get any attention at all is to get a review in a newspaper, magazine, or—God willing!—on television. Yet the problem is that these are precisely the works that most go begging for critical attention.

The music industry shows it doesn't have to be that way. There is a variety of levels of entry and opportunity, and a wide range of critical and commercial receptiveness. You have the Elton Johns who make mainstream music that is played on Top 40 radio.

And you have punk bands and minor jazz artists who play in base-ment clubs in New York or Boston. And what is wonderful is that there is room for all of them—commercially and critically. They are all accorded some degree of critical recognition and some chance to reach audiences, however large or small. But with film, there is effectively nothing *but* the Top 40, with the same ten mov-ies playing at every multiplex in the country and getting all of the critical coverage in the papers, which is why guerrilla groups have a far better chance of getting known than guerrilla filmmakers like Rob Nilsson, John O'Brien, Rick Schmidt, and Caveh Zahedi. There must be some way to make room in the distribution process for the garage filmmakers, the punk rock films, the jazz artists of cinema.

How about the serious film magazines? Are they any better than the newspapers and newsmagazines?

You mean *Premiere, Entertainment Weekly, Film Comment, Movieline*? Does anyone actually *read* those things? They're even worse than the Sunday *Times*, if that can be. They're print versions of *Entertainment Tonight*—glossy, four-color updatings of fifties movie-star fanzines, celebrity-gossip rags dressed up with zippy language and fancy photo spreads. There is no exercise of critical intellect or independent judgment, just a breathless rush to get an interview with the hottest star or to retail the latest factoid before it is reported in a rival publication. The studio publicists use them as part of a film's advertising campaign, and they are obviously glad to be used.

We complain that reporters are puppy dogs when it comes to asking hard questions of politicians, but the Hollywood hagiogra-phy of *Premiere* makes the Washington press corps look like par-agons of principle by comparison. When was the last time a studio director was grilled about the idiocy of the movies he makes, or an article told the truth about how silly most of the studio releases in a given year are? Of course, the reason they can't print the truth is that they need the studios for sources as much as the studios need them for publicity.

In short, it's all just PR, and the first principle of public relations is that you don't sell the steak but the sizzle, so it's not surprising that two-thirds of what appears in a given issue of *Premiere* or *Film Comment* is not actually about anything that is on the screen at all. As with any gossip column, almost anything else is more interesting than the film itself: its budget, its shooting schedule, the romantic relationship of the star and costar, self-serving quotes from the director, how the special effects were created, the trends, the buzz, the hype about Steven Spielberg's next piece of silliness.

How about the elite or high-culture institutions—museums, archives, and universities?

America is a culture of publicity, and there are very few institutions that successfully resist its pressures (or even attempt to). The museum film curators I know have no time for more important things because they spend all of it trying to get press coverage for the works they show so that they can justify their budgets. After a while, the tendency to compromise—to show works that can be depended upon to generate good reviews—becomes almost irresistible. The American university is not exactly a profile in courage, either. The Ivory Tower has always been a myth, as far as I can tell. Film professors' values are no different from those of the culture at large (though they invent terms like "pop culture genre studies" to give their taste for junk the appearance of intellectual legitimacy). The film programs at Ohio, UCLA, and Wisconsin embody more or less the same Hollywood values and priorities as American film reviewing does.

The whoredom after celebrity is as pervasive inside the ivy-covered walls as it is outside. How else does Spike Lee merit a visiting professorship at Harvard? If they wanted an African-American artist, Charles Burnett is ten times the filmmaker Lee is—but, of course, he's not a name to conjure with in *USA Today*. By what stretch of the imagination do schlock-meisters like Steven Spielberg and Oliver Stone deserve to be asked to address classes of film students at UCLA or USC? Are these the examples we want to hold up to the next generation of artists to imitate?

Are the American Film Institute and the Sundance Institute successfully counteracting these tendencies?

They're not even trying. The AFI and Sundance are in bed with Hollywood values and celebrities as much as the rest of the culture. When the AFI, which is explicitly chartered to devote itself to the *art* of American film, spends its money restoring *King Kong*, and Sundance picks former studio hacks to teach its seminars, what conclusion can you draw? Look at who the AFI gives its Lifetime Achievement Award to each year. They might as well merge with the Academy Awards and save both of them a little money. Or was I out of town the years Shirley Clarke, John Cassavetes, Morris Engel, Lionel Rogosin, Gena Rowlands, and Maya Deren were up on the dais?

How about academic film criticism?

When I've told you that *Cinema Journal*, the official scholarly film quarterly, runs articles about "I Love Lucy" and *Popeye the Sailor Man*, there's not much more to add. And since I recently wrote at length on this subject [in the "Polemical Introduction" to the Winter 1992 issue of *Post Script* magazine—DC], I'll spare you the gory details. Suffice it to say that there are two dominant schools of scholarly film criticism—the ideological and the formalist. The ideological approach basically represents a kind of affirmative action for the arts. The reviewer grades the work against a checklist: Are there enough female parts? What about minorities? What occupations do the characters have? Are women depicted as sex objects? Is sexist language used? The ludicrous critical consequences can be summed up with a story a friend told me at supper last night. She attended a university screening of Barbara Loden's *Wanda* (which is surely one of the greatest works in all of American film). After the movie was over, a Women's Studies professor got up and delivered a lecture on how the film "failed to provide adequate role models for women" and "failed to offer a solution to the central character's problem." The lecture was intended to be a more or less definitive critique of the film's artistic failure, but as my friend pointed out, all it ended up definitively proving was the absurdity of asking a work of genius to answer such kindergarten questions. Where in the world did this professor get the idea that this is what works of art do? Do we go to *Macbeth* to discover "adequate role models" for women? Do we read *Antony and Cleopatra* to find "a solution" to the title character's problems? Given such flat-minded standards of what constitutes artistic greatness, it's no wonder feminist critics prefer the triviality of *An Unmarried Woman* to the profundity of *A Woman Under the Influence*.

The formalists are at the other remove. While the ideological critics ask very little other than that their works of art have their political papers in order, the formalists offer a vision of artistic expression with stylistic razzle-dazzle a mile high and knowledge of life an inch deep. Meaning drops out of the account. Filmmaking and film viewing become a matter of "manipulating and decoding diegetic strategies."

It sounds sort of scary!

(Laughing) It's even scarier to see what it does to David Bordwell's writing! The vocabulary is an attempt to lend legitimacy to a field of study that is still too obviously an artistic and academic ghetto. But the result is to wall film into another kind of ghetto— a ghetto of semantically empty aesthetic effects.

What is the alternative?

To recognize that art is a form of knowledge or it is nothing. The formalists try to turn it into a stylistic game played off to one side of life, as if it were no different from chess; the ideological critics try to turn it into a shopping list of politically correct attitudes and positions, as if it were no different from the newspaper. The mistake both make is that neither takes art seriously enough. A work of art is the finest, most complex form of knowledge and communication of that knowledge that man has yet invented. That is not meant to be a flowery metaphor. When we watch *Killer of Sheep*, *Mikey and Nicky*, *Trash*, or *Milestones* we learn things— about our culture, about our relations with others—that we never knew, and that can't be learned in any other way. Art is a form of knowledge in precisely the same sense in which science, history, sociology, and philosophy are forms of knowledge. The only difference is that of all of the ways we can know, it is by far the most intricate and profound.

We feel this intuitively when we participate imaginatively in the greatest works of art—whether they are paintings, plays, works of music, dance, or film. We internalize new structures of understanding—not just new facts or observations or beliefs—but entirely new intellectual and emotional forms of awareness. Our consciousnesses are altered—as much as drugs or sexual or religious experiences can alter them.

I hope that doesn't sound like mystical mumbo jumbo. What I'm describing is a very practical thing, something the best students repeatedly experience in their course work, and I've often dreamed of a whole university curriculum organized around it. It would be a curriculum even more intellectually demanding than a conventional history, philosophy, or physics major, since the ways of knowing offered by great works of art represent knowledge even more subtle and intricate than the forms of knowledge already included in the curriculum. As a former physics and math major in college, I'm especially weary of scientists and mathematicians getting credit for being the only heavy thinkers on campus—or claiming there's some kind of knowledge gap if the Japanese have more years of math study in their schools than we do. If we want to turn out the deepest, most creative intellects possible, we should require the study of art from first grade up. Science and math are too easy. Anyway, isn't it about time America stopped worrying about its technological superiority and started grappling with its obvious emotional and spiritual immaturity? As the long-running national orgy of sex, violence, and consumption painfully testifies, we are a nation of emotional cripples and moral paupers.

Why do you say artistic knowledge is harder to master than physics or math?

Because it is much more complex. It offers sensorily thick experience in place of abstract intellectual analysis. Art gives us dense, lumpy oatmeal experiences—not a thin gruel of rules and formulas. More than that, it requires us to reconcile the truths of the body, the senses, the emotions with the truths of abstract ideas. It doesn't allow us to rise above the tangibility of space and time into a realm of conceptions, but forces us to express ourselves within space and time. Most challenging of all, it replaces static with dynamic knowledge. It provides examples of knowledge in motion that resists codification. It asks us to enter into continuously shifting states of awareness that won't stand still for analysis.

What do you mean when you say it alters consciousness?

The greatest works do brain surgery on their viewers. They subtly reprogram our nervous systems. They make us notice and feel things we wouldn't otherwise. One of the principal ways they do this is through the strangeness of their styles. Style creates special ways of knowing. Henry James and John Milton do it with sentences; Chantal Ackerman and Roberto Rossellini do it with pictures and sounds. Artistic style induces unconventional states of awareness and sensitivity. It freshens and quickens our responses. It limbers up our perceptions and teaches us new possibilities of feeling and understanding.

In this view of it, art is not a luxury, a frill, a pastime, a form of entertainment or pleasure (though it can be supremely entertaining and pleasurable). The greatest works of art are not alternatives to or escapes from life, but enactments of what it feels like to live at the highest pitch of awareness—at a level of awareness most people seldom reach in their ordinary lives. The greatest works are inspiring examples of some of the most exciting, demanding routes that can be taken through experience. They bring us back to life.

If film reviewers understood what you are describing, do you think that the major cinematic art works could reach large audiences?

No, I don't mean to give that impression. The ways of knowing that the greatest works cultivate are emotionally so demanding, intellectually so elusive that even at best only a minority of viewers are ever going to be ready to understand them. The major American cinematic art of the past thirty years will never appeal to the majority, no more than Picasso's paintings or Stravinsky's symphonies do. But that does not count against them. We don't measure the importance of a Rembrandt by how many people stop in front of it for how many minutes. What matters is that it is there waiting for the right person to come along. And one right person justifies a wait of a hundred years. Why do we expect great art to be popular, anyway? Leave that game to the Academy Awards and the Book of the Month Club. Why let business values creep into the analysis, when business values are one of the problems the art is a reply to?

Works of genius are always going to make demands that almost no one is ready to meet at first, and that most people are never going to be able to meet. Truly new experiences, new thoughts, new feelings are always going to be disorienting. They are going to be painful or seem threatening, because they *do* threaten our old ways of knowing. They require more of us than most of us are prepared to give.

Are you talking about avant-garde and experimental film?

I'm talking about any good film. The independent narrative tradition has always struck me as being more truly experimental, more genuinely avant-garde than the non-narrative tradition, but the category doesn't matter. As someone once said, all great art is experimental art. It attempts something that has never been attempted before, that's never even been dreamed of before. It gives us something we don't ask for, and tells us things we probably don't want to know. That's why it's always going to seem weird or ugly or scary at first. This is not a new phenomenon. Renoir's *Rules of the Game* was hissed at by audiences and beat up by reviewers so badly during its first week that it had to be pulled from circulation. Dreyer's *Gertrud* had half its audience walk out during its world premiere screening.

So you're saying that great art has to be unpopular?

I think it has to be in a minority position in our culture—and will probably always be created by artists who are part of a minority sensibility—though I'm talking in imaginative, not sociological terms. I wish it could be otherwise, and some days, for an hour or two, I convince myself that true artistic greatness is self-explanatory and self-evident to everyone; but my students keep me honest! They prevent me from having any illusions about the real effect of a first viewing of these works. They are a fair sample of the general public, and the greater the work I show them, the more confused or intimidated or dismissive of it most of them are. But that's not bad—it gives us something to talk about in class. And with a little luck and hard work, it's something both they and I can learn a lot from. And I don't claim to be different from my students. I was bored by *Chain Letters* the first time I saw it. I muttered under my breath at *The Killing of a Chinese Bookie*. I stormed out of *Faces*, confused and upset. I fought a number of other works tooth and nail before I gradually came to see that they were doing far greater things than I imagined possible.

That's another reason the whole instant analysis newspaper reviewing process is fallacious. Reviewers see a movie once and expect it to make sense, when in fact a film that is understandable after one viewing is probably not worth seeing at all. Like the most interesting people, the most interesting movies never yield up their secrets the first time we meet them.

Will you be writing more attacks on critics and films?

I hope not. If this hasn't gotten it out of my system, I don't know what will! I really don't enjoy being negative. I'd much rather praise than damn, which is why I confine the venom to a few essays. My books are all expressions of gratitude for the wonders that great art makes possible. But sometimes it is necessary to hack away at what's wrong in order to clear a little imaginative space for what's right. I remember something John Cassavetes wrote me at a fairly difficult time in my life. I had just gotten into one of my perennial scrapes because of something I had written that someone "important" had taken offense at. Cassavetes must have been aware of the hullabaloo, because he took a minute to jot a note to cheer me up. It began in a very gentle and kindly way, but the final words are the ones that have stayed with me: "Keep blasting through the concrete. Blast them. Then love them. Then be sure you blast them again!" It showed he understood that the blasting and the loving were really the same thing.

PREFACE

Hello, independent filmmaker, film student, film buff, video maker, and other media enthusiasts who have always wanted to direct and produce a feature film. With the help of this step-by-step guide to low-budget filmmaking, and the money it would cost to buy a used car (approximately $6,000), your dream is now within your reach.

Feature Filmmaking at Used-Car Prices has been written to teach the process of producing a "no-budget" feature film in the simplest and cheapest way possible. As you read through the chapters, from "Story Concept for a Feature Film" to "Scriptwriting for No-Budget Features," to chapters on preproduction, filming/directing, editing, and promotion, you will learn from my experiences in filmmaking during the production of my five features: *A Man, a Woman, and a Killer* (codirected with Wayne Wang), *1988—The Remake, Emerald Cities, Morgan's Cake,* and *American Orpheus.* Also included is valuable information from the production of *The Last Roommate,* created in a three-month collaboration with students at the California College of Arts and Crafts (Oakland, California).

You will learn how to select your story so that you can succeed in producing your feature within a strict low budget. You will be shown how to rally your filmmaking team around you through the use of "the contract," using deferred payment and percentage points of profit in your film instead of cash to pay all those people who help you complete your project. You will be taught my Fifteen Rules for No-Budget Feature Filmmaking (Rule #14—"Get as many charge cards as you can *before* you start making a feature!"). You will learn how to finally overcome your fear of equipment, how to operate even the most complicated 16-mm camera by pushing just one button. My "secrets of editing" will be revealed . . . secrets that will help you turn your filming "mistakes" into an innovative and original style. By reading how to promote your feature you'll understand how to use your first feature to help produce your second (you're hooked by now). Most important, this book is dedicated to helping you survive the difficult process of low-budget feature filmmaking and to create films that are original and meaningful as well as entertaining.

You may ask, "How do I go from what I'm used to doing [being a housewife, salesman, student, engineer, fry cook, artist, businessman, teacher, computer programmer] into being a film director/producer?" I'm not sure how *you* will do it, but I got into making films quite by accident. My story really begins when I was a dropout from the engineering program at the University of Arizona. I had married a woman with two children and was working as a fry cook at a local hamburger chain in Tucson. One day my first wife brought home some notes she had taken at the library about a college named the California College of Arts and Crafts (CCAC). She thought I might like to study industrial design, since I liked to make things with my hands and had taken engineering classes. Disgusted with life in general, I quickly crumpled up the paper and threw it on the floor. About an hour later, alone in the room, I got up and retrieved the notes. Calling CCAC the next day, I heard to my amazement that they would accept me "on probation" with my C– average. When they told me that tuition was $387 per semester (1966), that settled it, and we moved to California the following month.

At CCAC I found myself immersed in the world of professional art terminology—*form, texture, line, content*—with hotshot art students who had learned all the words in high school. Floundering and scared, I would have quit college again if it hadn't been for several teachers who took an interest in me. My first teacher, Marie Murelius, worked extra hard with me, helping me understand her assignments so that I had a chance to succeed. A later teacher, Charlie Simonds, taught me to ask two important questions of an art work: (1) "What is it trying to say?" and (2) "Is the message worth saying?" Charlie also reminded his students that if something had already been expressed in art, and expressed well, there was no reason to try to say it again.

My immersion into media came one day when teacher Phil Makanna decided to invite several painters and sculptors to take his experimental video class (1971). The thought of cameras, lights, and the harsh glare of examination was frightening to me, and I offered my place in class to another sculptor, who seemed happy to accept. After he took a few steps down the sidewalk toward registration I called him back, telling him I'd reconsidered and would take the class myself. I had just barely enough self-confidence to give video a try.

After I shot my first video with an early-model Sony portapack camera and recording deck, Phil suggested that I edit the footage. But since CCAC didn't have any video-editing equipment at that time, he told me I needed to transfer the video to film. For a couple hundred dollars I transferred the video to 16-mm and was handed an "original" copy, a "work print" (a low-quality contact print made from the original for editing purposes), and a "mag track" (sound track for editing). After asking a few questions of the employees at the lab, I found out that I needed to "sync up" the picture work print and sound track so that the picture would line up with its corresponding sounds. I rented a small editing cubicle and asked another employee to show me how to use the equipment, to make a "splice." Since I had rented an editing space that was generally used for cutting together original film for printing (a process called "conforming"), he assumed (wrongly) that that was my objective, and proceeded to show me how to use a "hot" splicer with glue that cut off a frame with every cut. The right tool would have been a "tape" splicer, which allows editing experimentation and reassembly without loss of frames of film. Screening my "rough cut," Phil was shocked to see glue splices, and thought that I had been so sure of myself that I had made permanent splices on my film. What a joke! But I was hooked. . . .

My little seven-minute black-and-white video film entitled *The Legal Operation* didn't show at any film festivals or win any awards (I never entered it) but I was thrilled to be able to put it on a projector and rain down the thunder of sound and images on my friends at school. It felt great to be able to shoot something very personal to me and then reveal it in such an immediate way to fellow humans. The process of video filmmaking seemed to connect me in some way to the rest of the world. I didn't consider myself a "director" or even a filmmaker at that time. I was just an artist who'd made a video film. I had no idea to what extent imagemaking would take over my life.

How did I go from making a seven-minute video (edited on film) to becoming a feature filmmaker? Certainly not through planning. It happened naturally as I shot longer videos, and then took the next step of shooting directly on film. About six months after graduation from CCAC, during which time I hadn't produced anything, I began to feel desperate to get back to work. While standing in front of a booth at the Alameda Flea Market on a Sunday morning, I made the decision to break my deadlock by just picking up a magazine, any magazine from the box at my feet, and shooting "a film." I didn't know what story I might pick and certainly had no idea how to get my hands on film equipment or even how to use it, but I felt I had to do something. I had also been stymied by the admonition of teacher Charlie Simonds to "say something worthwhile," because I didn't have any good ideas! I reached down into the box and pulled out a *True Confessions* magazine from 1933. Closing my eyes, I flipped open the magazine, then I opened my eyes to an article titled "What Flirting Cost Me." For the next six months I shot the film on weekends, using CCAC film equipment that my friends Wayne Wang and George Chang checked out for me when available. Each time I shot a scene I would simply hand the one copy of the magazine to the actors, Willie Boy Walker and Linda Egar, who would memorize their lines while I set up the camera and lights. Different friends helped me load the camera, take light readings, and record "sync" sound on location. On one evening I found myself without help, doing everything myself, from setting up lights and loading film, to blindly working the knobs on the Nagra sound-recording machine until I finally got it to record. The film ended with Willie reading the caption at the end of the *True Confessions* article: "to be continued . . ."

After a month of editing, the thirty-minute *What Flirting Cost Me* was completed, and with urging from Willie I entered it in the Marin Film Festival, where it was a prizewinner. Actor Bob Cummings presented the awards. My friend Wayne Wang said he had been surprised that I could edit a good film out of what he assumed to be a lost cause, and on that basis we collaborated on a short film with actor Bruce Parry. By the time our fourteen-minute film, *1944*, had won a first place at the Ann Arbor Film Festival (1973), Wayne and I were sharing an apartment and talking a lot about feature filmmaking.

While I was in art school I had inherited some money, which had mostly gone to supporting my wife and kids. I was now separated from them, baby-sitting the youngest ones—Heather, Morgan, and Bowbay—each Friday night to Monday morning; the two oldest daughters, Kathy and Lisa, stayed with their mother in Berkeley. I still had about $11,000 left when Wayne and I decided to go for it: to make a feature. Another friend, Dick Richardson, who had loved *1944*, joined us as a collaborator on the film. It was decided that we would write for two weeks and then film during the following two weeks, the entire process to be completed in one month's time.

I paid both Wayne and Dick $250 at the beginning of each week of writing, to assure all of us that the project was really happening. And during that period I ordered filmstock from Kodak, hired a soundperson with an assistant, helped select actors, drew up a profit-sharing contract with the help of an attorney, reserved equipment, arranged baby-sitting, did everything necessary to be prepared for the shoot. At the end of the month I had spent a total of $5,900 and had shot my first feature film (July 1973).

Of course, I didn't realize that once the film was shot the problems of production were only just beginning. During the next year and a half of what seemed to be insurmountable editing problems, I ran out of money and was very thankful that my mother decided

to invest in the film in return for a small percentage of the hoped-
for profits. Every weekend I would take care of my little kids and
every Monday I would return to my rented editing room and go
back to work. I was fortunate that the lab where I was editing
allowed me to charge the editing room ($320 a month) as well as
other editing costs (splicing tape, some sound recording for narrations, shooting and processing titles). At one point I had gone
almost six months without making a payment. On the home front,
my kindly landlord also let me go several months without paying
rent ($100 a month), and the corner store gave me thirty days to
pay for groceries. Although my life was in a complete financial
mess, the inspiration I derived from working with the footage kept
my spirits afloat through those difficult times.

In December 1974, I held the finished projection print ("answer
print") in my hands and was thrilled when I showed it to friends
at the Pacific Film Archive theater, which I had rented for $60.
The excitement generated from the screening helped me overcome
my exhaustion and gave me the energy to take the print to New
York, spending my last few hundred dollars to try to sell the film,
get a distributor and a showing, and find some way to pay the lab
the remaining $4,000 I had charged to complete *A Man, a Woman,
and a Killer* (75 minutes, Color/B&W).

Each day in New York I dropped off a print at some distributor
or showcase, and after each rejection I tried another possibility.
The film was rejected by the Whitney Museum, the Museum of
Modern Art, New Directors/New Films, Film Forum, Cinema 5,
New Line Cinema, New Yorker Films, etc. When I arrived at the
Bleecker Street Cinema and was asked by programmer Marc Weiss
what other response had been to my film, I listed all the rejections.
He screened the film and said he wanted to give it a show in March
(1975). Anne Wehrer, at whose loft in the Bowery I had been stay-
ing, had gotten herself drunk in order to tell me that I would fail
to get a New York screening with my film. She was dumbfounded
when I told her about the coming "world premiere." I didn't think
much of it, since it didn't appear to solve my immediate money
problems, but at the time I didn't know how difficult it was to get
any showing in New York. And considering that the independent
film program at the Bleecker Street Cinema folded a month after

my premiere, I had been exceedingly lucky to get any show at all.

Returning home to Oakland, I resumed the baby-sitting of my little kids Friday night to Monday morning, trying to keep up with feeding them properly and taking care of them (Heather was eight, Morgan was six, and Bowbay was three), and mostly lying on my bed, exhausted, watching TV and worrying about my avalanche of unpaid bills. What saved my spirit was the knowledge of the coming Bleecker Street show. I had also entered the film in the Ann Arbor Film Festival and looked forward to any positive results.

Around this time my filmmaker friend Bill Farley was applying for the American Film Institute independent filmmaker's production grant of $10,000 and kept insisting that I write up a proposal. I resisted, having little energy to expend, but he kept on my case, saying, "You have a feature film to use as an example of your film work [needed with the application]. . . . *You have to apply!*" I tried for several days to think up a good concept for a new film and finally, under pressure of the coming deadline, I thought up *Showboat 1988*, about my librarian friend Ed Nylund (an actor from *A Man, a Woman, and a Killer*) who sells his house when he finds out he has cancer and uses the money to give an audition for the classic American musical *Show Boat*.

Ed had always bad-mouthed the musical format to me, saying it was phony, and he said he wanted to bring the "stench of death" to the musical comedy. Ed's real life had been a series of "almosts." He had almost been a doctor, having had the distinction of being accepted twice at top medical schools during the 1930s before dropping out. He had also gotten close to receiving his master's in musicology from the Manhattan School of Music before his marriage broke up, destroying this second career. I liked the idea of Ed finally making a dream come true by staging the audition for *Show Boat*, at the same time giving all the troopers who performed the chance to "be a star" before the cameras. After I typed out the proposal I couldn't even afford the sixty cents of postage to mail it, and Bill Farley jammed the needed coins into my hand.

In March (1975) *A Man, a Woman, and a Killer* opened for a five-day run at the Bleecker Street Cinema during some of the worst weather New York City had ever experienced (hailstones, etc.), showing every day at 4 P.M. to a few scattered survivors and several critics the programmer had worked very hard to get to the theater. A review came out in *The New York Times* with the headline "FILM: 3 Interlocked Lives." Under that there was a caption: "'A Man, Woman, Killer' is Mildly Interesting." In the New York *Daily News* we did better, with critic Jerry Oster giving the film two and a half stars and calling it "one of the most absorbing films I've seen of what is generally called the independent film movement." A week later I heard that our feature had won Directors' Choice at the Ann Arbor Film Festival, and I was thrilled. On the film tour the festival sponsors yearly, the film won several first places in competition, earning me a couple of $100 checks, which seemed like a million dollars to me in my tough economic situation.

One day in early April, as I rounded the corner to my apartment, I met Wayne on the sidewalk, and with excitement in his voice he said, "Congratulations . . . you deserve it . . . you earned it." I had no idea what he was talking about. At the door I saw a telegram stuck into the crack. It was from the American Film Institute announcing that a panel of four, including King Vidor, had decided to award me $9,918 to make my next film, *Showboat 1988*.

I had been saved! For the first time in months I relaxed, not fully realizing the strain I had been living under. I was deliriously happy, relieved that I could now tell all those people to whom I owed money that I would soon be able to pay them back. All of a sudden everything was OK—great, in fact! But what was the difference between this week and last week? I still didn't have any cash in my hand. The difference was the *idea* of money coming. I wished that I could have just thought "Money" and received all the energy that the idea of winning the grant had supplied.

By the time I received the production grant money I was eight months behind in my rent. I promptly paid it off. And at the lab they agreed to let me charge my processing and work printing on *Showboat 1988* if I cleared my account. Although I wasn't really fully recovered from the workout of the first feature, with renewed energy and a full bank account I moved into production.

At this point the reader may ask what would have happened to me if I hadn't been lucky enough to receive the grant. After all, only ten such grants were given out from hundreds of applications. Well, since I was still in my late twenties and still had some youthful energy, I imagine I would finally have found some sort of job and begun slowly to pay off my bills. And of course any normal person who worked a regular job and used vacation time to shoot a feature would be able to return to work and pay off their accrued lab bills just that way. But I had begun without a safety net of any kind, and that added intensity affected my life and filmmaking in both negative and positive ways. For over a year I had spent much of my time desperately needing money for my film and living expenses. But, to paraphrase Mick Jagger, you can always get what you need. Somehow the fact that my life depended on getting help to live through my filmmaking process actually helped me overcome certain obstacles of shyness and reticence, enabling me to ask relatives, friends, even bankers, for their assistance in my struggle. And since I knew that I had only one "tool" with which to pull myself out of my difficult situation—the finished feature film—I was able to devote my constant attention to the project until it was completed. Of course, I probably would have done this if I *didn't* have a money problem, but I was certainly less apt to quit editing the difficult body of footage knowing that it was the only way to turn my economic situation around.

My friends and I had discovered early in our filmmaking careers that it seemed as difficult to make a five-minute film as a seventy-minute film, and it was often just as hard to get $200 as $2,000. The difference was that with a feature you had at least a chance to sell it somewhere and make some money back. The investment in months and years also made much more sense if the project had feature-length status. So although I hadn't been fully conscious of all the new editing skills I would have to learn to finally edit a feature to completion, I knew that taking the risk was the only really sensible step to take for my filmmaking career.

With the production of my second feature, *Showboat 1988*, I again ran into economic difficulties. Part of the problem was that I had needed to use part of the grant monies to clear up the past debt from *A Man, a Woman, and a Killer*, giving the lab $4,000 off the top of my budget. The next problem was that the *Showboat* audition grew so large that I shot over forty-five 400' rolls of filmstock to accommodate the filming of all the auditioners who crossed the large stage at California Hall in San Francisco, which I rented for three consecutive nights at a cost of $1,100. The grant money was eaten up with the production of posters and PR material, the hiring of lights for the large hall and "gaffers" to operate them, catered lunches for the fifteen friends who helped run the audition, a full video crew who interviewed each act as they walked off the stage, and a rented dolly for smooth camera shots for my rented Eclair camera. Once involved with the concept, I felt it was necessary to support the idea by supplying everything necessary to insure the highest quality production possible. Luckily, art patron Jim Newman rescued the last night of filming by giving me enough money for the additional filmstock needed to complete the shoot. But by the time I held the processed original, work print, and mag track in my hands I was at least $4,000 in debt to the lab.

Once again I was faced with the problem of being broke. Overcoming the fear of rejection and embarrassment, I called my uncle to ask for financial assistance to live on and to finish my film. On the phone he told me that once when he was a young man he had asked his father for $10,000 to start a small electronics store, and had been turned down. He decided to help me. Again I had put my life on the line and again I had been rescued by an understanding relative. Why had I done this to myself again? Was I a masochist? I knew I had the burning desire to create the best images, record the best sound, make the best film that I could in support of all the people who had given their time and energy to the project. I felt it was my responsibility to do the best job possible regardless of the limitations. And for that reason it was necessary to withstand the pressures of raising more money and occasionally being broke.

And it got worse before it got better. I suppose the lowest moment in trying to survive came when I found myself borrowing money from my daughter Heather's piggy bank. At the time my mother was sending me a check for $20 each week to make sure that I could feed myself and my kids (I was continuing to charge everything at the lab). Somehow I got $20 behind. With Heather's agreement to accept a fifty-cent interest on the loan, I would borrow her savings each Monday, live on it until the weekend came, and then return the twelve silver dollars, several quarters, dollar bill, and other change after cashing the check. This happened repeatedly. Finally, the teller at the bank asked why I always asked for the same amount of silver dollars and change. When I told her, she looked at me with disgust. A month later I received word that I had won a grant of $7,500 from the National Endowment for the Arts to complete *Showboat 1988*.

At another point of desperation, early 1977, I got a call from the programmer at the Bleecker Street Cinema saying that Hubert Bals, the director of the Rotterdam Film Festival, wanted to present *A Man, a Woman, and a Killer*, show my new feature, *Showboat 1988*, and fly me to The Netherlands. Somehow, with the help of my miracle-working friend Lela Smith, I was able to get a print in two weeks due to her night-and-day conforming of original (AB rolling) while I completed the edit and prompted the lab to meet my deadline. Suddenly I was jetted out of my Oakland apartment into the world of European international film festivals. At the festival I met Dennis Hopper in the hallway. *"Showboat* is a great film," he said. Being slightly delirious from exhaustion, I asked, "You mean the original?" "No, *yours!"* Hopper quickly returned.

And the struggle continued from there. After I completed the final version of *Showboat 1988* (in 1978) I was threatened with legal action by MGM concerning my supposed copyright infringement of the "Showboat" title and changed it to *1988—The Remake* to avoid a costly court battle. Fortunately, I was still able to earn about $6,000 on tour with the film and sold it for $13,000 to Channel Four in England after it had a successful showing at the London Film Festival. All this money—together with a second NEA grant, money from the sale of my 1939 Dodge pickup, and timely loans from friends—helped me pay off lab bills and shoot my third feature, *Emerald Cities*, the final film of the trilogy.

By 1986 I was back in serious debt with the lab ($10,000), immobilized at home while my wife, Julie, went off to work each day and I took care of our infant son, Marlon. It was then that I started to write about no-budget feature filmmaking, hoping to somehow sell the results and dig myself out of the economic pit again. Looking back at that time I see certain similarities to the tired old cliché of the criminal in his cell on death row, painstakingly penning his memoirs, racing against his predetermined appointment with the guillotine. But instead of racing the specter of death I was trying to avoid destitution. Julie was in a dead-end job (she supplied us with the monthly "nut" of food and shelter), looking more tired and irritated each evening when she got home, and I couldn't figure out how to earn a living, much less shoot another "no-budget" feature. Fortunately the book did sell, allowing her to quit her job while I was inspired to keep making films, completing *Morgan's Cake* in 1988, and *American Orpheus* in 1992.

There are many ways to alter your life in order to make your feature film. Perhaps your way won't be as stressful as what I put myself through. Maybe by having read my story you can get your feature production started on a firmer economic foundation, having a better overall plan for slow payback of lab bills from the money you earn at your job. It is my wish that in the following pages I'm able not only to supply you with the necessary skills to create an affordable low-budget feature but also to impart the feeling that regardless of your particular economic situation there is nothing that can stop you from making your feature-filmmaking dream come true. In an age where motion pictures are being called the major new art form of the twentieth century, I think it is important that many more of these "features" are created outside of the Hollywood system, by artists who have something to say with an original and personal point of view. It is my hope that you become one of these new independent feature filmmakers. Good luck, and see you at the festivals.

Rick Schmidt
lightvideo@aol.com

ACKNOWLEDGMENTS

Special thanks for the help I received in writing this book must first go to my wife, Julie Schachter, who continued to bring in the family paycheck while I toiled at home, at the same time taking care of our infant son, Marlon. It was definitely a team effort. And great thanks must be given to Jayne Walker, editor and agent, who first believed in *Feature Filmmaking at Used-Car Prices* when it was only a title and a loose collection of writings. She brought the project up to professional standards, encouraged me throughout the rewrites, taught me the basics of good writing, and gave me my first taste of what a great difference excellent editing can mean to a manuscript. Thank you, Gary Thorp, for bringing us together. Special thanks must also go to my first editor at Viking Penguin, Lisa Kaufman, for her belief that the book should be published, and for her inspired final edit that brought the manuscript to fruition. Thank you, Lisa, for that vital quality of yours: to be excited by and open to new ideas. And thank you Caroline White, the editor of this revised version, for your generous assistance and care with my latest manuscript additions. Also thanks to my agent, Carol Mann, who was indispensable in turning my work of writing into a second occupation.

I must also give thanks to the people who have helped me with my first occupation—filmmaking. My mother, Lura Janda, invested in my films and constantly offered her spiritual support throughout the rough times. And my uncle David Strawn deserves much thanks for his timely loans to my *1988* production during a period when I was basically homeless. Thank you, both, for your love and kindness.

None of my features could have been made without the help and full commitment of many talented and creative artists and technicians, who took time off from their own projects to see me through. Thank you, Wayne Wang, for sharing with me the first flush of independent low-budget feature filmmaking. Thanks to the cast of my feature trilogy, Carolyn Zaremba, Ed Nylund, and Dick Richardson, for putting up with ten years of my filmmaking with little or no pay. Thank you, Neelon Crawford, for showing me how great location sound can be recorded, and thank you, Nick Bertoni, for also delivering excellent recordings during the turmoil of low-budget production. Thank you, Kathleen Beeler, for giving me the gift of professional lighting during the production of *The Last Roommate* and *Morgan's Cake*. Bill Farley deserves special mention because he always seemed to have the right ideas for whatever film concept I was trying to work out and was always there to help me make my work better. Other friends, Lowell Darling, Willie Boy Walker, Ted Falconi, Phillip Hofstetter, Mike Church, Chris Reece, John Vargo, Henry Bean, and Nick Kazan, helped me script my ideas in spite of my own reluctance to give up any control. A special thank you to Lela Smith for AB rolling on my features, helping to meet my impossible deadlines. Thank you, all, for making such a big difference.

Other actors and technicians were also vital to my most recent films, each person a link in the chain of production. Thank you, Kyle Bergersen, cinematographer on *American Orpheus*, for your enormous energy, skill, and determination, helping me shoot the complicated full-color film in only ten days, even bringing in steadicam genius Troy Peterson for final "underworld" shots. And again thanks to Neelon Crawford, soundman, who came out of retirement to supply me with top-quality tracks. Paul Baker deserves thanks not only for his strenuous work as boom man, but for composing, arranging, and performing fourteen original and hauntingly beautiful songs for the sound track. And thank you, Diane Witherspoon, for composing and singing the exquisite title song, "Thanking You," and granting its use in the film, with additional permission from the record's producer, Art Maxwell, of Tonal Gravity Records (Berkeley). Jody Esther, lead actress in *American Orpheus*, has earned my highest admiration for her guts-out performance in the lead role as Fay. And Willie Boy Walker, a star in both *Morgan's Cake* and *American Orpheus*, deserves highest compliments for equally fine performances in both comedy and drama. Curtis Imrie must be greatly thanked for his excellent rendering of the risky role of an abusive husband, along with other fine performances by Karen Rodriguez, Jasmine Carver, Deborah Daubner, Tom Taylor, Katrina Eggert, Betsy Newman, Aaron Carver, Al Newman, Debi Hinton, Adrian Pike, Jan Burr—everyone who helped me pull off *American Orpheus*.

My son, Morgan Schmidt-Feng, deserves a most special thank you, for not only delivering a superb performance in the lead of *Morgan's Cake*, but assisting me with the production of that film and appearing in and helping me produce *American Orpheus*. I look forward to serving on *his* production crews in the future.

Thanks must go to my collaborators on *The Last Roommate*, Peter Boza, Tinnee Lee, and Mark Yellen, for believing that we could make a feature in three months using a college course film class (at the California College of Arts and Crafts) as our base. And thank you, David Heintz, Ian Turner, Jaime Oria, Ray Berry, and actors Jean Mitchell, Bruce Parry, Anita Forbus, Sarah Mann, and Marlene Ryan, for your help.

And thanks to my collaborators on the 1993 Feature Workshop film *Blues for the Avatar*—Eric Magun, Barry Norman, Anthony Pesce, Michelle Kulstad, and Trudie Dearinger, with help from cinematographer Kyle Bergersen, grip Karen Rodriguez, and sound man Mat Monroe—for working with me to shoot and edit a feature in ten days. Thank you, J. Cheyenne Wilbur, Mary Jane Knecht, Jane Holloway, Judy Goulder, Patrik and Tess Barr, their avatar baby Chyna, Stafford Decker, Tasha Roth McCormick, Donn Trethewey, Joe Calabrese, and Etta Roth, for acting and supplying locations for this breakneck production.

Many other people have helped me on my films, and I thank

you again for this assistance. Thank you, Michael Mideke, Kelly Brock Boen, Skip Covington, Lee Serie, Joe DiVincenzo, Mary Garstang, Jim Newman, Phyllis Richardson, Terrel Seltzer, Alan Shulman, Jim Summers, Bobby Weinstein, Fran Hawkins, Julie Schachter, Bill Kimberlin, Jim Mayer, Gary Coates, Flipper, The Mutants, Joe Rees, Liz Sher, Phil Schnayerson, M. Louise Stanley, Lee Chapman, Leon Kenin, Rachel Pond, John Claudio, F. Paul Hocking, Sara Rosin, Bob Arnold, Peter O'Halligan, Peter Buchanan, Judy Newman, Ben Goon, Bill Palmer, Brad Wright, Swain Wolfe, Bob and Judy Pest, Vic Skolnick, Charlotte Sky and Dylan, Fred Padula, Linda Egar, Jane Egar, Jim Maher, Gary Thorp, Lucile Fjoslien, John Corso, Murray Korngold, Elliot Rosenblatt, Alex Prisadsky, Anne Wehrer, Alex Feng, Johanna Feng, Gail Fisher, Katherine Sherwood, Leon Hayes, Billy Hiebert, George Manupelli, Bob Zagone, and Mary Ashley, every one of whom has helped me along the way.

Lastly, I want to thank Boston University professor Ray Carney, Cassavetes expert and author, for reminding us, in his ongoing articulate disputations against the Hollywood status quo, that our struggle to make personal feature films is a worthy and vital contribution to society.

FEATURE FILMMAKING
AT USED-CAR PRICES

INTRODUCTION TO LOW-BUDGET FEATURE FILMMAKING

I f you've looked over the table of contents, with its extensive chronology of the steps needed to create a feature film, you may feel a bit frightened by the seeming complexity of the process. And if you don't consider yourself a "technical" person, you may also have become worried that you don't have the necessary skills for making a film. This book, like other books that must include some technical information, may appear at first glance to be over the head of the novice who has always just had a *feeling* about making a feature film. But in this case that isn't true. Making something even as complex as a feature film can be accomplished if the process is undertaken in a thorough, step-by-step fashion. Each step in the process of making a low-budget feature is carefully outlined and explained in the following chapters of this book. And each step flows naturally to the next step, the final result being the creation of a feature film for $6,000.

Perhaps you don't even have an idea about what your feature film would be about. If you just have a *feeling* that you would love to make feature films, that is enough purpose with which to begin your project. In chapter 1—"Story Concept for a Feature Film"— you will be taught how to discover ideas in your own life as well as in outside news events that can be the subject for your film.

Most people don't place enough value on their own experiences, overlooking the incredible possibilities for feature film concepts relating to real life. By the end of the chapter you will have been taught how to expand your idea into a one-page "treatment" that can be registered with the Writers Guild for copyright protection.

In chapter 2 you will learn how to script your idea, whether it be a conventional story or a series of images and sounds that tells a different type of story. The emphasis of this book is on each person's striving to create his or her own original vision on film. If you don't consider yourself a writer, you will learn alternative scripting techniques that help you create a "menu" from which you can detail your shooting ideas.

Once you have formed a script or outline for shooting, chapter 3 explains how to write out a contract for the production, paying cast and crew mostly with hoped-for percents of profit or deferred salaries from money to be earned from the feature. You will learn how to follow the strict $6,000 budget, understanding the limitations of your low-budget enterprise. There is also information on raising money from investors and applying for grants.

In chapter 4, on preproduction, you will be taught how to collect the people, places, and things necessary to shoot your film. You will be shown how to locate the needed members of your cast and crew, find locations, and get the best deal on camera rentals, lighting kits, and other essential pieces of equipment. Different types of filming will be discussed, some that require only natural light to illuminate interiors, avoiding complex lighting systems by using faster filmstocks. At every turn, you will be taught ways to save additional money on your production. By using the preshoot lists outlined at the end of the chapter you will know when you are fully prepared for the next step in production—the actual filming of your feature.

Chapter 5—on production—begins by telling you my Fifteen Rules for No-Budget Feature Filmmaking. There really aren't any hard-and-fast rules to creative work, but I think you'll enjoy the food for thought. Once again the chapter is constructed in a step-by-step fashion, discussing each facet of shooting a film, from picking up cast and crew members to loading your rented camera—or just how to shoot it if you have been able to afford a camera assistant who can technically maintain the equipment for you. Here I encourage you to overcome your fears and just begin shooting, trusting intuition and honest intentions to help create an original and meaningful film. Steps are outlined that teach you how to set up lights and take a light reading, and I also offer suggestions for types of shots and techniques for shooting that save money and add originality. You will learn how to shoot titles on location and save hundreds of dollars. At the end of the chapter you are taught how to deal with the lab regarding processing and work printing of your footage, and how to check your film and sound for quality before completing the filming.

After the film is shot and the on-location sound has been recorded, the real alchemy of editing your footage into a film begins. Each step in the editing process is presented in chapter 6, from syncing up the picture and sound track so that the words spoken are lined up with the image of the mouth moving on film, through finding the best order of shots, refining the scenes, testing your edit, using music and sound effects to improve your cut, and adding needed pieces of narration or photos to complete your ideas. Once the final pacing and tightening have taken place, you are shown how to prepare your sound rolls for the "mix," in which every volume and tone is controlled in support of your story. You are also shown how to cut your original footage for printing at the lab, "conforming" the original using the identical images on the work print as your guide. Doing this process yourself saves you almost $3,000. I discuss how to order your print, making sure that the lab has the full, clearly stated instructions necessary for making a good first print ("answer print") on the first try. And finally you're shown how to assemble your feature and screen it for eager members of cast and crew.

Next comes chapter 7, on promotion, your lifeline to hopefully earning some of your production monies back, attending some glamorous film festivals in Europe, and getting your chance to make your second feature film. I show how to make your own pressbook, creating graphics (posters, letterhead) that will help sell your product. There is much information on how to enter film festivals in the United States and Europe, including addresses, and a listing of possible buyers for TV and several U.S. showcases that pay filmmakers to present their films around the country. Distribution is discussed along with alternative forms of getting your film into theaters. The final word in the chapter is to enjoy your accomplishment regardless of the acceptance or rejection of your feature film.

Next comes a dose of reality check, chapter 8, to help give the filmmaker a sense of purpose for making feature number two.

For those filmmakers who found it impossible to raise even the no-budget amount of $6,000 for a first feature attempt, chapter 9 offers the radical alternative of making super-low-budget features by collaboration: Five to ten people share the financial burden and create a feature film for as little as $1,000 each. And if you have already survived the hardships of producing that first feature, but were not fortunate in producing one of the few films that became critical and financial successes (*Clerks, Go Fish, Sex, Lies, and Videotape, Slacker*, etc.), then this chapter offers you a viable option for extending that one-shot feature attempt into a feature filmmaking career, by helping you afford to produce a new work.

Chapter 10 is devoted to the possibility of shooting your feature in video. Although I carefully budget out a video feature shoot at the used-car price of $6,000, it's still impossible to beat the quality of 16-mm for fine-grain images and high-quality sound at the same price. But my forecast is that with the advent of cheaper video equipment at broadcast quality, video will certainly be a viable means for producing features in the future.

Finally, chapter 11 explains how all filmmaking, from Hollywood big budgets to no-budget feature filmmaking, will be affected by advances in digital technology. From digital correction of a sound track thought to be ruined by excessive camera noise (the whirring sound of a camera can be totally removed without affecting the sound quality!), to digital editing (speeding up assembly and fine cutting which allows a hundred hours of rough documentary footage to be reduced to a finished cut in just six weeks), this technology is now becoming more affordable in its numerous applications. But regardless of the new technology or methods of production, what's most important is that each person take responsibility for making his or her feature filmmaking dreams come true.

1

STORY CONCEPT FOR A FEATURE FILM

To create a high-quality, low-budget, feature-length film, the film-maker must think of a film concept that not only excites his or her imagination, but that also can be made on, and that stands a chance of actually benefiting from, the severe restrictions of a used-car budget.

After each of my students and I had written treatments of possible feature film concepts for one of our collaborative efforts at the California College of Arts and Crafts (1984), I began the final selection process for choosing the one concept for our no-budget feature by withdrawing my own idea because it was obviously too big for our tiny budget. After two out of the three students also withdrew their story concepts, we were left with the one workable idea, which recounted the story of a woman in her thirties, living alone, who rents out a room to a male roommate (*The Last Roommate*). The story was about their relationship and how it developed with regard to the male partner's insane jealousy and her need to make a decision about aborting her pregnancy. This concept offered us (1) one basic location—her apartment, (2) only two main characters, (3) a straightforward narrative flow, and (4) a chance to discuss the timely issue of abortion. And by finding an actress who would be willing to let us use her apartment as the location for our movie, we would be able to save the cost of location rentals and benefit from filming in her private living quarters, which would undoubtedly reveal real aspects of her personality. The monetary restrictions actually inspired us to enhance our concept by including the extra touch of reality.

My first feature, *A Man, a Woman, and a Killer*, also benefited from the severe shooting budget of $5,900. Wayne Wang, Dick Richardson, and I designed a story that included three main characters: a young gangster holed up in a house with his girlfriend, and an older man who wanders into their lives and is mistaken for the hit man they are expecting. For the filming I was able to rent a house on the Mendocino, California, shore for two weeks, which housed our nine-person cast and crew. Because it was economically necessary for us all to live together during the shoot, we were quickly transformed from a group of perfect strangers into a commune whose members shared their most intimate secrets. One of the most original things about the film is that it interweaves the real love affair between Dick and actress Carolyn Zaremba with the scripted affair portrayed in the story. So in this case, the budgetary limitations not only enhanced the concept but expanded it and ultimately redesigned the entire structure of the film.

While budgetary restrictions may be a determining factor in choosing a film concept for production, the first step for the filmmaker is to begin searching for ideas, and defining personal attitudes, that will gel into an intriguing feature film concept.

WHERE DO IDEAS COME FROM?

Each person's life is littered with unrecognized stories and ideas that could be used to create fantastic feature films. Because we all get caught up in daily routines that camouflage the real dramas of just being a living human, it's easy to be unaware of the truly great stories we each already know. The concept for *The Last Roommate* came to us because a friend of my student Peter Boza told him the true story of how her jealous roommate terrorized her, becoming so crazy that he ended up in her backyard pruning her trees while completely nude to embarrass her with the neighbors. Although your life may not include this dramatic an episode, if you closely examine your life you may be surprised to find you hold within your memory an important story that should be told on film.

Perhaps there is a good story in how your parents or relatives immigrated to America. There have been a lot of films made that deal with a person's overcoming overwhelming odds to survive and win (*Rocky* and *Rocky II*, *III*, *IV*, and *V*, to name a few), and maybe you or someone you know falls into this category. I personally think that more films should be made that celebrate the silent heroism of people with disabilities, who must strive each day just to function, and that every Vietnam veteran has a moving story to tell. Everyone's life is heroic if placed in a proper dramatic structure. The play *Death of a Salesman* by Arthur Miller is a heroic story about an American salesman near retirement age who has exhausted himself in pursuit of financial success. Maybe your job offers some interesting filmatic possibilities for stories. Having been brainwashed by continual car crashes and murders on nightly TV, it's hard to see the simple, yet immensely vital, stories each of us live out in our quiet ways. These stories are the ones that the independent filmmaker should tell.

Many good films have been based on newspaper articles some scriptwriter noticed while in search of divine inspiration. Nick Kazan, a coscriptwriter on my second feature, *1988*, recently wrote the screenplay for *At Close Range*, based on a series of newspaper articles about the father of a crime family who is turned in for murder by his son. For several weeks before deciding to produce *The Last Roommate*, my students and I had worked on developing a story based on a newspaper article about a bully who had terrorized a small midwestern town and had then been shot to death, with the entire town refusing to divulge the identity of the killer. If you read your hometown newspaper every day, from front to back for two weeks, I'm sure you'll see some story that sparks your interest.

Sometimes an idea for a feature film comes to you in one line, or in a single flash of inspiration. My film *Emerald Cities* began with the single thought: What would it be like to watch the events of the modern world in 1984 on TV from a shack in the middle of the desert? It then occurred to me that maybe the TV would be an early color console in disrepair, that could only transmit green images. Comic Steve Martin has said that the premise for his first film, *The Jerk*, came from a line in one of his routines: "I grew up as a simple white boy born into a Negro family."

Film ideas can also arise out of those things you most value or enjoy. Frank Capra's movie *It's a Wonderful Life* presented the premise that each person's life is vitally important to all that it touches. If you feel that no one should go hungry in an affluent society like America, maybe you can expand this attitude into a full-fledged feature film concept. Maybe you can make a film that sheds some light on the modern victims of depression, as John Ford did with his film of John Steinbeck's book *The Grapes of Wrath*. The other day I saw a film on TV about the South Sea island pearl divers and thought this would be the perfect topic for an independent filmmaker who enjoys scuba diving and likes to travel.

But before making a feature film that explores your particular hobby or preoccupation, carefully check in a reference book to make sure there aren't films already made that sufficiently explore what you are interested in. The impact of your film depends to a great extent on the originality of your subject matter, and the power of your story will be diffused if it's too similar to an already-existing film. One good way to check out your idea for a feature film is to read through a book such as Leonard Maltin's *TV Movies*. Reading a short synopsis on each film not only lets you know what's been done, it also gives you a better understanding of the ideas behind the films you've seen. Reading the weekly film reviews in *Variety*—a film industry magazine—would give you the most current selection of movie concepts. Of course, even if you attempted to copy the story line of an existing Hollywood film, it's quite doubtful that anyone could recognize the similarity between your $6,000 effort and a big-budget film with millions of dollars' worth of production values. One of the greatest virtues of low-budget feature films is that most of them appear to be unquestionably original.

Not all ideas for low-budget feature films need to fall within the guidelines of traditional narrative structure. Many interesting features that challenge the way we see our world through the media of film and television have been made in the area of avant-garde filmmaking. James Benning made a feature film constructed only of one-minute static shots of industrial sites. Pop artist Andy Warhol made an eight-hour film that included only one continuous image of the Empire State Building over the course of a single day. Many film artists have used the essay format to speak about their world through personal observations. If you select this format for your feature production, you would first choose the theme of your film and then script the text for your narration and the images to illuminate your ideas. Some artists such as Bruce Conner have used "found footage"—film footage that they have acquired that was shot by others—and edited the pieces into new, original works.

Whether you choose narrative storytelling or more abstract means of speaking with film, I believe it's most important to respect your intuition and follow your instincts so that the final result of your film efforts will ring with a personal truth and originality.

SELECTING THE RIGHT CONCEPT

After you have thought of several ideas that appeal to you as concepts for your low-budget feature film, each idea must be analyzed in terms of feasibility within the severe restrictions of a used-car budget. In my earlier discussion of production on *The Last Roommate* and *A Man, a Woman, and a Killer*, I mentioned how each film made use of a few main characters and one central location. If your film concept demands the use of many characters, such as our "bully" concept did for the class production, it may be too expensive for the meager resources you have available. With a budget of only $6,000, there is little money to pay actors, and only a certain amount of percentage points of profits in the film that you can give away as enticements (see chapter 3). And since you are also very limited in funds for transportation to various locations, and cannot afford the additional days of shooting, with increased equipment rental rates and salaries that multiple locations would require, ideas that fall into these categories must be withdrawn from consideration.

When examining potential choices of ideas for your feature production at used-car prices, you must also evaluate all areas of your concept for costs that would be apt to destroy your chances for success. Does your concept require a great deal of voice-over narration or sound effects at costs that would exceed allotted funds for sound transfers to mag stock and sound studio time (see "Budget," chapter 3)? If you can't figure out a means of filming your extensive credits as part of the on-location shoot (see chapter 5), just this one extra expenditure could rob your production of precious production monies. Unless you are a skilled musician who can create original songs in a free recording studio, don't plan a low-budget *American Graffiti* around scores of popular songs for which you can't possibly afford expensive music rights. Obviously, don't consider making a low-budget "period" costume epic unless you have free access to the wardrobe of an opera company. Any deviation from the strictest limitations of story, location, and number of characters has the possibility of ruining your chances for completion of your production.

ELEVEN ESSENTIAL QUALITIES OF A NO-BUDGET CONCEPT

Before making a final decision with regard to your film concept/idea, consider its potential in terms of the eleven qualities listed below.

☐ *Originality*
   Have similar films been made?
☐ *Feasibility*
   Is your concept possible to produce given budget limitations (see chapter 3)?
☐ *Drama*
   Does your story have the possibility of human drama that will touch the audience's heart?

☐ *Responsibility*
Does your film concept add meaning or understanding, in a personal or universal way, to our lives?

☐ *Interest*
Will the audience be interested in the story you are telling?

☐ *Screenplay Potential*
Will your idea continue to grow into a feature-length script, or dry up in less than thirty pages?

☐ *Personal Choice*
Is this the kind of film you would go to see in a theater?

☐ *Notoriety*
Is this the kind of film for which you'd like to be known?

☐ *Richness and Complexity*
Is this a film that can be viewed more than once—that becomes *more*, not less, when seen again?

☐ *Timeliness*
Will your film concept quickly become outdated?

☐ *Critical Response*
What is the best—and worst—review your film could receive?

NOTE: To avoid possible legal problems it is vital that the filmmaker attain a release (see Appendix E) from any actors or people who will perform in a feature production. It is equally important to secure a release from an individual whose story you've derived from a newspaper article. If you use a newspaper story only as inspiration, changing the names and incidents into unrecognizable form, this release is no longer necessary. For our production of *The Last Roommate* we gave the real person upon whose story our film was based 1 percent of the hoped-for profits as payment for her idea. It is not wise to base your feature film idea on a published or unpublished book unless you are able to clear the legal rights with the help of a lawyer. And since the legal fees and "option payment" usually required for using such material may easily cost more than your entire used-car budget, it's best to avoid all these legal problems by thinking up an original idea derived from your own unique experience.

WRITING YOUR CONCEPT IN ONE SENTENCE

It is an old Hollywood adage that the head of a major studio will ask the producer who is pitching the idea for a new feature to "give me your idea in one sentence!" While it is not our intention to sell our idea to a studio, and certainly not necessary since we have the wealth and power to send our own idea into production (at used-car prices), it's definitely worth the time it takes to define your idea in the strongest sentence possible. Not only does this exercise bring about an increased awareness of the foundation of your story, but it gives you a chance to begin writing your movie. Below you will find several examples of how my class and I tried to define our idea for our "bully" movie in one sentence:

The Bully is a film about a small town that is terrorized by a bully, and then destroys him.

The Bully is a film about a group of townspeople who are terrorized by the town bully, and the moral dilemma they are confronted with of what to do about him.

The Bully is a film about the rise of a small-town bully whose victims reach their limits and take action to end the torment.

The Bully is about a bully who terrorizes a small American town and is killed by town consensus, the whole town refusing to reveal who actually killed him.

The Bully is a film about a town that worked collectively to kill a bully and then refused to reveal the individual responsible.

The Bully is a film about a group of townspeople who, after being terrorized by a bully, take revenge on him and hide the crime.

The Bully is a film about a group of townspeople who are being victimized by a bully, and the vi-

olent action they are forced to take after the legal system fails.

While each sentence describes basically the same story, the subtle shift in emphasis could account for seven different films made
from the same idea. In some descriptions the grammar or use of
words is poor and the idea loses energy. What do I mean by "energy"? If you read over the descriptions again you should find that
each one has a different ability to gain your interest. Most likely
the description with the most punch will be the one that is struc-
turally correct in grammar and concise in its use of words, giving
it the "energy" to grab your attention. By beginning your film project with a sense of accuracy with regard to each word expressed,
you are putting into motion the necessary care needed at every
stage of production. Whether you are writing your script, ordering
filmstock, renting equipment, directing actors, or editing your footage, the end result of all your labors will depend on your ability
to communicate your ideas to others as concisely as possible. So
by writing and rewriting your one-sentence description of your
movie concept until the words are at their best, you will clarify
your ideas to yourself and initiate a standard of quality that will
affect all aspects of your feature production.

EXPANDING YOUR IDEA INTO
A ONE-PAGE TREATMENT

Once you have settled on the one sentence that best describes the
film you want to make, the next step is expanding your idea into
a one-page "treatment." Below are two examples of treatments
written by students at CCAC for *The Bully*'s concept. You'll notice
that each student renamed the film, coming up with the following
titles: *The Round of Justice* and *Thou Shall Not Kill*. Although
neither of these titles is really dynamic enough to be a final choice,
at least an attempt was made to create an original title. Using their
imaginations, the students developed the bully as a character in
their story, inventing his past, his size and shape, his attitudes and
motivation. And each person tried his or her best to come up with

a beginning introduction, a middle development, and a suitable ending to the drama.

THE ROUND OF JUSTICE

The Round of Justice is a film about a group of townspeople who are being victimized by a bully and the violent action they are forced to take after the legal system fails.

The people of the town pride themselves on being a self-sufficient entity. The desire for a quiet life is something they share. Their tolerance and helpful concern for each other give them productive and useful lives. They all know why they are there; not because they are bitter fugitives from the outside world, but because they want to be in control of their lives.

Tobias Young, the catalyst of the action, a large-boned hulk of a man, is from a farm near the town. He served as an army supply sergeant in some recent war, where he developed a taste for personal power and dabbled in black-market goods. Now he works in a gas station by the highway. He needs respect, but doesn't know how to earn it until he discovers fear will get him what he wants. He uses his physical size to intimidate the townspeople. He stops paying for coffee, then for clothes; soon he pays for nothing, and when they complain, he breaks up their stores. After he has beaten up several people, one of the townspeople tries to teach him a lesson by burning his big pickup truck, but Tobias catches him and beats him nearly to death.

Tobias is arrested, and in the trial at the county seat he gets a minimal sentence for a first offense. When he returns from jail a few months

later he shoots one of the men who testified
against him. The town has a meeting to try to decide what to do. They know that even if they get
him put in jail again he'll return as soon as he
gets out. The next day they see his pickup truck
approaching the town and gather in a crowd around
him. A shot rings out and he falls dead.

The bully has been killed in a crowd of townspeople who all say they didn't see who did it. The
state can't decide whom to prosecute. The town
has gotten away with murder. They realize they
have to live with their guilt. Have they lost what
was good in the town? Have they gotten rid of the
encroachment of the outside world or have they
brought it even deeper into the town themselves
like a Trojan horse?

Although the basic story is outlined in the above treatment, it's
hard to get a specific feeling for the characters involved. Missing
from this treatment are the little details about people and places
that give life to the words. And there are some unanswered
questions—such as what the bully Tobias was like as a kid, some
history of his family that would account for his need for self-
respect at all costs. Also, what was decided at the town meeting
with regard to the bully? Did they *decide* to kill him? How have
the townspeople been affected by the death? Will the whole town
be prosecuted? These details must be filled in to complete the
story and fulfill the needs of the treatment.

THOU SHALL NOT KILL

This feature-length motion picture is a film
about a group of townspeople who are being victimized by a bully, and the violent action they
are forced to take after the legal system fails.

The bully has been getting away with terror-

izing a small town for the last two years, since
he returned from a job as a supply sergeant in the
army. It seems his self-esteem fell very low after returning to the town he grew up in when he
discovered there was no job waiting for him. In
the military he dealt with selling black-market
goods, special favors, etc., and he enjoyed the
power that went along with his position. But back
home he was a failure, a three-hundred-pound
''nothing.''

His mother, with whom he lived, was unable to
offer any positive support for his rage other
than her nightly reading from the Bible, and soon
he directed his anger and frustration on the town
at large. In the initial stages he was fueled by
an incident where he refused to pay for his coffee
after being angered by an inattentive waitress.
Getting away with the free coffee, he soon turned
to helping himself to free clothes in the town's
best men's store, bullying his way into the bar-
bershop for a free haircut, free meals at the
cafe. Everyone, including the one local peace
officer, looked the other way as this bullying increased like a type of fission. Everyone tried to
understand.

Finally, a well-liked member of the community,
eighty-five-year-old Mr. Ferguson, made a formal
legal complaint to law officers in Judson, the
town twenty miles east. The bully was brought to
court and Mr. Ferguston testified against him.
Through a technicality the bully was released
and, returning to the town, shot Mr. Ferguston in
the leg with a .38-caliber revolver. The bully
also broke several windows, cleaned out the
clothing store, and threatened several locals
with injury. It seemed nothing could stop him.

The townspeople decided to protect themselves, and fearing that the local justice sys-

tem would not help them in their defense, they decided they must destroy the bully. The next time he drives his mother in to church they (a group of thirty to forty people) circle his car, and a shot rings out. When the crowd clears he is found dead.

Questioned by authorities in Judson, the entire town refuses to talk about the killing. This film ends with the possibility of the whole town's being tried for murder and the changes that take place in the townspeople who were forced to take justice into their own hands.

Once again, the treatment does not quite meet the major requirements of storytelling. We are given a slightly more detailed description of the bully (a three-hundred-pound "nothing") and now know that his mother read the Bible, but what about his father? What were the ingredients of his childhood that prompted his behavior? It helps to see how a small incident such as "an inattentive waitress" began his reign of terror, and it is much more convincing to believe that he got off easy for wounding an old man than for almost killing him, as is stated in the treatment of *The Round of Justice*, but the treatment is not nearly as gripping as it should be, given the basic premise. Since the story must rely on the development of the bully's personality, it is vital that we learn about him through the use of "the characterization."

IMPROVING A TREATMENT
THROUGH DETAILED CHARACTERIZATION

To write a treatment that seems to describe a flesh-and-blood character, it is essential to understand the life of that character, from childhood through adult years. An example of the characterization of "Greg" from *The Last Roommate* is shown below. By understanding the physical attributes, education, social life, and work history of Greg, we were able to understand clearly how his character would relate to any given situation. Not only did this help to fuel additional scenes for scripting, it also aided the direction of actor Bruce Parry, helping him to attain a believable performance as the Greg character.

GREG

Physically:
Trim, well built, stands around 5'11", 175 lbs.; athletic-looking, brown hair, clean-cut. No physical defects. Goes jogging, eats health foods, but smokes grass and drinks.

Family Background:
He grew up in a small town in New Jersey. His home life was rather unhappy due to father dying of cancer at an early age. Mother then remarried to a man who disliked Greg, and eventually also died of cancer. Greg's mother had a difficult time raising Greg and his brother. In school Greg did well because he spent most of his time after school at home working on cars or studying. Did not date girls, although there was some interest in a girl who lived nearby. Most of the time if he went out, it was with the boys. His family was lower middle class, and lived in a modest home. The absence of his father caused him to withdraw some, especially with the arrival of his step-father. Greg valued the old-fashioned family unit and rituals his father practiced (togetherness at dinner table, respect for elders, family cooperation).

Education:
Graduated from high school with good grades. Attended college two years before going into the marines for a tour of Vietnam. He is well read; as a matter of fact, reading is a passion for him. Social subjects fascinate him. He is somewhat concerned with the struggle of poor people and the American drive to make money. He feels soci-

ety has lost its purpose of an ideal. He gradually
becomes anticapitalist in his beliefs. Vietnam
was a shocking experience for him, one that became especially difficult upon returning to American society.

Social Life:
Greg has always been single, one of those individuals who felt more comfortable with others of
the same sex. Not much on dating, he spent most
of his time working on cars with other friends,
or hitting the books. There was one female interest he saw at random. She was a neighborhood girl
who took more of an interest in him than he in her.
She turned out to be his senior prom date. The two
years he spent in college were more socially active with girls, but still mostly with the boys
and drinking. In his adult stage, Greg still was
not well adjusted with women, though he became
more outgoing. Insecurity plagued him and the
relationships he had. He has old-fashioned beliefs that run afoul in his encounters with the
modern woman. Because of this his last relationship ended when his girl walked out on him due to
jealousy. He has tried to come to grips with this
problem unsuccessfully.

Work History:
Steady and reliable. Since he was a kid, Greg has
had a good job background. As a teenager he worked
part-time in a gas station as a mechanic's
helper, doing tune-ups and other small jobs from
which he picked up enough knowledge to work on
his own car. While in college he held another
part-time job in an auto-parts store. After returning from Vietnam he taught for a while, but
the lack of good pay forced him to turn to private
business. Since starting a new position placing
executives with corporations, he has had diffi-

culty adjusting to the aggressiveness of private
business.

Reading the characterization for Greg, you should have the feeling that you know him as you would a relative or close friend. With this type of solid background, writing a treatment and script comes much more naturally. Here's another treatment for *The Bully*, entitled *A Time for Justice*, that benefited from the student's writing a short history of the "Ned" character, and then using the psychological and physical descriptions from his characterization to better understand Ned's motivation.

A TIME FOR JUSTICE

Synopsis:
This feature film is about a group of townspeople
who are being victimized by a bully, and the violent action they are forced to take after the legal system fails.

Outline:
The town of Eden is a small community symbolic of
small-town America. It is a town that prides itself on being self-sufficient enough to control
its own destiny and not be ravaged by progress.
The old values that founded this country, inde-
pendence, justice, religious freedom, hard
work, and respect for your fellow man, are
traditions that give Eden its character. Tolerance and concern for each other are virtues the
townspeople practice. Pursuit of the quiet life
is something they share. That is, until Ned
returns.
    Ned Tobias once was a teenager in Eden with a
reputation as an occasional hell-raiser whose
trespasses were taken as nothing more than grow-

ing pains. If anything, the townspeople ignored him. He reveres his mother, Hilda, a Bible-reading disciple, who tried to guide him, but could not control him after his father's death. His closest companion had always been old Billy, the retarded cartman who cleans up the town in his own way. Now things are different. Ned has returned from the service—the Marines, to be exact—a different man. For one thing, he's grown into a massive 6'2", 240-lb. man who's very aware of his strength. Attuned to power and manipulation, something he learned as a supply sergeant dealing in the black market, special favors, and simply getting whatever he wanted through intimidation, he's someone to reckon with. Since returning, his life has taken a turn for the worse. There is no job waiting for him except as a gas station attendant. The means to power and respect he found in the Marine Corps don't exist in Eden. His self-esteem reached bottom until he employed intimidation to get what he wanted.

It all started with an incident that took place his first day back. Feeling proud and worldly-wise upon returning to Eden, Ned walked into the coffee shop to have a cup of coffee as well as to be seen by the people there. Expecting clamor and attention, he was instead ignored. Resentful, he grabbed the waitress by the wrist and made a pass at her. When she pulled her hand away she accidentally spilled the coffee onto his lap and the uniform he proudly wore. Incensed and insulted, he used the moment to vent his anger at being ignored by breaking dishes and turning over the table before leaving. In time, one incident led to another as Ned gained strength from the fear he struck within the community. He manipulated the town through anger, threats, and violence. He interpreted their impotence as the respect he deserved. It became standard for him not to pay for meals, clothes, drinks, etc., if he chose not to. He beat up Kevin Kern, the town barber, for standing up to him. When Lyle Swanson refused him credit, Ned took all the clothes he wanted and vandalized the store. He disrupted church services. Finally, a well-liked member of the town, seventy-five-year-old Sam Ferguson, tried to teach him a lesson for stealing groceries by filing charges. But Ned got a suspended sentence and the sheriff was powerless to stop Ned from returning to town.

This final incident compelled the townspeople to meet. They realized that the sheriff was old and useless and the justice system ineffective. They knew that if Ned were jailed again, when released he'd return with greater vengeance. They tried to understand what had become of their lives and community. They discussed various solutions to the problem that gave rise to moral conflict amongst them. But their fears were great enough to reach a conclusion.

The next day, a Sunday, Ned drove into town for a drink. As he pulled up to the local bar in his pickup truck, a group of townspeople surrounded him. A shot rang out from the mob. The crowd then dispersed to the church for the Sunday service. After a moment, Ned's body slumped forward onto the steering wheel, setting off the horn in a final outburst of anger. There was no trace of the anonymous killer.

The state tried to prosecute, but there were no witnesses. The town maintained a silence over the incident. Their problem was gone, but will life be the same in Eden?

This treatment succeeds because it involves the reader in the drama, gives numerous details that enhance the story, and concludes the action. And most important, the story is told with the necessary energy to indicate the larger script that must flow from this beginning concept. The material seems to be begging for expansion. So it is worth the extra effort of writing a well-thought-out treatment in order to give yourself the best start possible for your feature project. Even with projects that don't depend on either character development or story—more abstract features that can't easily be defined—it's worth the effort to write out your concept and title in order to have the opportunity to protect your original work by registering it with the Writers Guild.

REGISTERING YOUR TREATMENT

After you have written the best treatment possible for your project, and thought of the most appropriate title for the film, you will want to legally protect your work by registering the treatment with the Writers Guild of America. On page 24 is an example of the title page form that must accompany your writing. Once your treatment is registered, you will have legal grounds for a lawsuit if someone tries to produce a film with either an identical story line or title after your registration date. It's even possible that you may be approached by Hollywood producers who wish to purchase your registered title for their big-budget project. Filmmaker Jon Jost sold the rights to his film title *Angel City* for several thousand dollars when approached by agents who needed the title for their movie.

To establish the ownership of your film concept, send a check or money order for $20, along with your treatment and title page, to Writers Guild of America, West, Inc., 8955 Beverly Boulevard, Los Angeles, Calif. 90048 ([310] 205-2540). There is no limit on the amount of pages you can submit, so if your treatment has run to fifty pages, that amount of writing can still be registered for the $20 fee. Within a month you will receive a slip of paper from the Writers Guild that shows your date of registration and your registration number. This information should be transferred to the title page of your treatment for future reference. Once the filmmaker has written a treatment that not only conforms to the rigid demands of a used-car budget, but also excites the imagination, the next step is to expand the concept into a full-fledged shooting script.

Use this title page format when registering your treatment with the Writers Guild:

THE LAST ROOMMATE

Feature-length Motion Picture Treatment
by Peter Boza, Tinnee Lee,
Rick Schmidt, and Mark Yellen.
Copyright 1984.

(Registered by Writers Guild of America, West, Inc.,
on this date _____, registration # _____.)

2

SCRIPTWRITING
FOR NO-BUDGET FEATURES

f this is your first film venture, or if—film being basically a visual
medium—you've never before needed to write a script for previous short films, you may be quite surprised to find yourself
confronted with the task of writing a feature-length script. Maybe
you found it exceedingly difficult to arrive at a one-sentence description of your concept, and took weeks just to write a one-page
treatment for your story. Maybe during this time you kept
repeating to yourself: "I'm not a writer . . . I'm not a writer . . .
I'm not a writer . . ."

It's true that not everyone is a writer in the grandest sense of
the word. Not everyone can use words to bring ideas and characters to life. But almost anyone can write out a recipe for choc-
olate chip cookies and list the ingredients that must be purchased
from the store. A script is like that recipe. The simplest form of a
script could be a list of scenes, or just shots and accompanying
sound track, that are the desired ingredients for your film:

INTERIOR—JEAN'S HOUSE—DAY.

1. (Wide shot)
   JEAN enters house and locks front door. (CUT
   TO)

2. (Wide shot)
   JEAN walking away from camera down hallway
   toward the dining room. She notices a trail of
   clothes leading from GREG's bedroom entrance
   to the kitchen. She stops at bedroom door:
     JEAN (knocks on door)
     Greg?
   Getting no response, she opens the door and
   looks in. (CUT TO)

INTERIOR—GREG'S BEDROOM—DAY.

1. (Wide shot)
   From inside GREG'S bedroom we see JEAN open
   the door and look in.
     JEAN (looking about)
     Greg . . . ?
   (CUT TO) . . .

A more complex version of a script might include pages filled
with thoughts, essays written in loose form, with none of the
speakers of the lines identified, as was the case for *A Man, a
Woman, and a Killer:*

''What do you want?'' I asked.
''You mean you want me to lay you,'' I said.
''No, I don't want you to lay me. I just want you
to love me.''
''Yeah. But what do you want me to do?'' I said.
''I want to be happy.''
''Tell me what to do and I'll do it.''

```
''I want you to take care of me,'' she said
(pause).

Long still shot  fade out
```

Thanks to my professional scriptwriting collaborators Nick Kazan, Henry Bean, and filmmaker Bill Farley, I was supplied with writing for my feature *1988* that closely resembled the traditional form of Hollywood scripts, as on the next page.

Just as each person is able to think up original feature film concepts, each filmmaker will be able to arrive at a scriptwriting format that best suits his or her needs and the needs of the project. Since you are producing your own feature film at used-car prices, you don't have to conform your filmatic recipe to standard script format, which would normally be necessary for acquiring major studio funding. You can structure your script so that it best helps you prepare for shooting your film. Although it is generally considered taboo to include instructions for camera angles in a "professional" script, any notation you decide to add to your script is entirely appropriate if it helps you realize your goals. Even if you aren't a writer, it should at least be possible to list the ingredients (scenes) of your film, and then describe the action that takes place with regard to your story.

If you are still hesitant about trying to write your film, one possible way to break the "block" is to speak about your film into a tape recorder. Once you have described your concept and talked about the characters, location(s) you envision, and mood you'd like to achieve, remembering to give your story a beginning, middle, and end, spend $50 to have a typist transcribe your words on paper. When the typist hands you twenty pages of rough "scripting," you will realize that you can create a recipe for your feature film.

WRITING SCENES ON INDEX CARDS

Writing for a feature film is done in stages, each new stage bringing the ideas of the film more into focus. After writing one sentence

                    ED
      I don't want big names. I don't want
      Zanuck and I don't want Bette Davis.
      Hollywood would poison this film. I
      want a sidewalk Showboat.

Skip shakes his head helplessly; he tries to impress
on him realities.

                    SKIP (slowly)
      Do you want a movie, Ed? Or do you
      want to sit around this ridiculous
      hotel suite and pretend for another
      couple of days until they throw us
      out. LOOK...
               (he takes some money out
                of his pocket)
      I've got about six bucks. You want
      it? Here.
               (he puts it on the table)
      That's not ~~going to cover the phone~~   *enough for the breakfast!*
      ~~bill.~~ You're ~~talking about~~ a movie, *Sweetheart.*
      ~~Show me the family.~~

                    ED
      ~~IXXXXXXXX~~ Skip, I'm going to have ten
      thousand dollars by lunch.

                    SKIP
      Where from?

ED holds up a hand telling SKIP not to ask.

                    ED
      We're going to make this with
      ~~XXXXXXXXXXXXXXXXXXXX~~ our own money.
      I want a film that comes out of America,
      a film America gives to herself, instead
      of buying one pre-fab from Hollywood.
      I'm going to give the means of image
      production back to the people.

The phone rings. Skip answers and begins talking in a low
voice. ED ~~XXXX~~ goes on talking to DICK or, perhaps, just to
the room.

      SKIP (background)   ED (foreground)
Hi, yeah, great. (laughter) Right   Everyone - every one is a
I think it'll be very hot   star, and I'm going to give
word-of-mouth. We open in colleges   them a chance to show it
and the cities, score the hip-   and find out for themselves
liberal press, then sell to Corman   I'm going to let them write
or somebody. Right. Yeah. We   their fantasies in celluloid.
forget the south, Midwest, the   My producer tells me it's
hicks. Yeah, fourwalling is a   impossible. My assistant
posso, but...right. But you   director tells me it's imposs-
figure the budget's under a   ible, and the money men say
hundred and we spend raisents   I'm out of my mind. And that
on promo. No, we want twenty-five   convinces me, that it is not
grand minimum investment for   only possible - it's necessary.
twelve and a half percent. Right.

Page of script from *1988—The Remake*.

that best described your film concept, you expanded the idea into a treatment, adding some character development while envisioning your story. The next step toward completing a shooting script is to once again expand the writing, using the treatment as a source of inspiration for thinking up as many scenes as you can for your film. A method that's worked for me in creating scenes for a feature is to change the size of the writing surface from 8½"-by-11" paper to 4"-by-6" index cards, using one card per scene. This format helps me overcome my fear of large blank pages and gives more presence to the one-sentence scene descriptions written on each card.

After you've written down as many scenes as you can, read the cards in order and see if you get a complete feeling from your story. It should be easy to determine where scenes are missing. By being sensitive to the flow of your story, you should have the ability to create new scenes that will make transitions between the scenes you've already written. By filling in these structural holes, you can quickly add many new scenes to the film.

EXPANDING CARDS INTO SCRIPTED SCENES

The final stage of writing the first draft of your script is to expand the idea on each card into a living scene. This means that you need to describe the location where the action is taking place, perhaps provide some background information on the emotional mood of the characters, and actually create the dialogue spoken. Let me mention once again that it isn't necessary to write your scenes in any particular professional scriptwriting format. What's most important is that you are continuing to develop your ideas and concepts as freely as possible. And if you have any confusion about the structure of your story, it may help to list your scene ideas on a single piece of paper and then shift them around to get a renewed sense of the beginning, middle, and end you are trying to achieve. Here's how we listed our scenes (out of order) for *The Last Roommate:*

Scenes for The Last Roommate

1. First dinner Greg & Jean/dishwashing/begin romance.
2. Jogging . . . Jean meets Greg . . . surprise.
3. Jogging . . . Greg's jealousy of Jean's jogger friend.
4. Jogging glimpses . . . sound effects, breathing, steps.
5. Jogging . . . Jean's fear that she is being followed.
6. Bookstore . . . jealousy . . . Jean leaves before Greg jealous.
7. Interviews with selection of roommates at restaurant.
8. First meeting of Nancy with her girlfriend (about new roommate).
9. Second girlfriend meeting (Greg real possessive, etc.).
10. Third girlfriend meeting (Jean is scared).
11. Jean moves into girlfriend's house.
12. Abortion clinic sequence.
13. Driving (Jean) from SF to clinic (credits?).
14. Ride home from clinic.
15. Greg moves in (boxes, etc.).
16. Answering service jealousy (in bed).
17. Answering service messages from Greg.
18. Greg nude in backyard.
19. Jean gardening.
20. Greg . . . drugs . . . drunk.
21. Greg moves back into his room (after argument).
22. Greg cries (Jean watches?).
23. Jean back home after abortion (catharsis?).
24. Billy and computer.
25. Typing and bulletin board.
26. Greg complains about money, job, etc.
27. Greg goes through Jean's purse.

28. Greg punches holes in diaphragm.
29. Greg gets angry and breaks something.
30. Greg shows up outside Jean's girlfriend's house.
31. Police scene . . . evict Greg.
32. Jean alone . . . Greg bangs on door (night).
33. Jean reads letter about Greg wrecking diaphragm.
34. Greg and Jean have a good time.
35. 4th of July fireworks.
36. Lovemaking collage Greg and Jean night to morning.

Some books on scriptwriting, such as Syd Field's excellent *Screenplay* (New York: Delacorte Press, 1982), discuss the concept of "plot points," which are special scenes that drive your story into higher drama. These scenes, occurring at the tail of the beginning section of your film, and just before the start of your film's ending section, should throw a monkey wrench into the regular flow of events, adding new spice to propel the story forward. Something unusual should happen, something ironic or surprising that changes the basic way in which the audience perceives the story. A film may have many plot points, each one shifting the context and energizing the audience's interest. As Field says, every film has plot points or the audience would probably walk out from boredom. In your list of scenes you may already have created moments in scenes that are, in fact, plot points. Look over your most exciting and interesting scenes. Do these high points generate a rebirth of interest in your story? Do they twist the story around, adding new insight into your characters?

Field says that the first plot point usually occurs about twenty minutes into the film. In our film the first plot point is probably in the abortion sequence, when Jean discusses abortion with a nurse at the clinic. This scene fills in the gaps of information from the beginning flashback, and propels the film forward as Jean is prompted to tell her story. Another plot point occurs when Jean discovers her roommate Greg standing nude in the backyard, pruning plants. This scene signals to the viewer that Jean's moody boyfriend is perhaps also a psychopath. As Jean runs out of the house, terrified by Greg's erratic behavior, the film jumps into a higher dramatic level. Relating with the character Jean as she tells about her problems with Greg, the audience now is doubly frightened for her, and doubly interested in what happens next. The next time you watch a movie, look for the plot points. How many plot points are there in *Citizen Kane?*

While Field's book on scriptwriting is mainly directed toward the writer whose primary goal is probably to script a commercial feature, his advice regarding the structural creation and plot points of a script is also of great interest to the independent filmmaker and avant-gardist. *Screenplay* would be a worthy addition to your reference library.

If you continue to have a problem writing your scenes, sit back and try to identify what's wrong. If you're having problems breathing life into your imaginary characters, it may help to think of real people you have known, writing some real events and observations into your scenes. Or maybe you've been working too hard writing your script, and desperately need to give yourself a break. Take a week off in search of rest and new inspiration. See three movies in a row, or read a good book from cover to cover. If, on the other hand, you have been lazy and sluggish, it may be time to apply the needed pressure of a deadline on your writing. On our production of *A Man, a Woman, and a Killer*, we decided that the only way to actually produce a feature film, given all the daily pressures of just living, was to work within the strict deadlines of writing for two weeks and then filming the next two weeks. All systems for the shooting of the feature were set into motion at the same moment that the scripting began. We made the commitment to film with whatever we had at the end of two weeks, with added writing completed during the shoot. *The Last Roommate* was mostly scripted from index cards during the shoot, with each collaborator often writing into the night for those scenes to be shot and directed the following day.

If you're in the enviable position of having thought up a great feature film concept, and find that you still can't begin scripting no matter what approach you take, it is probably time to consider working with a collaborator.

SCRIPTING BY COLLABORATION

If you are able to remind yourself that all films are a collaboration in some capacity, dependent on cast and crew working together toward the common goal of a completed feature film, it shouldn't be difficult to imagine the possibility of sharing the job of scripting your feature with a friend or professional writer who believes in your concept. Although it will be necessary to pay your coscriptwriter with either money (if available) or percentage points of future profit in the film, as well as share the glory if the film is successful, you'll quickly discover that the price you pay a collaborator is small compared to the overview he or she will offer. Once you have decided that you absolutely can't do it alone, you will want to carefully begin your search for a coscriptwriter.

One of the most serious and wide-ranging decisions you will ever make in your creative life is whom you choose for a collaborator on your project. This decision can make, or break, your film. Not only must you exercise extreme business acumen, but you must intuitively select a talented individual who will enhance your original concept without trying to own it, at the same time freely giving the best of his or her abilities toward your project. You want to pick a person who is as different from you as possible, with different experiences and insights, and who is at the same time compatible with you and your story. If you select someone outside of your small group of friends or associates, what you're basically doing is creatively marrying someone you know only from appearances and a few conversations. If you have a friend, male or female, who is not only very sympathetic to your concept, but also talented and available, you must still use extreme caution in making your final selection. If you fail in *any* way to define any aspect of your relationship, from amount of potential payment if the film succeeds to which name appears first on the film poster or credits, you stand a good chance of losing that friend during or after the production process. Before you choose a collaborator just because he or she is a friend and available, you may want to make an attempt to stretch your limits—by considering the possibility of working with a professional.

If you are a member of Film Arts Foundation (346 9th Street

[2nd floor], San Francisco, Calif. 94103, [415] 552-8760) and have paid your $35 yearly dues, you are eligible to place three small ads in their *Release Print* newsletter for free during the period of one year. It is not unusual to see ads from filmmakers who wish to collaborate on scripting of feature productions. You may want to advertise for a few months in order to see if you can meet a compatible scriptwriter by this means. FAF also offers an extensive file of filmmakers and their various skills, which you may want to review in search of potential collaborators.

911 Media Arts Center in Seattle (117 Yale Avenue North, Seattle, WA 98109, [206] 682-6552) also offers its members free listings in the extensive resource guide they put out each month. So if you are searching for a collaborator, rustling up filmmaking equipment (or selling it), ready to enter film festivals with a completed film, or interested in a wide variety of workshops and screenings, give them a call and join up ($35 per year). You will also be eligible for discounts at many Seattle-area media companies and labs, quickly earning back your membership fee if you are actively making films.

On the East Coast, the Association of Independent Video and Filmmakers (AIVF) publishes a magazine called *Independent Film and Video Monthly* (625 Broadway, Dept. E [9th floor], New York, N.Y. 10012, [212] 473-3400), which offers advertising for "Freelancers" and "Opportunities—Gigs" in its classified section. Your ad in this magazine for scriptwriting assistance would surely reach someone who would enjoy collaborating on a feature-length project. And if you don't live on either coast you might try advertising in your local alternative newspaper or local film society newsletter.

Once you are satisfied that you have found a coscriptwriter who will satisfy your needs both spiritually and technically, you will want to write out a simple contract that clearly states the facts of the collaboration. Appendix A shows a contract I wrote for my script collaboration with Mike Church on *The Attraction*. In this case, Mike approached me with a body of essays he had written with my style of filmmaking in mind. I liked the writing very much and decided that the best way to proceed with a collaboration on scripting a feature film from the writings was to pay him a small option payment that I could afford ($100 a year) as his salary for the work he had already done. I also stipulated that an additional payment would be given to him if the film was produced, with a sliding scale of increased payment depending on the final shooting budget. I then outlined how our names would read on the credits ("Script by Michael Church and Richard R. Schmidt") and that he would receive an additional credit for his initial writing ("Original story by Michael Church"). In the last paragraph of the contract I stated that Mike would receive 10 percent of the profits of the film if I was producer, outlined when each option payment would be paid, and stated clearly that I had purchased the right to direct, film, edit, and produce the film (originally titled *The Monopole Verification Experiments*) without restriction. With our signatures legally binding our collaboration, we wrote together for a year before completing the script at 118 pages. I greatly enjoyed receiving Mike's latest writing breakthroughs in the mail, working with the new ideas, and then sending him my new writing. And whenever I was creatively stymied, Mike was able to resuscitate the script and vice versa. If you have emerged from a shared writing venture with a finished script, and your friendship is still intact, then you can definitely consider your collaboration a success.

FINALIZING YOUR SCRIPT

Often a commercial scriptwriter must rewrite his or her script several times until it satisfies his producer, agent, and possible stars of the production, but when you write for a feature that you will produce (at used-car prices), the only one you have to satisfy is yourself. Since you will continually be able to make contributions to your film throughout the filming and editing, your script need not be complete in every detail. If you have been honest in your feelings toward your subject matter, and truthful to your intuition while writing, you probably have created at least a viable outline from which to shoot your feature.

After you have completed the first draft of your script, place it aside for a few days and give yourself some distance from the material. Then read it over with an eye toward possible improvements you could make to increase the power and clarity of what you've already written. During this review process you may also think up new scenes, but your main focus is on finalizing your script.

If you are not a professional scriptwriter, it's probably not worth having someone else read your work at this point, since your writing most likely only reveals a tapestry of your ideas and feelings that will be made complete during the remainder of the production process. If, on the other hand, you desire to create a fully commercial script, incorporating all elements of dialogue and story necessary to fulfill a reader's needs, then you must understand that you have actually embarked on the career of a scriptwriter instead of that of a filmmaker. You may see the years slip by as you change a line here, a word there, fine-tuning your script into oblivion. Don't let the writer in you forsake the need to shoot the film. If you are the rare individual who can not only write a commercial script over a several-year period but also take the chance of shooting the script on a hairline budget, then I applaud you. What usually happens, though, is that the several years of scripting somehow work to convince the filmmaker that he or she must go for a bigger production budget. I've seen friends spend several years trying to sell their commercial script, even getting their project to the point of being listed for the next year's production by a major studio, only to see their title erased from the blackboard when their contact at the studio was fired. While creating a finished script in any form is quite an accomplishment, it is important to withhold some measure of self-satisfaction until the film has actually been produced.

Strangely enough, at this final stage of writing a script you also need to ask yourself the same question that readers at major film studios ask: "Do I love this script enough to recommend it for actual production?" Certainly many no-budget scripts written in unique styles, with "no story," wouldn't seem appropriate for production at a major studio whose audience must be derived from a huge cross section of America. Someone at the studio has to love the script being considered for production, love its potential for monetary success. In your case, as a no-budget feature filmmaker, you must be much purer in your demands on the scripted materials. You should love the story, dialogue, characters, locations, the way that the writing touches upon important truths that you want to share with the world. You can love your script because it is uniquely funny or fascinating. You can even love it because it will lead you into new worlds of people and places where access wouldn't normally be granted if you weren't shooting a film. But as a final verification, to make sure that you didn't write your script for the wrong reasons, read over your writing to see if it truly comes from your heart.

In parts of East Africa, when people see each other on the street, they grasp hands and give the familiar greeting, "Do you love yourself today?" If one answers "no," then the other person keeps a firm grip on his or her hand and asks a laundry list of questions. "Is it your husband or wife? Your children? Money? Health?" The questioner holds tight until he or she gets a suitable response. So ask yourself, *"Do you love your script today?"* If not, why not? Is there something wrong with your choice of story? Is the dialogue clunky? Did you write it with a conviction worthy enough to put yourself and your family through the hell (and expense) of production? Now's the time to face your work and make sure that your writing is worth rendering into film. Even if what you've written isn't, in itself, great, you may have a strong enough personal motive for making the film that your drive to express these feelings will override any and all logical reasons for abandoning the project. If that is the case I say, "go for it." Only doubt yourself if your intention is just to earn money or to elevate your status to that of "film director." Tell the truth. I'm holding your hand firmly in mine. Soon we'll be past this uncomfortable moment. Do you love your script today?

THE SHOOTING SCRIPT

The final step toward more completely visualizing your script as a movie is to add instructions for the shoot. You will want to add notes regarding camera angles and movement, possible cuts, needed sound effects, anything that will help you make these important decisions during production. Don't worry if you aren't experienced enough as a filmmaker to be able to write this information down at one sitting. Not all filmmakers can totally visualize their entire film before they shoot. The process of developing the shooting script can take several months as you work in preproduction to find locations and select actors. Rumor has it that Orson Welles screened John Ford's movie *Stagecoach* fifty times before going into production with *Citizen Kane*. We all need inspiration for our work, so if you don't have any idea of how or what to shoot, start by seeing some of the classic movies that are available on videotape. Go to your nearest video store and rent films such as *Grand Illusion, L'Atalante, Zero for Conduct, Le Testament d'Orphée, Modern Times, Metropolis, 8½, Battle of Algiers, Wild Strawberries, Citizen Kane, A Bout de Souffle (Breathless)*, and any film by John Cassavetes. Watch the use of the camera, the framing, the cuts. Listen for the sounds and music that create the atmosphere for the story to unfold. With inspiration high, it's time to move into the world of production.

NOTE: Your final script or creative outline should also be registered with the Writers Guild of America, West, Inc., for copyright protection. Cost for script registration is $20. As with the treatment registration, you should include a title page listing the title of the script, author(s), and blanks for registration date and number.

3

BEGINNING

In the world of big-budget feature filmmaking, only a few of the many hundreds of scripts optioned each year by film companies are chosen for actual production. In 1994 the Writers Guild of America, West, Inc., received more than 27,000 treatments/concepts/scripts to register for copyright protection. Given the fact that less than 500 feature films are usually produced in the United States each year, one can see that the odds are very high that most scripts will remain only scripts. Instead of fighting these nearly impossible odds, the low-budget independent filmmaker has the power to take a script or outline right into production, without anyone else's approval. For the price of a used car—plus enormous amounts of determination, hard work, and enthusiasm—you can make your idea for a feature film into a reality.

For the low-budget filmmaker, the first and most crucial step is telling yourself and your friends that you are going to make a feature film. Because the idea of making a film always generates excitement, you'll probably find that people around you will respond with laughter, amazement, and then great enthusiasm. For a while, you may feel that your friends believe in your film more strongly than you do, but as you go on talking about it, the project will start taking on a life of its own. When people start volunteering to become involved in your production, you'll realize that by wishing out loud you've already come a long way toward willing your feature film into existence. At that point, you'll need to do a little reality check.

DEFINING YOUR PRODUCTION LIMITATIONS

Is it really this easy to begin your feature film production? The answer is yes—as long as your film concept and script are tailored to the limitations of a used-car budget (see chapter 1) and both you and everyone involved in the film are prepared to work within the special constraints of a super-low-budget production.

If you're making a feature film at used-car prices, almost all of your budget will be eaten up by the irreducible costs of renting equipment and purchasing and processing enough filmstock to produce at least seventy minutes of usable footage. Even with every price break imaginable from the lab, you shouldn't expect to be able to shoot more than fourteen 400' rolls of film. This means that you will be able to shoot two and a half hours of film, out of which you will cut a feature somewhere between seventy and ninety minutes long. Because of this two-to-one shooting ratio, you must attempt to shoot every scene right on the first try and then move on to the next shot. If there is a technical problem or a disastrous mistake by actors, then and *only* then can you afford to reshoot the scene. You and everyone who works with you must be prepared, both psychologically and practically, to do the best possible job with this nerve-racking shooting ratio.

To be able to afford to rent a high-quality 16-mm camera (Eclair, Aaton, Arriflex, CP-16) that delivers the sharp and consistent image necessary for potential sales or possible blowup to 35-mm, you'll probably have to do most of your filming on weekends when special rates are available. Many equipment-rental outfits will offer weekend rentals (from Friday afternoon to Monday noon) for a one-day rental price. If you're shooting on weekends, your location must be easily accessible to all the people involved with the production. And you'll have to use your shooting time on location very efficiently to minimize the costs of travel, food, and equipment rental.

Even with all these economies, you'll have very little (if any) money in your budget to pay actors or a production crew. Is this an insurmountable problem? Not at all. But it does require some careful planning—and some powerful persuasive techniques—from the beginning.

The most minimal crew for a feature film that requires lighting and sound recording will have to include the filmmaker/cameraman (and after reading chapter 5, you should have gained enough confidence to shoot your film yourself), a good soundperson with sound-recording equipment, and a camera assistant to help the filmmaker place lights and take light readings, sync up scenes with a clap board, load and clean the camera between takes, and cope with dozens of other production chores. The sound recordist is usually the most expensive member of a low-budget crew, and he or she shouldn't be expected to work on anything except getting the best possible sound. It would be nice to be able to afford a production manager to organize all the details of the shoot for you, but in this super-low-budget situation, you'll have to do this yourself, perhaps with the help of your camera assistant. You'll also have to edit your feature yourself, with some input from other people you invite to view and critique your rough cut.

Fortunately, many professional actors, as well as most amateurs, are willing to do almost anything, including paying their own expenses, to star in a feature film of any budget—as long as they respect the story and the filmmaker. Still, it's wise to pay each of the cast members, as well as every member of the crew, at least a small daily stipend of $20 or so to help insure that they will take the production seriously enough to show up on time every day, with their equipment or costumes, ready to work hard for the production.

This small daily stipend, which doesn't even approach the minimum wage, will not in itself be enough to convince expert cast and crew members that they should give all their energy to your production. You'll have to give them a share in the potential profits of the feature so that they'll at least have the assurance of being well paid if the film is a success.

PROFIT SHARING

Profit sharing is the most powerful persuasive tool of the film-maker whose budget lacks the vital ingredient of ready cash. Once you realize that the only way you can make your film is with the help of talented people you can't afford to pay, you should be able to give away a large percentage of your potential profits and feel good about it. If you are receiving all or most of your small budget from one or more investors who have demanded 50 percent of the profits from the film, you may have to give away half or more of your remaining 50 percent. But if this is what it takes to make your film, you should have no qualms about doing it. Profit sharing is the only financial incentive you have to offer potential cast and crew members.

And it can be a powerful one. When I assigned my soundman friend Neelon Crawford 5 percent of the profits of *1988—The Remake*, he was very impressed, because he'd never heard of a soundman receiving even 1 percent of the profits of a feature. And I felt good about giving him a generous share of the film because I knew I would have to depend heavily upon his expert sound recording for that production.

It's fun to be generous with numbers on a piece of paper, but keep in mind that low-budget features have been known to earn millions of dollars. If yours is next year's big hit, all those points of profit will turn into cash. My friend Wayne Wang gave most of the profit points from his hit feature *Chan Is Missing* to the cast and crew, leaving himself with under 20 percent of his own film. Be careful! But if you are the kind of filmmaker/director who believes in working your cast and crew until they are ready to drop, you had better be prepared to give away a lion's share.

DEFERRED PAYMENT

Some professional cast and crew members may request that you pay them their usual high salary in the form of a "deferred payment," so that they will be guaranteed their salary from first monies received from the finished film (see Appendix C, deal memorandum for *Morgan's Cake*). Contracts vary as to exactly when the deferred payments will be forthcoming. The best and most honorable way for a producer to regard these payments is as real debts of the film, to be paid out of first monies received by the film company, without any deductions subtracted for various distribution or operating costs. If the producer/director has worked for free alongside everyone else, he or she would not want to spend weekends writing checks for everyone while sitting penniless wondering how to pay the rent, and must include his or her own deferred salary in the contract. Once the schedule of payments is agreed upon, and it is written in the contract that your soundman/woman will receive $750 per day for on-location recording (the going rate for top sound people), the cameraman/woman $1,000 per day, and so on, you should be able to afford the best technicians and actors that money (or, in this case, lack of money) can buy.

Sometimes you will want to write a contract that includes a combination of deferred salary and profit percents as incentives for working on your production. Looking over the contract for *Emerald Cities* (Appendix B) you will notice that not only is there a list of percents to be paid in the event that the film is profitable, but also that deferred cash salaries are indicated for some members of cast and crew. Had I not been able to pay less than half of the camera rental fee up front to Bill Kimberlin, I couldn't have afforded to shoot on location in Death Valley. And in some cases, like the deferred salary for soundman Nick Bertoni, the small amount of payment reflects my need to give him a monetary "gift," not the actual salary he could command on another production. He was helping me out of his love for a friend, and money was never an issue. At best, the writing of your contract will be an outpouring of love and thanks in the form of monetary rewards for those people who help you make your film become a reality.

Some film producers would rather not deal with the idea of being caught in a situation of paying percents of profit from their film, writing checks quarterly, and at times getting phone calls in the middle of the night from workers wondering when they will be paid again. If you don't like the idea of being the focus of cast and crew members for the rest of your life (if your film is a hit), then assign "top dollar" amounts for their deferred payments, and honor these production debts from first monies earned by the finished feature.

THE CONTRACT

The best tool I know for beginning the process of willing your feature film into existence is the contract. Writing a contract forces the filmmaker to start making the kind of decisions that will result in a concrete plan of action. What will be the name of the production company (under what title will you be doing business)? How much will the film cost to shoot on location? What will be the total budget, including editing and print costs? What cast and crew members will I need and what payment will they receive, in cash or percentage points, for their participation?

By thinking seriously enough about all these issues to be able to draft a contract, you will be forced to develop a detailed plan for organizing your film project. And once it is written, the contract will become a powerful force for conjuring the film into existence. By transforming your hopes and dreams into a legal document, the contract will help generate the momentum that will carry your film through to completion. Here's an example: When I wrote the contract for *Emerald Cities*, I didn't actually have the $5,000 I'd committed myself to raising in order to begin production with a five-day shoot starting on or about December 15, 1979. As this date approached and the pressure on me increased, I worked harder and harder to raise that money, asking everyone I could think of for help, even selling my used car to force a cash flow. Amazingly, a series of minor miracles eventually brought me the money I needed to begin production by the deadline. Without the self-created but very real pressure exerted by that contract, *Emerald Cities* might have remained only a dream.

Besides serving as a powerful incentive for the filmmaker himself, the contract is also a very effective device for persuading other people, from potential investors to prospective cast and crew members, that the film is a viable project, not merely an idle fantasy. When I came to the first class of my CCAC Feature Filmmaking at Used-Car Prices workshop with a contract that every class member was to sign, it immediately convinced them that, although we were meeting as a class, we were actually agreeing to collaborate in the serious endeavor of creating a feature film (see Appendix D). A carefully drafted contract will have the same effect on all the people you'll need to help you make your film.

Each contract for a feature film must be carefully designed to fit the particular needs of the production. For a low-budget film, the contract should be simplified to be as straightforward as the production itself. Although each contract will reflect a different set of production needs, all have a number of important features in common.

CONTRACT CHECKLIST

☐ The contract uses legal terms that are universally accepted.

☐ The filmmaker is identified as *doing business as* a "film company" for the production of a feature film *tentatively entitled* _____ (*name of film here*).

☐ The film is described as 16-mm gauge (or other applicable format), color or black and white, and as a feature-length motion picture film.

☐ Everyone who will participate in the production of the film is listed by name and job title, and the amount of payment to each person is clearly stated.

☐ The contract stipulates that those people working on the production will *not* receive any payment unless they complete their jobs.

☐ Usually the length of the shooting schedule is declared and identified by dates, as is the total amount of time needed to complete the film. It is important to state this timetable so that members of the cast and crew will know when their participation in your project is required, and it's also important to any investors who must know the (tentative) release date of your film for tax purposes. The word *approximate* is used when describing these dates so that the filmmaker is legally protected from being overly optimistic.

☐ Each person who commits to becoming involved in the production has signed the contract on the line with his or her name printed below, and has written the date and location of signature.

☐ The contract lists the order of payback to investors, lab, cast and crew, etc.

The most important words in a contract are *upon completion of services* and *gross* or *net*. You must include a clause stating that if the work isn't completed, then the person who fails to do the work will not share in the rewards. And if your cast and crew are to receive a percentage of the *gross* profits, they will receive their money from the total amount of dollars earned, before any is spent on overhead costs and other expenses. If your helpers receive a portion of the *net* profits from your film, then they receive their percent of profits after you deduct reasonable expenses for such things as limited promotion and advertising, travel to a few film festivals, and replacement print costs.

If, as I've suggested, you are drawing up a contract as your first major step in the filmmaking process, your first draft will have to approximate some entries such as the length of the shoot and the budget for the film. You will probably begin with a list of job descriptions and rates of pay for cast and crew members, with blanks left for the names of the people you will later find to fill these roles in your production. If you decide to use my contracts as models for your film, you should still consult with a lawyer who is knowledgeable in motion picture law or at least in contract law. Tell him the amount of your budget and ask if he can help you draw up a very basic contract. Or at least let him review the contract you draw up on your own using my examples. Because a contract must stand up to the possibility that a film might earn hundreds of thousands of dollars, it is very important that every point accurately reflects your wishes.

The contracts for my first two features were drawn up by a lawyer in San Francisco who specialized in motion picture law. When I first went to him and announced that I was planning to produce a feature film for $11,000, he was shocked, saying that he had never heard of such a low budget. He then helped me with the contract, for a token fee of $100 (a portion of his hourly rate).

BUDGET

After you have drawn up your contract, the next step is to prepare a detailed budget, so that you will be able to plan exactly how much you can do—and how many corners you will have to cut— to produce your film with the amount of money you have or can raise. To help you see how to fine-tune the budget for your own film, I'll take you through the various steps I went through with my CCAC class in the summer of 1984, before we finally settled on a production plan that would allow us to do our film within our $6,000 budget.

Film production prices are continually subject to change, but one thing never changes: To create a feature film at used-car prices, you *must* get the maximum price break from your lab. To do this low-budget filming you must let people know you are making a feature film for the same price as the average American used car—$6,000. After they stop laughing, they will probably do everything in their power to help you succeed.

FILMING COSTS

As I've mentioned in earlier chapters, most of your used-car budget will be eaten up by irreducible costs: equipment rentals, minimum salaries, food and transportation costs, and filmstock, with the biggest bite out of your budget coming from lab expenses. While filmstock may be purchased from the lab, a large savings can be made by dealing directly with the distributor (Kodak, Fuji, etc.) unless the lab offers a blanket deal on all lab costs for your project (discussed later in this chapter). After the lab develops your footage, charging you the "processing" fee of so many cents per foot, you will probably need to have them print another copy of your film, a low-quality "work print" from which you can edit your feature without the risk of scratching or damaging your precious original footage. Because the lab must supply filmstock, make a contact print from your original, and process the results, the work print is very expensive.

There is also some expenditure required for the production of a high-quality sound track. After the soundperson records your location "sync" sound on ¼" tape using the high-quality Nagra recorder, these tapes must be "transferred" to 16-mm gauge sound track ("mag track") for editing purposes.

Here's our first estimate for the filming costs alone.*

SHOOTING BUDGET (16MM)

14 rolls (400') Color Negative filmstock ($102/roll) $1,428.00
14 roll ¼" sound recording tape ($4.59/roll) .... $ 64.26
Camera rental package (2 weekends @ $250 ea.) .... $ 500.00
   (includes camera, magazines, battery belt, lights,
   light meter, lenses, power cables, tripod, everything
   needed to shoot)
Soundperson with Nagra recorder ($200/weekend) ...... $ 400.00
Camera assistant ($100/weekend) .... $ 200.00
Actors' fees ($100/weekend for 2 actors) .... $ 400.00
Food for 2 weekends for cast and crew (60 meals) ..... $ 250.00
Transportation (gas) .... $ 30.00
Processing of filmstock ($.15/ft.) 5,600' .... $ 840.00
Work print for editing ($.215/ft.) 5,600' $1,204.00
Transfer cost from ¼" tape to mag track ($50/hr.) .... $ 150.00
5 1,200' rolls mag track for ¼" transfer ($50/roll) .... $ 250.00
                                                        $5,716.26

Just to complete our two-weekend shoot and process the results we would have already spent $5,716.26 of our $6,000 budget. And we haven't begun to budget editing and determine final projection print cost, which usually alone runs above $2,000. Even with actors handling their own makeup, costumes, and props, we are at

---

* Prices quoted in shooting and editing budgets represent "rock bottom" costs that the filmmaker must fight for, especially at the lab, in order to afford to produce a future film at used-car prices.

least a couple thousand dollars over our budget even before we add in editing costs.

Could we retrieve the $1,000 total we assigned for the sound-person, camera assistant, and actors and still have a production? Only by deferring these salaries could we hope to complete such a low-budget feature film. And if each person brought his or her own lunch and ate breakfast before leaving home for the filming, so the production only paid for a good dinner and beverages on location, we could probably reduce the food budget to four dinners for five people (twenty meals) at a cost of $7 per dinner and save $110. Each person who worked on the production could still receive a $20-a-day salary so that at least the filming wouldn't cost them money out of their own pockets. For the four days of filming, that would cost the production $80 per person. Two actors, a soundperson, and a camera assistant would then cost the production only $320 for two weeks, saving $680 from the $1,000 originally allotted for salaries. With this savings of cash from the salaries and food costs ($680 + $110 = $790) plus the initial remaining funds ($6,000 − $5,716.26 = $283.74), we would still have only $1,073.74 remaining from our $6,000 budget, not really enough to complete the film.

If each person in the cast and crew was generous enough to forfeit his or her salary and work for the $20-per-day stipend, then they would each deserve to share in the profits of the film. Each of my features abounds in examples of this type of profit sharing, and I'm sure the reader will be able to offer his or her helpers a generous share of the pie. I gave 60 percent away on *A Man, a Woman, and a Killer*, 82 percent on *1988—The Remake*, and 75 percent on *Emerald Cities*. Without my friends' help on each of these features, I would not have been able to make any of my films.

With lab and filmstock costs rising all the time, it's obvious that the first-time no-budget feature filmmaker can't really afford to shoot in color. With Kodak 7222 black-and-white negative stock ($56.80/400' roll), the cost of fourteen rolls is reduced from $1,428 (color negative) to $795.20, saving the production a crucial $632.80 (lab fees of processing and work printing are relatively identical for black and white or color). This raises our sum of available funds to $1,706.54, at least within range of our $2,000 needed for editing costs.

Another possible way to reduce our budget is to forgo our work print, saving $1,204 (5,600' @ .215). If your film will be made up of several long takes, which reduces the actual handling of the negative film, this option could be seriously considered. (Because long takes can be pieced together into a film without the considerable handling that scenes with many short takes require, there is less risk of damage.) But if your first-time effort will require a lot of editing to overcome the vast quantity of unknowns you will most certainly face, then you should spend the money on a work print to avoid damaging the original footage. Another possibility is to make your work print only after you've eliminated all the original footage you know is unusable. This could save close to a third of the work print budget. Using this projection, we could add another $400 to our production budget, giving us up to $2,106.54 for editing and final print costs of a black-and-white feature.

EDITING COSTS

Once you have in your hands the work print and mag track from your film, you should feel confident that it will be possible to edit your feature together regardless of the obstacles that lack of money can present. After you learn how to make a tape splice and are able to "sync up" your picture and sound track (see chapter 6 on editing), you should have identification numbers printed on your sync rolls ("edge numbers") to insure that you can't lose your sync during editing. With a number at each foot of synced up film and mag track, you have the capability of shifting footage without worry. Unless you have shot your film in long takes that require little or no editing, I recommend spending this money for your peace of mind. The greatest expense of editing may be the rental of a flatbed editing machine if many months are needed to figure out your complicated film. This machine shows you your film on a screen and plays your sound track, so that you can see how your edit is progressing. Once your film has been edited into the most cohesive and dynamic form possible you will need to "mix" your sound track, adjusting the volume (sound level) and tone (equal-ization) of every shot. This procedure can also become very ex-pensive, but with the help of this book you should accomplish the mix in around seven hours for a feature-length film. This mix pre-pares the sound track for your *projection print*, referred to by the lab as your "answer print." The picture is prepared for printing by matching your original footage to each piece of edited work print and splicing the original together in a "checkerboard" pattern on two separate "A" and "B" rolls, using black leader between shots (see the section entitled "Conforming Original for Printing" in chapter 6). The answer print is the final result of your best picture and sound quality, ready for projection, and is usually the largest lab expense.

Now that you are somewhat familiar with the terms used for editing procedures, let's look at editing costs we would normally encounter after shooting is completed:

EDITING BUDGET (16MM)

Edge number 5,600' picture, 5,600' mag track .... $ 168.00
   ($.015/ft.)
Flatbed editing machine ($600/month for 3 months) $1,800.00
Titles (shot on location while filming) .... $ 0
Editing tape (10 rolls picture tape @ $6.50/roll) .... $ 65.00
               (10 rolls sound tape @ $9.50/roll) .... $ 95.00
Sound mix (7 hrs. @ $125/hr., plus $150 for mag) $1,025.00
Conforming (matching original to work print $2,700.00
   @ $30/hr.)
Black leader (3000' for conforming "AB" rolls) .... $ 300.00
Answer print ("A" and "B" rolls, sound, 80 min., ... $1,396.80
   2,880' B&W @ $.485/ft.)
                                                                   $7,549.80

Again it is all too obvious that we are way over budget. And while there is no way to erase the cost of our answer print, there are, fortunately, ways to reduce some of the other editing costs.

We really can't afford to pay $1,800 for the rent of a flatbed editing machine for three months. One way of reducing this cost might be to edit at a nearby art school or college film department by enrolling in a class. Hopefully, you will be able to complete your feature film by editing on the school's flatbed machine after hours while, at the same time, getting college credit to satisfy parents' or career demands. You may be able to book time at "alternative" editing facilities such as the Film Arts Foundation in San Francisco, where you could edit on a flatbed for a half day (twelve hours of day or night) for a fee of $25 if you're an FAF member. By grabbing small amounts of affordable editing time you would be able to constantly refine your film as your budget permits.

BUILD AN EDITING BENCH

Another possible solution is to build an editing bench in your house for a cost of about $150. The drawing on page 54 shows the dimensions of an editing bench I built to fit in a space usually reserved for a washer and dryer. This 64"-long editing bench represents the shortest-length bench possible that can still accommodate the largest 2,000' reels along with editing equipment (synchronizer, Moviescope, sound reader). The simplest way I found to build my bench is to make careful measurements of the space it will occupy and have the 2"-by-4" structural boards precut at the lumberyard. (Make sure your measurements are, if anything, ⅛" larger than the space, to insure a tight fit. If your editing bench isn't enclosed by two walls, you will need to add a support leg; see photo on page 54.) After the boards are cut, lay them on the ground as they will be nailed together, to check them for overall measurements and to make sure that boards with the same length are cut correctly. Once home, you can nail your 2 × 4s together with glue on each joint and nail the whole structure to the walls. If you set the height of the 2 × 4 structure at around 34", then your countertop will be about 38" from the floor. This has been a good position for me (at 6' tall) for either sitting on a stool or standing at the editing bench.

Once your 2 × 4 structure is nailed into place, the next step is to laminate the Formica top onto your precut plywood top (most

Rick Schmidt's editing bench built into washer/dryer alcove.

2" × 4" wood structure for "do-it-yourself" editing bench.

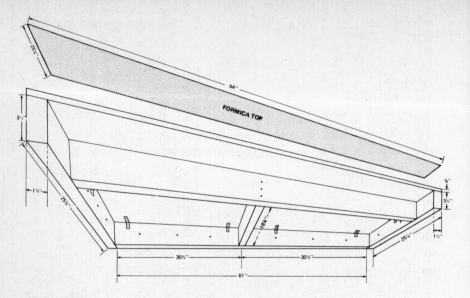

Editing bench.

Sound speaker, Moviescope and sound reader, synchronizer, rewinds—everything needed to edit at home.

lumberyards recommend "pressboard" for lamination). After applying contact cement to both the bottom of the Formica and the top of the pressboard (make sure there is adequate ventilation—working outside with a strong fan blowing the fumes away from your face), let the glue dry to the touch, then carefully fit the pieces together, making sure that there is an overlap of ¼" to ½" of Formica all around the edge of the pressboard. After the glue is dry, trim around the Formica with an "edge trimmer," making the Formica's edge flush to the shape of the pressboard. Place the laminated Formica countertop on your structure and screw together with brackets from underneath. All that's left to do to complete your editing bench is to drill holes for screwing your rewinds to the surface, placing them at least 10" (to their center measurement) in from the side walls, and nail on trim to the counter edge.

LIST OF MATERIALS (EDITING BENCH)

1-¾" pressboard sheet 25¼" × 64"
Board lumber (No. 2 and better grade):
   2-2" × 4" × 61"
   2-2" × 4" × 25¼"
   1-2" × 4" × 16¼"
1 Formica sheet (white) 26" × 65" (trim to pressboard)
Contact cement (1 quart), cheap brush
"Edge trimmer" (cost approx. $35) for Formica
3½" nails, white glue, brackets for top
1-½" × 1½" × 64" (wooden trim for front of counter)
1" finishing nails and filler for nail holes
1 pint white acrylic paint for trim and 2" × 4" structure

If you don't like carpentry, then perhaps you could purchase a sturdy table that would satisfy these needs. To edit with this kind of arrangement you would need to purchase (or rent) rewinds to reel the film from head to tail; a Moviescope to view the images on a small, 4" screen; a sound reader and small speaker to hear the sound from your mag track; a "synchronizer" to keep picture and sound track synced up; reels to hold the film and mag track; locks to keep the reels together while rewinding; spacers between reels; and small accessories such as a marker pen, grease pencil, razor blade, and a tape splicer. I edited my first two features with this basic equipment, screening the footage as often as possible to check my results. You should be able to purchase the equipment listed above, in used condition, for about $400 to $600. Check ads in film newsletters and magazines (*Release Print, Independent Film and Video Monthly*) and on bulletin boards at your lab, nearby film school, FAF, AIVF, or 911 Media Center in Seattle, to find the best deal on equipment.

The cost of a sound mix is an expense that is almost impossible to avoid. I've found that sometimes the cheapest mixing can end up costing you more money and aggravation in the long run. I'll discuss this whole topic more fully in the editing chapter, but for now I want to emphasize that a high-quality sound mix is vital to the film you are producing. Sometimes it is possible to gain access to a mixing studio in a film school, but without the help of some-one who is a skilled technician, your results will surely be disappointing.

One large cost that we *can* radically reduce is the $2,700 budgeted for conforming the original for printing. Although cutting the original film and splicing it together for printing is a task that requires careful attention to detail, and usually takes a couple of weeks to accomplish for a feature-length film, it is certainly within each person's reach to learn the process. In the editing chapter I'll show you how to do it yourself—and save almost $3,000.

Working within our total used-car budget of $6,000, even with the reductions of cost in flatbed editing and conforming, the $2,106.54 allotted for editing our film barely covers the cost of a sound mix and one answer print. It's time to take another look at the total budget, including the cost of the shoot, to determine what other reductions we can make without jeopardizing the success of our project. If we only shot twelve 400' rolls of film instead of the fourteen rolls as budgeted, the savings from two fewer rolls (800') of filmstock, processing, and work print would be $405.60. And with this twenty-two-minute reduction in footage we could cut back on mag track needed for transfer from ¼" sound rolls, saving another $50. Some money would be saved from edge numbering cost, now that there would be less work print and mag stock. Also, if we budgeted only one roll each of picture and sound splicing tape ($16) instead of the total ten rolls possibly needed during editing, we would release $144 to the overall budget. And while it's almost impossible to edit a feature in a couple of weeks, let's budget some twelve-hour "half days" on a flatbed machine, giving the opportunity for syncing up and rough assembly of the footage. One final saving can be made if we reduce the length of our answer print from eighty minutes to seventy minutes, the minimum length most film festivals regard as "feature length."

Although these savings can't help us to afford the full price of an expensive, high-quality sound mix, the little bits of added cash should supply an "emergency cash fund" during the shoot, using cash that remains as a savings for the mix or additional flatbed editing time. What's important is that the budget allows the film-maker to shoot the film and reach a point in the editing where the rough assemblage can generate the necessary inspiration needed to combat financial and creative problems ahead.

At this point let's take a look at our reworked budget:

SHOOTING/EDITING BUDGET (16MM)

12 rolls of B&W Negative 7222 stock (4,800')	$ 681.60
Processing/work printing ¾ of the stock (3,600')	$1,314.00
12 rolls of ¼" sound tape (1 roll per filmstock)	$ 55.08
4 rolls (1,200' ea.) of mag track	$ 200.00
Camera package rental (lights, etc.) 2 weekends	$ 500.00
Soundperson with Nagra recorder/mikes (daily stipend)	$ 80.00
2 actors' fees (daily stipend)	$ 160.00
Camera assistant (daily stipend)	$ 80.00
Food (4 dinners for 5 people)	$ 140.00
Transportation (gas)	$ 30.00
Edge numbers (3,600' work print, 3,600' mag track)	$ 108.00
Flatbed editing machine rental (10 12-hr. sessions)	$ 250.00
Editing tape (1 roll picture tape, 1 roll sound tape)	$ 16.00
Titles (shot on location)	$ 0
Black leader for conforming	$ 300.00

Conforming (done by filmmaker) .... $ 0
B&W answer print (70 min./2,500') $1,212.50
                                                                 $5,127.18
Sound mix, miscellaneous costs, taxes* .... $ 872.82
                                                                 $6,000.00

The creative filmmaker/scavenger should be able to reduce this pared-down budget even more by gaining free access to needed film equipment (camera, Nagra, lights, mag transfer machine, flatbed machine, splicer, etc.) that sits unused 95 percent of the time in film schools, art schools, in closets of individual owners. If one of your collaborators is currently enrolled in a school or college that offers film classes, then it's a good bet that you can shave another $1,000 off your budget, making money available for a good sound mix. At our CCAC Feature Film Workshop we were fortunate to have the use of an Eclair camera with extra magazine, 12–120 lens, Lowel lights, Tota kit lights, Nagra recorder and microphones, transfer machine for resolving ¼" sound tape to mag sound track, Showchron flatbed for editing, and free help from fellow collaborators. CCAC also supplied us with free mag track and ¼" sound tape, splicing tape for editing picture/sound, screening facilities, and conference room. Although the students had to pay a hefty tuition and a $650 lab deposit for the project, there was an obvious advantage to collaborating on a feature at a well-supplied film department such as CCAC's. Whatever your circumstances, the important thing is to get a good start on your feature with whatever funds you can raise initially and take each stage of the production as it comes.

RAISING MONEY FOR YOUR FEATURE

After you have a clear idea of the financial needs of your project, you may want to start looking for some investors. When you ask people to invest money in your feature film at used-car prices, usually it takes a few moments for the laughter to stop and the

* Except in states such as Montana, which don't have a state sales tax, the filmmaker must be prepared to pay taxes on goods and services.

questions to begin. Is it a *real* film? It's so low-budget! How will your film earn money? When will I get my money back? If it *is* good, will I get my name in the credits? And so on. I've found that the best policy is *the truth*. Yes, it's a *real* film. No big stars, no expensive car crashes, but a sincere attempt to portray something important on film. The film will earn some money by being shown at the several film showcases and museums across America (see lists in chapter 7). And if we're very fortunate, the film will be shown at European film festivals and will then stand a chance of being purchased by more progressive television programmers such as those at Channel Four in London. Yes, we'll be happy to put your name in the credits if you invest a major amount of the needed budget.

Any prospective investor should be reminded that filmmaking is, and always has been, a form of gambling. There is no way to know ahead of time if a film will be a financial success or not, but even if it fails, at least they'll come out with a tax deduction. For family members and friends, a more important point is that they are helping you create a unique film that may help expand the understanding of people on this planet. You are willing to perform the service of producing a film with minimal resources, and you are asking them (your parents, friends, guardian angels) for their support.

If you are approached by a serious investor, that backer will want to know what he or she will get in return for financial risk. If the investor gives you the entire budget for your film, the usual agreement is that he or she receives one half of the profit points (50 percent) in the film as well as being paid back for the investment plus 10 percent interest per annum. For investments of less than the full amount, it is up to the filmmaker/producer to set a price for each percentage point of the profits. For smaller investors such as family members and friends, you can give 1 percent of the film away for each $500 invested and only spend 12 percent to get your $6,000.

If an investor wants to put up the entire budget of your used-car production, then it is important to add back into the budget the salaries of the actors, soundperson, cinematographer, camera assistant, and probably yourself. Otherwise, if the investor gets half of the percentage points, you could be left with few points after you've paid your cast and crew with points instead of cash. If an investor is receiving 50 percent of the profits of your super-low-budget feature, you would have to raise the budget amount to the $15,000–$25,000 range to pay everybody something and still have 25 percent of the profits for yourself.

For our film *The Last Roommate,* we set a price of $650 for each percentage point of profits. Since the four directors were splitting whatever points were not given away to the cast and crew, there were very few points left to sell (see Appendix D). We were all working for free and the students were investing lab fees of $650 in the project, so it was necessary that each person be given a suitable amount of percentage points for his or her labors.

If you have drawn up a professional contract, worded properly, that clearly states your plans to produce a feature film, family, friends, or other interested investors will look at this document and see that you are serious and businesslike. You should also meet with someone at your lab and have him or her write out a commitment to an estimate of prices for your film. This price quote from the lab will give the interested parties the impression that you are moving ahead on the project, with or without them—and they will be right. You may also want to take pictures of your prospective actors and use these photos, along with a copy of your script, contract, lab quote, projection of earnings from showcases and possible TV sales, and background information on qualifications of key members of cast and crew (yourself included) as part of your "presentation package." While it is impossible to afford the cost of an expensively printed cover with professionally designed graphics for a presentation folder, you should be able to at least have the title of your project typeset (cost: around $20) to add some zip to your letterhead when presenting your project to an investor. All these things help to give the impression that you are a professional, so don't show anyone poorly typed pages or out-of-focus photos. Make sure that everything you present is absolutely as impressive as you can possibly make it. If you are able to present your film project as a legitimate investment, an investor might be able to write off a trip to a European film festival where your feature is being presented and recover some of his or her small investment in tax deductions.

The most essential principle of making a feature film at used-car prices is that lack of money shouldn't be able to stop your production. If you can afford to drive a car, you should be able to make a feature film. By persuading friends or relatives to part with a couple of $500 investments, perhaps selling your car and taking the bus or car pool to work, and sprinkling money toward the project from your salary over the next year, you should be able to produce your feature cheaply, with your own resources. And don't worry about not having the entire budget in your hands when beginning the project. Once you have a work print—something concrete that you can show to potential investors (relatives, friends) —you'll probably find it much easier to raise the money you need to complete the film. Also, by making a high-quality video copy of your work print and synced sound track (see sections on VHS and ¾" video copies, chapter 7) you could apply for grants and enter competitions that offer completion funds as well as support for new works.

NOTE: For even feature film projects at used-car prices, investors may require a "limited partnership agreement" that includes "purchase offer" papers, so that you and your film attorney can supply him or her with a K-1 form at tax time. While it will cost the film-maker around $100 to file the partnership papers, and up to $700 for a certified public accountant knowledgeable in film law to prepare the tax returns each year for the partnership (based on your declared costs of the film and any money earned over the years), you should save thousands of dollars by making a copy of the California limited partnership papers I used to raise three $5,000 investments for the $15,000 budget of *Morgan's Cake* (see Appendixes H and I). Be cautioned that the partnership and purchase offer papers *must* be revised by a lawyer in order to conform to current federal and state requirements, and should only be used as a time-saving model for the lawyer to follow when drawing up new agreements for your particular project.

GRANTS

Many organizations offer grants for production of independent films. These funding bodies usually require a sample of your previous film work, or at least a script of the proposed project. Check out your local and national filmmaking magazines (the *Independent Film and Video Monthly*, FAF's *Release Print, 911* in Seattle) for lists of foundations that fund independent works, and apply to as many as possible.

The National Endowment for the Arts (NEA) has grants for film/ video production, in the range of $5,000 to $35,000, offered through their Media Arts program.* Write to the National Endowment for the Arts, Media Arts, 1100 Pennsylvania Avenue, N.W., Washington, D.C. 20506, or call (202) 682-5400. The deadline for this grant is September/October of each year, so it is important to write for applications early. Listings of other sources of grants are also available in most public libraries, and many large university libraries offer computer searches of grants in every discipline, including film, for a small fee. I highly recommend checking what sources of funds are available. But be careful that you don't become a professional grant writer instead of a filmmaker.

I have been fortunate to receive grants from both the NEA and the American Film Institute (its Independent Filmmaker's granting program is now discontinued). Without this support I would have taken quite a bit longer to finish my features. *1988—The Remake* was begun with a grant from the American Film Institute for $9,918, and the film was helped to completion with a grant for $7,500 from the National Endowment for the Arts. By the time I was struggling to complete the feature I owed so much money that the grant from NEA was completely swallowed by the lab, but without the money I would have had to stop working. Still, you can't depend on winning these grants, even when you have an earthshaking concept. Thousands of filmmakers apply each year for the few grants offered. Apply, and then continue to battle your low-budget feature into existence with your own resources.

* The NEA's value as a funding source for the arts has fallen under attack in the 1990s. Hopefully this vital program still exists by the time of this publication.

I can truthfully say that money has never really stopped me from making my features. I've been slowed down at times almost to a dead halt, but once I've begun shooting (and editing) I find I can maintain the push to complete the task. To make films, I've used money I've earned, sold family antiques, received grants, borrowed money from relatives and friends, charged many thousands at the lab. I've even gone a year without paying rent (thanks to my generous landlord). If you believe that nothing can stop you from making your film, not even money will hold you back.

EMERGENCY SELF-FUNDING

NOTE: If you are the type of super-logical filmmaker (film buff, scriptwriter, producer-to-be) who can now talk yourself out of your feature filmmaking fantasies because the whole idea seems just too complex and expensive (even $6,000 is a big chunk of money), you may want to override the negativity and jump start your production now by following the steps listed below:

Step #1: Phone Kodak "Film Center" at 1-800-874-6867.

Step #2: Order twelve 400' rolls of either Kodak 7276 B&W Plus X reversal or 7222 B&W Negative filmstock (Kodak offers an all-night filmstock ordering service called "Shoot Saver" which guarantees delivery of filmstock by 10 A.M. the following day for all orders charged by phone before 2 A.M. Eastern time. While stock and shipping costs are more expensive, make the nighttime call if it helps to overcome inertia).

Step #3: When the shipment of filmstock arrives, immediately place the rolls in your refrigerator to assure cool storage, and place a note on the outside of the refrigerator with the date, one year hence, inscribed in bold letters.

Step #4: Before the stock spoils (Kodak guarantees stock for one year), get an idea, write a script, round up a cameraperson, sound recordist, and actors, select locations, confirm shooting dates. You *will* shoot your feature before the expiration of that filmstock. (No logical person would ever allow more than $600 worth of filmstock to go to waste!)

4

PREPRODUCTION: PREPARING TO SHOOT A FEATURE

Preproduction begins the period of time when the filmmaker turns his or her *idea* of making a film into a *reality*. While most Hollywood productions can afford to spend many months in preparation for their expensive productions, the independent, no-budget filmmaker must gather all necessary components for the shoot in a matter of weeks. The activities of preproduction include, but are not limited to, the following: final selection of cast and crew, signing the contract for profit sharing, rewriting and rehearsing the script or improvisational outline, reserving all equipment (camera, sound gear, lights, etc.), purchasing filmstock, scouting and selecting locations, gathering props and other production accessories, cementing the schedule for shooting, last-minute money raising, and making sure that *everything* you need to make your film is in your hands by the morning of the shoot. All these details of the filming must be nailed down within a short period of time so that you will be able to shoot your feature before the talented members of your cast and crew are lured away from your production by "real" jobs (jobs that pay). If your actors and technicians are crazy enough to have already agreed to work on the deferred-payment plan, then maybe there is hope that they will also be crazy enough to turn down a good paying job to help you shoot your film . . . but I wouldn't bet on it. The filmmaker who is attempting to make a feature film on very little money must limit the period of preproduction to a month at most, so that his or her intensity of purpose keeps all the core members of the production interested in the project. It is also through this intensity and desperation in light of a quickly approaching deadline that the filmmaker is best able to create the miracles of preproduction that are necessary to every no-budget feature.

Each one of my feature projects has benefited from last-minute miracles that occurred during the month of preproduction. On my first feature, *A Man, a Woman, and a Killer*, my collaborators, Wayne Wang and Dick Richardson, and I found no houses available for rent in Mendocino, California, where we planned to shoot. I had already spent half of our shooting budget of $5,900 paying Wayne and Dick $500 each for two weeks of scripting, purchasing forty-five 400' rolls of Plus-X Reversal filmstock, and making a deposit to soundman Neelon Crawford and his assistant, Lee Serie, and felt desperate to secure this location with only a week to go before shooting. I suggested we drive to the ocean side of town and look for For Rent signs. As we passed a red-and-white Victorian two-story house at the edge of town, I told Dick to stop the car. In my intense state I decided to just approach the people on the porch and try to rent their house for our movie. To make sure they wouldn't think "Hollywood" when I mentioned we were making a feature film, I told them we had gone to California College of Arts and Crafts. Hearing this, the owner of the house said she had taken a class there once, and agreed to rent the house for two weeks for $450 if I would pay for her hotel room during production ($280 for two weeks). The filmmaker must be incredibly persuasive during this stage of preproduction, able to convince anybody to do (or give) anything he or she needs for the upcoming shoot.

During preproduction of my second feature, *1988—The Remake*, the entire scope of the concept changed drastically. I had originally envisioned conducting a small audition as part of my movie, perhaps renting a small stage at a recreational center. But my advertising friend Joe DiVincenzo offered to design a poster if I would pay him $1,000. I had a $10,000 grant from the American Film Institute and decided to pay Joe for the graphic promotion.

While I was searching for a suitable location for the audition, someone recommended California Hall on Polk Street in San Francisco. I ended up renting the large hall, complete with a fifty-foot-wide stage that included several hand-painted scenery backdrops. And with every new decision, the event of the audition leaped onto a grander plateau. Friend Bill Farley insisted I hire his two script-writing friends (and himself) to help me write my script. These friends—Nick Kazan and Henry Bean—have since scripted major Hollywood movies. When Joe's designed poster, letterhead, and press release reached the press, the audition became a hot item on two network nightly news shows. My filmed audition for *1988—The Remake* became one of the largest ever held in the history of San Francisco. In this case, preproduction completely reshaped the filming and final film result.

Preproduction for *Emerald Cities* was accomplished totally by phone, since there was no money for the shoot. Without a budget, all I could do was call previous members of my cast and crew to see if they could afford to work without salary for five days. Actors Ed Nylund and Carolyn Zaremba agreed to help me complete the film trilogy, with Ed offering me a loan for the production. After a friend convinced me that my idea of camping out for the five-day shoot would be a mistake for morale and creature comforts, I looked up motels in Trona, Death Valley, at the library (the extent of my "location scouting") and called to reserve four rooms sight unseen. With each phone call, I was able to make the production more real to myself, adding fuel to the idea that it was really going to happen.

As soon as you make a *real* commitment to shoot your feature, you will discover that you have the power to solve all the needs of your upcoming production. These needs for the shoot fall into three major categories: *people*, *places*, and *things*.

PEOPLE

It is almost impossible to create a feature film without some help from fellow humans. Most stories need actors to play out the roles, and most filmmakers need at least a few helpers to light their scenes and record their location sound. Some exceptionally gifted filmmakers are able to do everything themselves, shooting the camera while recording sound with a microphone either attached to the camera body or placed near the actors. But in terms of the most minimal low-budget crew for a feature film that requires lighting and sound sync recording, a filmmaker will usually have to hire a soundperson and an assistant who can help set up lights, take light readings, "clack" the clap board, carry equipment, do errands, maybe load the camera and keep it clean, and other things. Without this assistant the filmmaker will need to have a great deal of stamina to keep up with all the physical work required to shoot on location. Often through listings at film schools and organizations such as FAF in San Francisco and AIVF in New York you can locate an eager assistant for your shoot who will work for free just for the experience of getting his or her name in the credits of a feature film. Since the full burden of organizing all aspects of the shoot is on the shoulders of the filmmaker, "hiring" someone to help with errands and heavy equipment is the least you can do for yourself. You may also be able to locate a production manager and even a soundperson who would be willing to work on your production for the experience, but usually these professionals can't afford to work without at least a minimum salary and some profit sharing. While you look over every man and woman you pass on the street, wondering if they might be suitable actors for your story, the first concrete step you should take is rounding up the crew for your production.

CASTING THE CREW

It is very important to know you have a crew who will help make the film a reality. After you have met with some prospective sound-people and possible production assistants and been shown either examples of their technical abilities or résumés of their past achievements, you will want to ask yourself if you feel you can get along with their particular personalities on a shoot. It is vital that you don't feel extra pressure from your technicians during filming, even if they know more than you about how to make a film. Explain to them that this is your first feature (if it is) and that you will appreciate any help they can give you, but that they may need to exercise some patience as you feel your way along. When selecting the people you will be working with and depending upon to make your film (and spend all your money), it is critical that you find people with whom you can get along.

When you have made your final selection of soundperson and production technician you will want to have them sign your contract to confirm that they will indeed be part of your production. Since the contract clearly states the amount of deferred salary and percentage points of profit for each job, with the stipulation that these crew members will receive nothing if their jobs aren't completed, the act of signing clarifies the business of making your film. After the crew members have signed the contract, you should feel the added energy that comes with knowing that you are a major step closer to shooting your film. The next step, once the crew is set, is to begin the search for your "stars."

CASTING "REAL" ACTORS

For some types of low-budget stories you will want to cast trained actors who can be depended upon to deliver the same high-quality performances on each take. There are always many unemployed actors who are excellent at their craft, but who don't fit the mold of whatever Hollywood film is casting at present. If you can afford the time and money to search for your actors, maybe the best way to proceed is by putting an ad in the classified section of your local newspaper, describing the parts available. For between $50 and $100 you should be able to reach a large pool of talent in this way. Talent agencies may also be able to supply you with photos and résumés of actors and actresses who fit your bill, but there is usually a fee for this service. Without any money it is impossible to conduct an audition for your cast, so your next best way of scouting for professional actors is by going to plays in your town and watching the actors. And acting schools or theater departments at local colleges and universities may have bulletin boards that advertise actors looking for work.

When you interview prospective thespians for a part in your movie, let them know immediately that you are producing your feature at used-car prices. And if there is no money for salaries, let them know that you'll be paying per diem stipends (if this is possible) so the shoot won't cost them money. Explain to them that you will be sharing the profit points of the movie with the cast and crew. They may respect your story, your low-budget daring, and agree to perform in your movie on these terms.

Before a highly trained, highly professional actor agrees to perform in your low-budget "first time" feature, it is also important to inform him or her that you have no training in "traditional" directorial techniques (if this is true). In a large sense, you will be depending on the actor's ability to "self-direct," to control his or her own performance. You believe this person is right for the part in your movie, and to a certain extent you will be able to spot the moment when he or she fails to act the role in an honest and believable way during the shoot. But because you are responsible for many facets of the production (shooting, directing, managing the details), you will have to depend heavily on the actors' ability to create their own performances. Some actors demand constant pampering, "directing," and need several takes to get "warmed up." If you select this type of actor by mistake, you will waste at least your first roll of film, if not sink your entire production. A good rule of thumb is that if the actor is down-to-earth, without affectations, likable and intelligent, and can talk intelligently about your story, then perhaps he or she might also be right for the part. Observe the actors carefully when you mention your shooting ratio of one take per scene with few retakes. If this small shooting ratio scares them (and why shouldn't it?), there is no real comfort you can supply. You must be able to depend on your actors to *at least* complete the filming so that you have a chance of creatively editing away their, and your, hopefully few mistakes. Sometimes it is actually easier to shoot one-to-one using untrained nonactors.

CASTING NONACTORS

The essence of the performance of a nonactor in a film is the natural, raw quality that he or she is able to project on the screen. And, obviously, with each repeated take the naturalness diminishes. So it is the job of the filmmaker to catch the fleeting moment of the nonactor's best performance on the first or second try. Since most nonactors are not trained to memorize pages of dialogue and instruction, it is not even worth trying to proceed in this way. An intelligent nonactor (like the best actors) can often take the concept of a scene and explode it into dazzling runs of dialogue you could never write in a lifetime. For most of my feature productions I have used nonactors with great success, selecting people who *are* my characters. And many of the scenes in which they perform are scripted directly from some story or event I have observed or been told about that actually occurred in their real lives. What I'm really asking them to do is relive part of their lives before the camera. Or I may place them in a certain situation that is new to their experience and film them reacting in an honest way.

I still can't help laughing when I think of the looks on actor Dick Richardson's face when I shot scenes for *Emerald Cities* of Dick pulling off a rubber Martian mask, sitting next to Ed Nylund in a Santa Claus outfit, and being past-life hypnotized by Freuda Morris in front of her real class of future hypnotists in Berkeley. No writer could script, and no actor could duplicate, the looks of puzzlement, suspicion, disbelief, and fear that crossed Dick's face during these scenes.

While your mind is totally set in search for your needed actors, you might spot someone on the street who perfectly resembles your mental picture of one or another of your characters. Don't let these people get away! Overcome your shyness and approach them, being as polite as possible while you explain your problem. Tell them that you only have a few weeks left to find your actors for your low-budget feature and you think that they may be right for one of the parts. If they respond positively to the idea of being in a movie, let them know just how low-budget your production is, and see how they react. If they enjoy the idea of acting in a film, and have the time to accommodate your shooting schedule, you may have hit a jackpot. We found our actress Jean Mitchell for *The Last Roommate* in the cafeteria at the California College of Arts and Crafts around eight in the morning while my group of collaborators (Mark Yellen, Peter Boza, Tinnee Lee) and I were worrying about finding our actors for the upcoming production. And don't forget the possibility of using your friends as actors.

Occasionally a location will supply you with additional actors for your film, when you make use of the people who live and work there. When we needed a "hit man" for the final scene in *A Man, a Woman, and a Killer*, Wayne Wang, Dick Richardson, and I drove into the town of Mendocino, California, to find someone we could ask to play the part. We spotted a large man dressed in white pants, white shoes, sort of a "Las Vegas" look. He agreed to drive up in his station wagon, pull his rifle out of the backseat, get out of the car, and aim it at Dick, who would be standing on the porch. After he did the scene for us he told us he was a deputy sheriff from Nevada and showed his badge. We were very lucky that the nonactor we chose for the part was an expert in firearms, because that authenticity carried to the screen. And during the filming of *Emerald Cities*, the owner of the motel we stayed at for three days unlocked the church next door and with his wife became an audience of two while Ed Nylund rehearsed the upcoming Christmas pageant. Using local nonactors in your movie always brings an added richness to your production.

NOTE: Whether using actors or nonactors, remember to get releases from all performers *before* shooting your scenes (see release form, Appendix E). Even if a clerk in a store speaks only one line of dialogue for your movie, you must have him or her sign a release. And if the actor or "extra" is under eighteen, the release form must be signed by his or her parent or legal guardian as well. Your lead actors with whom you are profit sharing must sign a contract *and* a release before the shoot.

PLACES

To film your feature you need special places called "locations" where you will bring your story to life. Often Hollywood films spend months "scouting locations," but with your nonbudget (and probably little gas money) you need to be much more inventive than the usual Hollywood production. Maybe your overgrown backyard will double for the African wilds. Maybe not. But there may be suitable locations within a few miles of your house that might work perfectly for your story. Within twenty miles of my former home in Point Richmond, California, I had access to ocean, beaches, San Francisco, Oakland, hills, country, desert, swamps, islands, Berkeley street people, the University of California, punk music, outdoor concerts, and so forth. Perhaps a friend's apartment, or the house of your actor or actress (or their parents' house), would be right for your story. If you need a restaurant or other public place for some scenes you must once again overcome any shyness and just *ask*. Most people will be happy to have been chosen for the honor of being involved in a movie. And if you experience resistance from the location's manager or owner, try to offer a small sum of money ($20 to $50) and maybe that will change his or her mind.

While filming *Emerald Cities*, I encountered a desk clerk who would absolutely not let us shoot a scene in the driveway of his motel, where I had spent $100 putting the production up for the night. I begged, I offered money, I explained that our movie was ultra-low-budget. Nothing seemed to change his mind. Finally I told him that making films was, for me, the same as working on his car might be for him. It was my hobby, my love. And here I finally hit the right button. He said he worked on his car and understood, and told me to go ahead and shoot my scene. The moral is don't give up when someone says no if you feel your blood rush at the sight of a great location. At least don't give up until you've explained who you are and why you need to film at that location. If possible, get a commitment in advance for your filming at a location to avoid wasted time and effort.

To shoot on location without a snag demands that the filmmaker think like the genius production manager he or she can't afford to hire. The filmmaker must anticipate problems before they happen. During my shoot of scripted scenes for *1988—The Remake*, I had rented a hotel room to film a banquet scene. At the last minute I was told by the management that I couldn't bring the already cooked (and paid for) catered meal for the shot into my room. Luckily, my production manager, Bobby Weinstein, who was working for me for three days at a salary of $250, was able to get around this problem by working out a deal with the kitchen to use their plates and silverware (at a nominal cost) with our food, thus conforming to hotel regulations. This creative solution not only saved the $150 worth of elegantly prepared food created by culinary expert Ruth Reichl, but also saved the momentum of the filming. It's always best to review any plans you have for a certain location with the owner or manager before the day of the shoot so that this kind of problem doesn't arise. And if you sense resistance during your discussion, it is probably best to change locations.

As a low-budget filmmaker you can't really play by the same rules as Hollywood when securing locations. City regulations in most large cities such as San Francisco require a filming permit to film on their streets. I know many people who have never paid such a fee and don't intend to in the future. They have just gone ahead and shot at these locations, and have succeeded in getting great shots without being bothered. Some risks will be necessary when shooting your low-budget feature on location, but try to nail everything down that you can.

NOTE: The safe filmmaker will get a location release signed at each location, so that when he or she has a big hit on his or her hands the choice will not have to be made of either paying an unreasonable fee for the image of someone else's property or refilming. (See location release form, Appendix F.)

STORYBOARDING

Once you have a firm commitment from a particular location you may want to finalize your vision by making a sketch of how you see your actors in the scene. This drawing, detailing how the camera will frame the shot, including size and position of actors and specific background elements, is called a storyboard.

An average-length feature film would require hundreds of such drawings, one for each cut. I'm sure that some filmmakers swear by the process of knowing every shot down to its exact composition, as did director Alfred Hitchcock, but I believe that the filmmaker is wisest if he or she is able to enter the filming with both eyes open, feeling special compositions, inventing ways of shooting based on the emotional network of the moment. During the shoot I believe in placing the camera in the spot that feels right, instead of trying to determine that special location for the camera beforehand. Also, the obvious fact is that without any real budget the filmmaker can't completely control all the facets of filming and must be able to take advantage of unexpected moments and events while filming.

LONG-DISTANCE LOCATIONS

When Wayne Wang and I planned the shoot for our first feature, *A Man, a Woman, and a Killer*, in 1973, it was clear to us that if we could get our cast and crew out of the familiar surroundings of our hometown (Oakland) we would have a better chance of making a good film. We had learned on shoots for shorter films that a great deal of effort is spent just rounding up all the members of cast and crew and equipment for a day's shoot. Also, if you are able to bring your cast and crew to some new place to live together as a sort of "film family," there is a "high" created that stays with you for years after the film production has ended. This special emotional energy created by the teamwork of making a film on location always adds something special to what you see on the screen. If your film demands an exotic location, as did my *Emerald Cities* feature, which was partly shot in Death Valley, it is important to be true to your concept and somehow raise the additional funds to travel and live at that special place.

Often the free availability of a mountain cabin or other types of housing will help the low-budget filmmaker to get the inspiration for a story he or she wants to shoot. The only problem the small production has is transporting the cast and crew to the location (gas credit cards) and feeding everyone during filming. While shooting *A Man, a Woman, and a Killer* in Mendocino, I paid for breakfast at a restaurant each morning for nine members of the cast and crew, supplied cold cuts for lunch, and gave each person an "allowance" of $4 for dinner. I actually handed out four $1 bills to each person on the production, which was the price of the basic dinner offered by the Mendocino Inn (in 1973). Only if you are making a feature film at used-luxury-car prices can you afford today's prices for food and shelter on location. But if you limit your long-distance shooting to a five-day trip with three days for actual filming, as I did on *Emerald Cities*, you may be able to afford the special images that come from such an adventure. Carefully budget your food money and call ahead to a motel, making a deposit if necessary to give yourself the security of shelter during the few-days' shoot you will attempt. You may find that food prices are greatly reduced, from what you expect to pay in cities such as San Francisco and New York City, when you travel to rural settings. The air is fresher, the food is home cooked, new vistas await the daring no-budget filmmaker who takes his or her show on the road.

THINGS

Things for the production include every piece of equipment (camera, lenses, sound recorder, light meter, lights, batteries, power cables, tripod, etc.) as well as props, food, clothes or costumes, filmstock, sound tape, and all the accessories that you will need to have on location for the filming. It is very important to decide what items you need for the shoot and either reserve them for renting or purchase them in advance. Since you can't afford to hire a production manager whose job it would be to make absolutely sure you had everything when you needed it, you must keep a notebook to organize these needs. As the date of the filming approaches, each day will add new things to the list. Part of the list will indicate members of the cast and crew the filmmaker must call by phone to discuss shooting schedules, revised script concepts, etc. The other part of the list will reflect which pieces of equipment are needed, when and where they must be picked up for the shoot, with additional notes on food and transportation— everything the filmmaker must remember if the shoot is to be successful.

CAMERA EQUIPMENT

One of the most vital pieces of equipment (as well as the most expensive) that the filmmaker must acquire for the shoot is a camera. Although we have chosen to shoot our feature in 16-mm instead of 35-mm for the obvious reasons that 35-mm filmstock and Panavision equipment are many times more expensive than our used-car budget could afford, we are still committed to producing the sharpest images possible, to insure the potential for blow-up to 35-mm in case our film is theatrically distributed. And while 8-mm film and equipment are much cheaper than 16-mm, the smaller-gauge film offers an image only half the size of 16-mm, causing much more grain buildup when quadrupled in size for 35-mm blow-up. To protect our own investment of time and money, not to mention of any investors' dollars, it is essential to our production that we shoot our film with the best 16-mm camera and optics available. A high-quality 16-mm camera (Eclair, CP-16, Aaton, Arriflex) usually rents for between $70 and $275 per day. Each filmmaker must get the feel of these cameras in his or her hands and choose the one that seems best and is affordable according to the budget of the feature. The rental price on each should include a battery belt or some type of battery power, two film magazines, power cables, crystal sync motor, lenses, and a camera case. Most rental houses carefully check their equipment after each rental before sending it out again, and this should insure a smoothly running camera for your shoot. If you decide to rent your camera from a rental house, ask them if they have checked the magazines for quiet running. Ask them if the lens has been calibrated lately. Look at the camera and get an impression of how new or old it is. It should look clean instead of banged up. You will want to reserve the equipment as early as possible, phoning at least two weeks in advance to set your reservation for the camera, sound gear, and lights you will need. And if you have decided to shoot on weekends, then make sure you request the special weekend rate (if available) of one day's cost for a Friday-night-to-Monday-morning rental. It is worth spending the few extra dollars for equipment insurance when renting your gear (most rental houses require insurance and include it in the rental price), since you are legally responsible for damage and loss when you sign the rental agreement.

It is possible to save money by renting a good camera from someone who has advertised equipment for rent on a bulletin board or in a filmmakers' newsletter. The owner may refuse to rent precious equipment to you unless he or she is present at the shoot (with an extra fee included), but this may be to your advantage if the person knows the camera and can help load it and clean it between shots. I rented my camera and sound gear for the *Emerald Cities* shoot from a friend who greatly reduced my work load with his attention to the camera duties. As the video revolution gathers steam, I imagine that more and more filmmakers who invested heavily in expensive 16-mm cameras will be anxious to rent their equipment on feature projects whenever possible. Even if their rental price is the same as that of a rental house, if the price includes their help, you are getting a good deal. Just make sure they aren't the type that will bully you or intimidate you on location. You will want to make your own filming decisions, shoot your own film, with their assistance.

WHICH LENSES?

If you are renting your camera from a rental house you will need to choose the high-quality lenses that are best for your shoot. The 12–120 Angenieux zoom lens ($40 per day) and the wide-angle

9.5–57 Angenieux lens ($45 per day) are both excellent choices because from wherever you place your camera you can zoom in to select your framing of the shot. The Angenieux 9.5–57 is a good choice for wide angles since its lens allows for very close-up, in-focus shots. And this lens is indispensable for keeping all your titles in focus if you use the low-budget method of shooting titles made with stick-on letters on clear acetate placed in front of a lit scene (see chapter 5). So that the on-location filmmaker still has the wide-angle capability with either choice, I recommend renting the 9.5–57 lens, or a 9-mm or 10-mm wide-angle lens ($30 per day) along with your 12–120 lens for the shoot.

SOUND GEAR

Usually, a good soundperson will have his or her own Nagra sound recorder, which he or she will have pampered by resoldering any loose connections over weekends. This type of soundperson is most certainly out of reach financially for the low-budget or no-budget filmmaker, unless he or she has such a sound expert as a best friend. You will probably have to hire a soundperson and rent the necessary sound equipment for filming. There is no question that the Nagra is the best quality workhorse recorder for on-location sync sound, and it usually rents for around $50 a day. Rents are higher for newer Nagras that record time code on audio tracks for eventual transfer to video, but if you intend either to complete your production on video, or to edit on video or digital equipment, then you must secure this special Nagra T recorder with SMPTE time code ($70 a day). You will also need to rent microphones, which will add another $60 per day to the cost. The Sennheiser #416 is a fantastically high-quality mike ($20 per day) that is very sensitive to sound and must be used with a very quiet-running camera at an equally quiet location. This mike can literally hear through walls. (While I was filming a scene in a restaurant the soundman informed me that his #416 was picking up the motor sounds of what was probably the refrigerator of the store next door.) For outside recording you will want to have rented a Sennheiser #816 shotgun mike ($25 a day). This directional mike allows

Arriflex 16SR-2 camera. Photo courtesy Arriflex Corporation.

CP-16R/A camera. Photo courtesy Cinema Productions
Corporation.

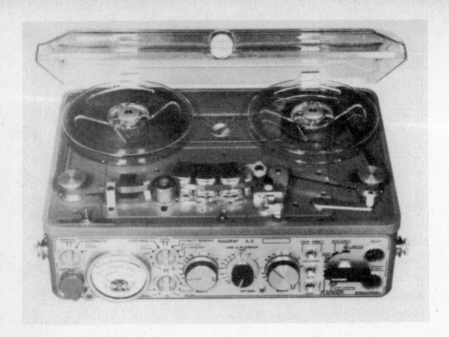

Nagra 4.2 recorder. Photo courtesy Nagra Magnetic Recorders, Inc.

the soundperson to pick dialogue out of the mouths of your actors without recording all the interruptive outdoor sounds nearby. And if a large portion of the filming involves dialogue between several actors in different parts of the room, you will probably need to rent several lavaliere mikes ($12 each per day), which pin onto the inside of a shirt (like those seen on TV newscasters). For sound recording on location there will also be the need for several recording "accessories" such as a 4' to 15' fold-up extension "boom pole with shock mount," which gives the soundperson the ability to hold the mike high above the actors or low below the frame line of the shot for the best possible position for recording (well worth $20 a day).

As you can see, when renting sound or camera gear all the necessary "extras" quickly raise the overall price per day to a barely affordable rate. So once again it might be to the filmmaker's great advantage to hire someone with his or her own equipment. Some rental houses will also require that you buy the $25 of bat-

Filmmaker Jon Jost's standard equipment—CP-16 400' magazine camera with highly portable sound-recording gear: a small recorder, 60-cycle sync pulse generator, and directional mike.

teries needed to power the Nagra, which easily brings the total rental price for the Nagra into the range of $100 a day. If you can hire a soundperson for $200 (including equipment) for the weekend, you are doing very well. Check the lab bulletin boards and the FAF listings, looking for a reasonable sound package with perhaps a soundperson attached to the deal.

Another option for the filmmaker who needs sync sound recording on location may be to purchase a Sony Walkman Professional recorder. It is possible to purchase this recorder for under $500, and it is very close in quality to the $12,000 Nagra. My soundman expert, Neelon Crawford, checked the Sony recorder against his state-of-the-art Nagra and found that it was quite comparable in quality. By hooking up a special box of electronics (about the size of a pack of cigarettes) that supplies one channel with a 60-cycle sync pulse, and connecting a high-quality mike to the other channel, one can record excellent sync sound onto audio cassettes with this lightweight, compact recorder. A Sony TCD-5 recorder is also excellent for on-location recording, but this model is about twice as expensive ($900) and not pocket-size. So if your Nagra rental will be more than $500 for your shoot, you should definitely consider the purchase of one of these Sony recorders.

LIGHTING KITS

Unless you have chosen very fast filmstock, you will need some sort of lighting kit for your shoot. These kits range from the diffused lighting of Lowel "soft lights" ($20 each per day) to the more hard-edged lighting of Tota kits ($45 a day) and "spots" ($25 a day). The rental of lights must also be accompanied by the rental of necessary accessories to make each type of lighting effective. Soft lights need only what comes in their cases (stands, diffusion cloth backing, bulbs, electrical cords with on-off switches). Other types of lighting will require support gear such as stands, "C" clamps, "scrims," "barn doors," "snoots," expensive color gels, diffusion "cotton," reflectors, etc. And for any set of lights, a rental "must" is at least three 50' extension cords ($1.50 each per day) so that you can avoid blowing fuses on location by plugging lights into different outlets around the house.

Before committing yourself to a certain type of lighting, you should add up the total cost of various lighting concepts, taking into consideration the difficulty of and time required by each process versus the desired results. For each of my features I have tried to simplify as much as possible the process of lighting my indoor scenes.

EXAMPLES OF LIGHTING ON
RICH SCHMIDT FEATURES

In my earlier features a very direct, improvisational method was used to light the scenes. In *A Man, a Woman, and a Killer* all our lighting was supplied by three 1,500-watt Lowel soft lights that were aimed directly at the characters. George Manupelli, who ran (and founded) the Ann Arbor Film Festival in Michigan, and who has directed/produced five features himself, had told me about the soft-light method just before we were to shoot. Without really looking into the subject, I just took his recommendation and rented two soft lights. Fortunately, our grip, Jim Mayer (now a video producer in San Francisco), brought a third soft light along for the shoot. By aiming the diffused light from our three soft lights directly at the actors, and underexposing ½ stop for our black-and-white filmstock, we were able to achieve a very luminous quality for the film. (We used a filmstock called Plus-X Reversal [Kodak 7276], with very fine grain due to its low 50 ASA, which was capable of producing very rich blacks.) And so this first feature had a feeling that many foreign films have—dramatic and very beautiful to watch.

My second feature, *1988—The Remake*, was also shot on Plus-X Reversal using soft lights in combination with diffused lighting for large areas in the audition hall. Grip Jeff Gilliam brought large banks of lights to California Hall (San Francisco), where the audition was conducted, and these, combined with the illumination from the stage floodlights, were able to achieve the desired lighting. For smaller, scripted scenes, soft lights were once again used to diffuse the light on the characters.

Emerald Cities, my third feature, was shot on Color Negative stock (Kodak 7291). This color sort of bursts at the seams, very bright colors, no grain, with super definition. Not all films can handle the almost cartoony color of this stock, but for *Emerald Cities* it was perfect. For the interior scenes I bounced some light off the ceiling until I got an f-stop reading between 2.8 and 4. This approach worked well for the subject matter, and instead of spending many hours lighting each scene I was able to move quickly, set up the lights, and get good improvisational performances. Using a "Lowel D kit," which consisted of four 1,000-watt lights with "barn doors" (metal flaps that fit in slots in front of the lights, used to control the "edge of the lighting" and the brightness, $50 a day), along with a soft light for fill ($20 a day), I was easily able to reach a good f-stop, even when I had to light a large stage area in a church.

For *The Last Roommate*, Color Negative stock was again used, mainly at the prompting of Monaco Lab in San Francisco, where the manager convinced me of this decision by offering me the stock at their cost for my project. Kathleen Beeler, bi-city cinematographer (L.A./Bay Area), signed on as our director of photography, and applied her techniques of lighting to the shoot. This was a big departure for me, having to wait a long time between each shot while the lights were set up and tuned. Also, because of the difficulty and amount of time it took for each lighting setup, it was necessary to shoot all the scenes that took place at that location at the same time. This made it necessary to shoot some scenes as it is usually done in Hollywood: out of the natural order of the story. It is always my desire to shoot a dramatic story so that the actors (or nonactors) can live through the drama in a realistic progression of events. But because of this attitude I have often settled for less-than-adequate lighting. In my features I have created my moods through the improvisational power of catching special moments of light and shadow while I film. For each filmmaker a balance has to be struck between improvisation and carefully crafted lighting.

SELECTING YOUR LIGHTING

Occasionally, the low-budget feature filmmaker will attempt to give a big-budget Hollywood look to his or her film. The commitment to this idea must be very strong, because to effectively use these techniques requires many hours of setting up hot lights, much less improvisational flow for the actors, and quite a bit more expense added to the production because of the added time required to shoot the feature. Although it is very difficult to imagine a no-budget filmmaker's being able to convince a cast and crew to abide by the extra days this type of lighting will add to the shooting schedule of a feature, it is possible that if that filmmaker were in collaboration with a skilled director of photography he or she might consider the possibility. I include some in-depth information about the Hollywood system of lighting as used by Kathleen Beeler for our production so that the reader can make a wise decision with regard to lighting his or her feature. I also include information on shooting without any lights at all, making use of fast filmstock. Since the entire schedule for shooting a feature depends on what approach the filmmaker takes in terms of lighting, this decision must take place in the preproduction period. With no lights, or few lights, a filmmaker can shoot a film in under a week. With Hollywood lighting, the filmmaker would be working night and day to complete the feature within a two-week period, at least doubling the cost of the shoot.

HOLLYWOOD LIGHTING

The basic groups of lights used by Kathleen Beeler for *The Last Roommate* were as follows:

1. Tota kit (Lowel), which included three 650-watt lamp heads.
2. Two baby spots, each with 1,000 watts (1-K) of light.
3. Two 200-watt midget spots used for pinpointing light on objects or actors.

These lights are used in combination: to cover the light directed toward the actors, the background light, and the highlights. By bouncing light from a baby spot off a piece of white foamcore board onto the actors at a 45-degree angle, the filmmaker can achieve a beautiful diffused light (as is created by the use of soft lights). During the filming of *The Last Roommate*, we often used orange gels (called CTOs) on the lights, which gave a warm, fresh glow to the actors. And we used blue gels (CTBs) for the background to visually pop the actors forward, giving them a more 3-D look. This is the type of lighting structure used on Hollywood pictures by cinematographer Vilmos Zsigmond, and it gives a coral color and fresh ocean feel to each scene.

To give a "natural" feel to a scene set next to a window, the Hollywood cinematographer would light his or her scene in such a way as to direct the main light source from the window's direction. The "key light" would be set on the side of the room near the light source (window) aimed at the actors. Then a light reading would be taken by aiming the white bulb of the meter toward the camera position. This incident reading would represent the average light reading. Using the focusable spots as "key" and umbrellas (umbrella-shaped reflectors) as "fill," we complete the lighting by adding a "back" or "rim" light to the subject. This gives a 3-D feeling to the image. Gels and diffusion materials would be held in front of the lights using clothespins to clamp them on the barn doors. Specially bright bulbs called "practicals" might be screwed into a lamp fixture to give additional illumination to the existing amount of light in the room. For this "natural" look, the Hollywood cinematographer would also usually tone down a plain white wall, adding color to avoid the starkness. And an "85 gel" would be used to cover the glass of the window, filtering out the blue color that would occur on the Tungsten balanced filmstock without such protection. Just like the 85 filter used for outside filming, the 85 gel balances the color difference.

The essence of the "Hollywood look" is the concept of "painting with light." Have you ever seen an Edward Hopper painting? Look at the values of light and the different colors that collide on his canvases. For some cinematographers, such as Kathleen Beeler, Hopper is a prime example of what they would like to achieve in their lighting of scenes. By using a spot meter, the cinematographer can check the density of light in each area of the scene, adjusting the illumination until all the values are as rich as he or she desires. Black and white areas are checked so that details aren't lost because of either extreme darkness or hot highlights.

LIGHTING FOR LOW BUDGETS

Many low-budget filmmakers tend to reject Hollywood-style lighting, preferring to invent their own lighting style. By using the garish colors of reality, white highlights and deep shadow blacks, the filmmaker can "paint with light" by how he or she selects compositions with the camera. By shooting fast and spontaneous scenes with minimum lighting interference, one can create scenes of great dramatic power, with a greatly reduced rental cost.

For a first low-budget feature film, I recommend using either fast ASA 400 color film with minimum lighting and natural light or shooting black-and-white Plus-X or Tri-X stock and lighting with three 1,500-watt Lowel soft lights for diffused light, to avoid the problems of color balance and grain buildup. If you must shoot color film, then use Color Negative stock, but without worrying about achieving a Hollywood look. Because there are so many details for the filmmaker to juggle on location, it's especially important to reduce problems associated with lighting.

NATURAL LIGHTING WITH ASA 500 FILMSTOCK

One way to shoot scenes inside and maintain the highest degree of improvisational energy with your actors is by using a high-speed filmstock that doesn't require artificial lighting. Although these fast stocks often add to the amount of grain visible when your film is projected, they sometimes allow you to shoot interior scenes with just the available natural lighting. Both Fuji and Kodak now offer ASA 500 color stocks in 16-mm, each claiming to have scientifically reduced unwanted grain buildup in images produced by these ultra-fast stocks. The filmmaker must test these stocks to determine which nuance of color and texture works best for his or her project. If you call the Fuji representative [1 (800) 326-0800] and let him know you are considering using Fuji stock for your feature, he may be able to send you both a 200' roll of ASA 250 Color Negative and a 200' roll of ASA 500 Color Negative for you to "test." Of course, with your small budget, it is necessary to treat this free stock as potential footage for your film, and shoot it carefully as part of your movie.

You must place your actors in advantageous natural light situations to get the best results from this method, and you may need to supplement nature with one soft light and a few 250-watt practical light bulbs to get a suitable f-stop for interior filming. If your actors are placed near a sunlit window, the natural light should be sufficient to shoot them with a very interesting lighting mood created. And the ability of the filmmaker to move the actors from one emotional sequence to the next without lighting-change interruptions will give him or her much more control over the performances. Instead of spending an hour setting up each scene with artificial lights, you will be able to film your movie four times as fast—meaning you will save money, time, and energy. If the mood of your film is enhanced by this natural lighting, and won't suffer with the addition of a grainy image, then I highly recommend shooting without lights using fast film.

While working carefully to use dramatic areas of light and shadow for your shots, it is important that you continue to keep your main focus on the actors and the story you are trying to tell. For a first feature it may be wise to use Tri-X black-and-white film to eliminate the problems with color under low-light conditions.

NOTE: To make sure that a "fast" stock is correct for your movie concept, it would be a good idea to shoot a couple of 100' rolls of film using the stock you are considering. Since this is just a test, borrow a friend's Bolex camera and shoot test lengths of perhaps ten seconds at those locations you have selected. Get the film processed and project the results under good screening conditions. And if the feeling of the stock appeals to you, then you have been blessed with the ability to shoot your film in the easiest, most straightforward manner.

SOFT LIGHTS

The most basic way to light with soft lights is to place one light on each side of the camera, aimed directly at your actors, using a third light to add illumination to the actors and background, and then take a light reading. Using your Spectra light meter with inserts for each ASA, you aim the white cone back at the camera from where the actors are located to measure the incident light. (See chapter 5 for more information on using the light meter.) If you are shooting Plus-X Reversal black-and-white film, and want a rich, luminous, European look, underexpose ½ stop (as an example, close down the exposure from f-4 to a setting between f-4 and f-5.6) and have the lab print it as normal, without timing changes. With three soft lights you won't blow fuses as long as you use your 50' extension cords to plug into outlets in different locations in the house where you are filming. If you can light your scenes to get your f-stop readings between 4 and 5.6, you should be able to shoot quickly with elegant results.

SAVING MONEY ON
FILMSTOCK AND SOUND TRACK

Sometimes, if you check the bulletin boards at the labs or look through ads in filmmaking newsletters, you can find an offer for inexpensive filmstock. The price may be greatly reduced because the filmmaker needs money back for stock that wasn't shot on location, or because the filmstock is outdated. In either case, it would be extremely unwise to purchase any stock until you shoot a short test (20') to see if it's OK. And check with your local lab to see if they still process the type of stock you are considering. In the last few years many beautiful and interesting filmstocks such as Kodachrome 2-A have been discontinued, and soon it seems only Color Negative stock will be available. Perhaps the video revolution will push the entire 16-mm film industry into the drink, but for now the filmmaker can take advantage of lowered prices, unused equipment, cheap editing "packages," and unwanted stock to complete his or her low-budget features.

If you buy your filmstock directly from a lab, make sure that your price for the stock included in the overall deal you cut with that lab (for stock, processing, print cost, sound mix if possible, work print if necessary) approaches what the stock would cost you if you bought it directly from Kodak or Fuji. And to insure consistent color values, you must request all rolls of stock be from the same batch of emulsion numbers. (This will be apparent when you examine the cans of filmstock and see that the numbers on the labels are the same.) If you weren't able to make a package deal with the lab for all your processing and printing needs, then definitely purchase your ten or more rolls of stock directly from the Kodak or Fuji distributor in your area, since this (small) bulk purchase will save you several dollars on each roll.

It is not worth purchasing either ¼" recording stock for your Nagra, or sound cassettes for your Sony Walkman Professional recorder, from individuals at "discount." The regular prices are low enough so that the filmmaker should make sure he or she gets top-quality tape for on-location sound recording.

For each low-budget feature production, the filmmaker should purchase a case of ten 1,200' rolls of mag track directly from the 3M supplier. This purchase will save the filmmaker more than a hundred dollars. Phone 3M in Minnesota (1 [800] 752-0732) and order your case of sound track, giving the name of your production company and a request that they bill you for the delivery. They will ship it to you within a week, sometimes giving you a few months to pay. This mag track will be used for sound transfers from ¼" recording tape from your on-location recordings, as well as for all other needed sound transfers, including sound effects, music, narrations, dubs, and possibly the final sound mix (3M Company, 3M Center, St. Paul, Minn. 55144).

SUPPORT EQUIPMENT

Various other pieces of equipment must also be rented or obtained for the successful on-location shoot. A tripod will be needed to support and smoothly move the camera. I recommend the Miller Pro fluid head tripod ($25 per day), and for shots that require a lower vantage point you will want to rent "Baby Legs" ($10 a day), with their shorter tripod legs. To keep the tripod legs from slipping on a slick floor, a "spreader" is essential ($5 per day). A changing bag ($5 per day) will be needed to load and unload the filmstock in the camera magazine. And if you plan to shoot over four 400' rolls of film each day you will need an additional battery belt ($15 a day) to keep the camera running. Sandbags ($1.50 a day) are helpful to weigh down the base of the tripod to light stands, but not all rental facilities have these in stock. Of course, if the film-maker has some idle time and lives near the coastline, he can fill up some durable cloth or plastic bags with sand from the beach and save some money. Also, apple boxes, sturdy boxes about one foot tall, are excellent for standing on while working at high tripod settings when shooting the camera, or for adjusting lights above your head, and recording sound from above the actors heads ($1.50 a day). Reinforced orange crates or plastic milk cartons may do the job without the cost. To insure that good, clean sound is recorded on location, the noise from a running camera must be silenced with a "barney" ($10 per day), which surrounds the camera with sound-resistant padding. And several filters, including an 85 filter for outside filming, and a polarizer filter to avoid glares and enhance clouds, must be rented ($4 each day) for the camera. You will need a clap board ($5 a day) for striking sync before each scene, and a light meter (Spectra or Luna-Pro) is a must for setting f-stops ($10 a day).

It will also be necessary to purchase "shooting aids" such as gaffer's tape (large roll, $19), which you will quickly discover is indispensable for securing tripod legs, sealing up camera magazines, holding lights, repairing costumes—the list goes on. You will need a bottle of compressed air for cleaning out the camera magazines after shooting each roll of film ($8), and some orange sticks to scrape out dirt from the camera aperture ($1). Lens tissue is a must ($3), and a few Sharpie permanent marker ink pens ($1) will be needed to identify magazines shot, etc. If there will be a lot of setting up of lights then some sort of work gloves ($7) will be necessary to protect your hands from the hot light heads. And if you will be doing a lot of painting with light, you'll need to purchase a collection of different gels, which could easily run you over $100 for the assortment. All these costs add up quickly, but if the low-budget feature filmmaker is able to simplify his concepts of lighting (leaving "Hollywood" lighting to Hollywood) he or she can afford these prices.

EQUIPMENT CHECKLIST

- ☐ Camera body
- ☐ Batteries and battery pack
- ☐ Extra magazines
- ☐ Power cables
- ☐ Lens mounts
- ☐ Lenses
- ☐ Filmstock
- ☐ Barney

☐ Light meters
☐ Tripod
☐ Baby legs
☐ Hi-Hat (tripod mount to shoot from floor, other surfaces)
☐ Spreader
☐ Spreader dolly
☐ Wheelchair (for no-budget dolly shots)
☐ Apple boxes
☐ Sandbags
☐ Ladder
☐ Gloves
☐ Plug-in electrical boxes with four outlets
☐ 3-prong adapters
☐ Foamcore board (for reflecting light)
☐ Reflectors
☐ 1-K baby spots (including scrims, barn doors, snoots, to aim light)
☐ Midget spot
☐ Stands and clamps for lights
☐ Tota kit
☐ Soft lights
☐ Gels, diffusion
☐ Orange curtain, neutral density curtain, black cloth, black backdrop, other lighting accessories
☐ Changing bag
☐ Accessories for unloading camera (small cores, reels and black bags, empty cans)
☐ Compressed air, orange sticks for cleaning camera
☐ Gaffer's tape, camera tape
☐ Filters, filter rings/85, diffusion, polarizer
☐ Clap board
☐ Marking pens, chalk
☐ Powder pad for makeup

PAPERWORK/ERRANDS/LISTS

The four weeks of preproduction are like being on a roller coaster, cranking up the large first hill before being released toward the dips and curves ahead. As you continue to try to remember everything important for the shoot, the juggling of so much information makes you feel like an overworked computer. Even in your sleep the wheels continue to spin. Small details merge with major concerns. Each morning you must rely on your large organizational calendar to keep the shoot in perspective and in control. This wall calendar is made out of 4"-by-6" index cards Scotch-taped together, each card representing one day, a countdown until filming is completed. With deadlines for reserving equipment, meetings with actors and technicians, other production details, you will watch the calendar fill up as the shooting deadline approaches.

In the last two weeks before the filming there will be many small errands to run. You will need to make copies of your revised script/outline and mail them (E-mail, FAX) out to the cast. And you will need to make copies of your release form for the actors or anyone who happens to appear in your movie. Searching for props, costumes, locations, maybe even lead actors, will keep you constantly on the move. On your calendar you need to remind yourself to keep in touch with the key members of your cast and crew, keeping their energy high for the forthcoming shoot. Every day you will make lists on your calendar of things to do, and every night you will cross off what you've accomplished, along with putting an X across the day that has been spent. You will need to write a schedule of what scenes will be filmed, at what locations, on what day, with which actors in attendance. As you do this last-minute schedule you may find that you need to write more scenes to complete the transitions. Working under pressure always seems to open up new thoughts and ideas. When you hand out the shooting schedule to your cast and crew a few days before the shoot, they will get the feeling that you do, indeed, have everything under control.

It is very difficult to be responsible for everything connected to making a feature film, but this is what every filmmaker who has attempted such a low-budget project has endured. Soon the air will clear, and even though the next phase of production—*the shoot*—is the most intense, it will be a relief to be able just to focus on actors, camera work, and constructing scenes that tell your story. Before we begin the tasks of directing and filming on location, let's review what must be readied for the shoot.

PREPRODUCTION CHECKLIST

☐ Reserve all equipment at least two weeks in advance, after first checking with the rental agency to find out when they recommend you make your reservation. Request the special rate for weekend shooting if applicable, or request a "filming package" rate from an individual. In either case, make sure the lens has been, or will be, calibrated for sharp focus. Review your equipment checklist to make sure you will have everything you need for the shoot.

☐ Select the cast and crew as soon as possible and have them sign contracts (and releases for actors) before the shoot. Hire as good a soundperson as you can convince to work on your project.

☐ Order filmstock from the lab (as part of your "lab deal") at least two weeks before the shoot, requesting all rolls be from the same batch of emulsion. Or purchase rolls directly from the Kodak or Fuji supplier. Keep rolls cool and dry.

☐ Buy sound tape (¼" or sound cassettes) and order a case of mag track directly from 3M.

☐ Select locations for filming and, whenever possible, nail down agreements with responsible parties to insure no last-minute snags, getting signed location releases in advance.

☐ If you have decided to purchase your filmstock from the lab, make sure that you talk to the manager about a "lab deal" involving their best price breaks on stock, processing, work printing (of usable scenes), sound transferring from ¼" tape or sound cassettes to mag track, final print cost—after making them aware that you are producing a feature film at used-car prices.

☐ Budget your money for the shoot ahead, making sure that there is enough cash for equipment, accessories of the filming, small per diem salaries, and food that will be provided by the production. Have at least an extra few hundred dollars in your wallet (if possible) for unexpected needs during shooting.

☐ Spend as much time as possible going over your story, thinking hard about what you will film, what you are trying to say.

☐ Give a copy of the script or outline to the actors.

☐ Talk to your cast and crew members occasionally during the last week before filming, keeping their energy and commitment high, making sure everything is still "go."

☐ Schedule the scenes to be filmed, at which locations, involving which members of the cast and crew.

☐ Organize transportation for the cast and crew to the locations of the filming.

☐ Mentally prepare yourself for the jump into the unknown of filming; ready yourself to work to exhaustion (and convince others to do the same) until the filming is completed.

☐ Get some exercise (swimming, running), eat some good food, and grab some rest, to prepare yourself for the hard work ahead. Good luck!

5

PRODUCTION: FILMING AND DIRECTING

Although lack of money is generally thought of as the major problem for not getting a feature film into production, I believe *fear of the unknown* is the primary reason why so many productions collapse just before the shooting is scheduled to begin. And the biggest unknown is: Will the film be any good? No one wants to be associated with a failure—not a Hollywood studio, not an independent filmmaker. At this point in production, everyone realizes that his or her self-esteem is on the line. Last-minute doubts flutter in the face of the filmmaker. He or she wonders: Can I really shoot a feature? Is my story really worth telling? Will my actors (or nonactors) be convincing? Can I direct? Will I have enough money to finish my film and also pay my rent? Will I fail? You are certainly aware that all your friends are watching, with attitudes that range from scorn, jealousy, and disbelief to pride, encouragement, and love. Everyone will be waiting for the results of your "folly," and although you are trying your best to ignore the negativity, you must admit you have your own (well-hidden) doubts. You can still back out, cancel the equipment rentals with a phone call, call the cast and crew and tell them that the production is "temporarily" postponed until . . . The fear of failure has reigned supreme. Or has it?

To overcome the gut-ache panic of taking this last step of commitment to your feature film project, it is important to remember the role fear plays in the creation of art. This final bout with the fear trapped inside the gut of any self-respecting filmmaker is no different from the last-minute butterflies most of the best actors feel before they walk onstage. It is this fear that fuels greatness. As every cell in your body becomes aware of the intensity of the risk you feel you are taking, your focus narrows down to meet the challenges of the production. Your energy is stronger, your creative powers never better. The complexity of being an adult has been replaced by the simplicity of purpose. You're scared, but also excited. Instead of being bothered on a daily basis by mundane worries, bills, small talk, lightweight games and hobbies, you are on the threshold of taking back some control over your life.

Just before shooting was to begin on *The Last Roommate*, my collaborators experienced a severe case of last-minute jitters. They couldn't believe that I was serious about shooting with "no script" (we had only completed five pages of scripting, but had a very clear outline, detailing the incidents of our story). I convinced them to just jump in and begin, scripting each night as we shot the film. After they saw the beautiful results from the first 400 feet of footage, the doubts vanished and the work carried us through. To successfully shoot a feature film, it is important to open yourself up to the possibilities, as expressed in my Fifteen Rules for No-Budget Feature Filmmaking.

FIFTEEN RULES FOR
NO-BUDGET FEATURE FILMMAKING

1. Script . . . but go with the flow.
2. Don't overlook miracles around you while filmmaking.
3. Use available people you know (actors, technicians, extras).
4. Use all problems to *benefit* the film.
5. Try to pay people who work for you *some* money so you won't be embarrassed when you take control of their lives for a film.
6. Contractualize everything.
7. Don't skimp on getting good recorded sound.

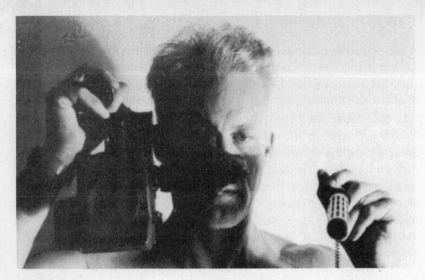

Jon Jost—a crew of one—shooting CP-16 and recording sync sound for a feature.

8. Don't be too cheap to get the best camera.
9. Be creative and original while shooting; find your own way of seeing.
10. Don't get discouraged. You can fix it in the editing (even if some say you can't).
11. Don't turn your back on the ideas and resources of your actors (change the script instead).
12. Say something with your film—action is not enough!
13. Pick a location that offers great visual possibilities.
14. Get as many charge cards as you can *before* you start making a feature.
15. If you don't quit, you *can* finish your no-budget feature before you die.

Because it is such a complex task to film/direct a feature film with no money, it is absolutely vital that the low-budget filmmaker simplify, as much as possible, the problems of the shoot. When I was a sophomore in engineering at the University of Arizona (Tucson, 1964), I took a course called "Statics and Dynamics." This course was designed to confuse, discourage, and weed out the uncommitted engineers, and it did just that. The class started out with a hundred students coming to lectures, and after the teacher filled four large blackboards with mathematical equations in vector calculus (which none of us knew anything about) only eighteen students bothered to show up for the following session. I tried to do the twenty problems assigned at the end of each chapter we studied, but after spending eight hours on one problem and not getting the answer, I gave up. I doubted if there were enough hours in a month to complete the weekly assignment. So I decided to spend my time trying to understand the one sample problem of each chapter (though it still took hours and hours). I would go over the mathematics and keep checking myself against the numbers in the sample. When I took the final exam for the class (having done only twelve problems in the book) I achieved a 33 percent—which was graded on the curve as a solid C—and passed. So what I'd like to do in this chapter is give a "sample" of how to film/direct with actors, shoot the camera, record sound, and light the scene. Hopefully, with the strong foundation created by this sample shoot, the reader can apply this knowledge to his own situations of low-budget feature filmmaking.

PICKING UP RENTAL EQUIPMENT

Rental equipment will usually be picked up either late in the afternoon on Friday, for the special reduced weekend rate of a one-day rental, or on the morning of the shoot. As the filmmaker carefully checks off on his or her list the pieces of equipment that have been set aside for the rental package, he or she is most careful that nothing vital to the filming is missing. The filmmaker double-checks for the power cables that run the camera. He or she makes sure the extension cords have three-prong adapters for plugging into household outlets. And after the filmmaker is satisfied that all pieces of equipment have been accounted for, he or she packs everything carefully into the car, making sure *never* to leave it unattended, even for the few seconds it takes to go back into the rental agency for the next load. Then, with the Nagra recorder specially cushioned on a seat where it can't be damaged by bumpy driving conditions, the filmmaker either drives the equipment to the location for filming or drives it home, to wait for the next morning's filming.

MORNING OF THE SHOOT

You get up around six, shower to wake up, get something to eat, and go over your script for that day's filming one last time before facing your cast and crew. Perhaps, under the pressure of knowing you will be filming in a few hours, you think of some new dialogue to add, or maybe cut some extra dialogue out. The pressure of actual filming will generate new ideas and crystallize ideas that needed to be improved. On your front door you notice the note in large print that says DON'T FORGET BATTERY BELT, and you unplug it from the outlet where it has been charging overnight. If the folks from the rental house had already charged it, they probably recommended that you give it a quick-charge for about an hour before shooting. It is always worth leaving this note to remember the battery belt, since the morning will be filled with distractions. You were, of course, smart enough to carry all the heavy equipment into your house for security overnight. You knew it wasn't worth risking having $35,000 worth of equipment stolen from your car by someone with a coat hanger. And now it's time to load it back in again.

LOADING EQUIPMENT,
PICKING UP ACTORS AND CREW

It is now eight in the morning and it's time to begin loading equipment into your car or van. Starting at eight will give you twenty minutes to lift the heavy equipment into the car before leaving to pick up your actors and crew members at the appointed times you have prearranged. Either you live in a safe neighborhood and have no fear that the equipment already loaded in your car will be stolen between trips back into the house for the next item, or you have hired a production assistant to help pack and guard your car. The last pieces of equipment you load should be the camera and the Nagra recorder, being careful to strap the Nagra on a cushioned seat with a seat belt holding the delicate machine tightly in place. If you have a production assistant, then he or she can hold the machine on his or her lap for the ride over to the location.

You have promised to pick up the lead actor around 9 A.M. because his car is broken, and you arrive on time. He is still eating breakfast, saying he got up late, so you decide to review your script out in your car where you can guard the equipment. He takes about twenty minutes to consume his cornflakes, while you worry about being on time for the other people you are to pick up. When the actor finally arrives at your car you are too relieved to scold him about his tardiness, and you don't want to start off the day on the wrong foot, but if it happens again or you feel yourself losing your temper, you must let him know he'd better knock it off. If you are already in an irritated mood then you'd better talk to him now and get it off your chest. You tell him that he has made you late in picking up the other members of the cast and crew. You tell him he must be on time tomorrow and for every deadline during the shoot. You have said this before it builds up into a big emotional thing. He says, "Sure, sorry," and everything is cool. If he has become irritated by your scolding you had better have a talk with him *now* before you waste your valuable filmstock on a problem actor. Clear it up before it gets worse.

ORGANIZATION ON LOCATION

After you have picked up your cast and crew members who needed a ride (and who were able to squeeze into your car along with all the equipment) and arrive at the location for the filming, the first thing you do, if you haven't done so already, is select a small room or corner where you will bring the equipment. Pick a place that is out of the way of any shots or heavy foot traffic. This way you won't have to keep moving the equipment around the space you're using, losing valuable time for filming. A small room is best, since you will also use the space for loading and unloading your filmstock into the camera. It is important that you are able

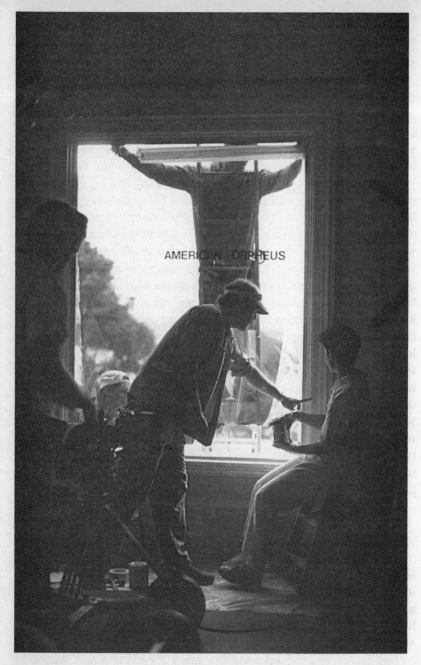

AMERICAN ORPHEUS

Rick Schmidt directs lead actress Jody Esther for the opening shot of *American Orpheus* (1992). Photo by Julie Schachter.

to concentrate on loading without outside distractions, so that you don't accidentally open up the wrong side of the film magazine, exposing the film you just shot to the light. Also, it will be very important to correctly mark for the lab each can of exposed film with your name, the number you designate for the roll, and type of stock, indicating if footage shot is either a partial or full roll. A mistake in this procedure could cost you eleven minutes of shots (one 400' roll) and maybe demoralize the entire production.

While you load your magazines you will want each member of the cast and crew to keep busy in preparation for the shooting of the first scene. If you are lucky enough to have a director of photography, then he or she will begin to set up the lights in the room where the first shot will take place. If you must light the scenes yourself, then your assistant can unpack the lights and assemble them on their stands. The actors may also want to help with setting up the lights because the physical work may ease their tension just before filming. Or it may be necessary for them to review changes in the script. As soon as everyone knows what to do, you let them know you will be loading film in the storeroom and ask them to please not come in for equipment until you are done. You may want to make up a sign that says FILM BEING LOADED—STAY OUT! Make sure everyone understands that you must be left alone, with no one bothering you with questions, until after you have removed the exposed 400 rolls (done inside a light-tight "changing bag") and reloaded the magazines. At later stages of the shoot you may decide to load magazines with people around, but for the first attempts you need privacy.

LOADING THE CAMERA

Hopefully, the clerk at the rental agency has shown you how to load a magazine on your rented camera. And ideally you have had a chance to practice a few times. A manual for the camera you have chosen will be available as a backup guide (check places that sell motion picture cameras; or your rental agency can supply one or tell you where to find one), but no guide can replace hands-on practice using exposed film. Or maybe you rented your camera from a private individual who will load the magazines for you. When I was preparing to film *A Man, a Woman, and a Killer* in 1973, I had many doubts about my ability to use the Eclair NPR camera. All I knew was that it was a very good (and expensive) camera and that I should rent it for our two-week shoot. When I picked up the equipment the day before we were to leave for our location in Mendocino, California, 150 miles away, I had never even held the camera and had no idea how to load it. The manager of Adolph Gasser's rental facility pulled out a roll of exposed film and quickly showed me in about five minutes how to thread the film through the magazine. I remember concentrating as hard as I absolutely could, because I knew that this was my one chance to learn the routine. After I had shot forty-five 400' rolls of film and was preparing to return home to Oakland, my soundman, Neelon Crawford, told me that this was the first shoot he had been on where an Eclair NPR camera had not jammed at least once! I guess my constant fear of failure with regard to loading the magazines correctly prompted me to double-check each sprocket and roller for correct threading.

Don't wait until the last minute like I did. Request a demonstration on threading the film through the magazine as soon as you have selected your camera for the shoot. And if you aren't sure you know the correct procedure after one demonstration, ask for another.

As soon as you have loaded the film into your camera, your next step is to focus the eyepiece for your particular eyesight.

FOCUSING THE EYEPIECE

Before you can shoot sharp images for your movie, you need to adjust the eyepiece on the viewfinder of your camera. To accomplish this task you first need to adjust the lens to infinity and loosen a small screw on the viewfinder that locks the focus into place. Focus the eyepiece until the grain of the glass is in sharp focus and the center crosshairs are perfectly focused to your eye, tighten down the lock-screw, and you're ready to go.

CAMERA MAINTENANCE

A final word on the camera: Don't forget to check your camera for particles of dirt that may build up on the pressure plate and aperture as you run rolls of film through the magazine. An "orange stick" should be used to scrape away any buildup of emulsion dust and dirt inside the camera. The cameraperson must also check the camera's aperture for hairs and dirt particles that would ruin the shots. A good practice is to use compressed air to blow out the camera magazines after each 400' roll is filmed, to insure that no dust will interfere with clean images. And if this entire process of loading, unloading, assembling, and cleaning your camera has worn you out (before you've even shot a foot of film)—don't worry—hire a camera assistant from a local film school who knows how to load the camera, operate it, and clean it between rolls, while you just push the button after framing your shots. Or rent a camera from someone who will help you shoot on location. Remember, your main job is to think about what you are saying in film.

PLACING THE CAMERA FOR YOUR FIRST SHOT

You must now select the placement of the camera, that spot from which your first shot will be filmed. Sometimes this decision will have already been made and drawn on a storyboard card, but for the director/filmmaker who works in the style of improvisation, this decision will not be made until he or she gets the actors together at the location and gets a feeling for the scene about to be shot. Because of the heightened sense of urgency when on the threshold of filming, you will find that ideas and feelings about the story will seem to come into focus as never before. And with this new insight you will place your actors in the scene in a way you hadn't considered at the time you first scouted the location. It is possible that you hadn't been able to see the rooms for the filming except in late afternoon, and now you are affected by the early morning light that covers the walls and windows. And maybe the weather is different, and this also affects your decisions. Also, you may notice something different about the chemistry between your leading actors when they are together the first day of the shoot, and decide to film an unplanned scene to capture this spirit.

While the members of the cast and crew wait for you to decide the first placement of the camera, you feel the pressure that comes with being the leader of the project. Even if you are not absolutely sure, you must break the ice and make the decision of where to place the camera so that you don't stall the filming and undermine your self-confidence. Unless you are shooting with angled shots as Orson Welles did in *Touch of Evil*, either place the camera on a level surface or attach it to a tripod and level your shot by loosening the large wing nut below the mount and lining up the bubble at the center of the bubble gauge before tightening down. Look through the lens and use the zoom to (tentatively) set the framing, with your actors in their (tentative) positions. You will want to readjust this framing just before shooting, once you've observed how the lights affect the actors and background. After the camera placement has been set for the first shot, you and your helper(s) can begin to light the scene.

TIPS FOR LIGHTING ON LOCATION

Whether you have chosen to light your scenes with soft lights aimed directly at your actors, Tota kits in combination with spots to create a complex zone system for painting with light, or just a couple of 250-watt Practical light bulbs with natural light, there are similar lighting problems to watch out for during the shoot.

☐ Watch out for reflections in the shiny surfaces included in your shots. Look through the lens of the camera and closely examine mirrors, glass objects, and windows for reflections of cast and crew members and film equipment you might overlook during the excitement of the filming. Request that everyone behind the camera remain still during each shot; even if you have missed the reflection of a helper it probably will not be noticed if he or she doesn't move.

☐ While looking through the lens, check for light flares (obvious bright spots of light that will disrupt the look of your shot) on walls, edges of chairs, and on shiny surfaces. If you slightly change the position of your lights, most flares will disappear. Another solution may be to use black paper tape to cover reflected highlights on small areas such as metal chair tubing or edges of wooden counters. Of course, make sure that the tape isn't visible when looking through the camera.

☐ Also check the faces of your actors for shiny highlights that may detract from their performances. Although the low-budget filmmaker usually doesn't have a makeup person on the set, someone should have a powder pad for this purpose.

☐ Always use your 50' extension cords to plug in your lights at electrical outlets at far corners of the house in which you are filming. This procedure guards against unnecessary blowing of fuses during your big scenes. And after you have checked your lights for f-stop and placement, turn them off so you don't waste the life of the bulbs. If you are unable to have all the necessary lights for your shoot turned on without blowing fuses, it is possible to "tie in" directly to the source of electricity for the house on the pole outside, but *don't attempt this without the aid of a professional gaffer*.

☐ Try to maintain your light as constant as possible around an f-stop of f-4 to f-8. For some reason, most lenses function best in this range, giving clearest, sharpest images there.

☐ Try not to adjust your lights between shots that you will want to cut together. If the lighting direction changes radically between a close-up and a medium shot while two people are talking, it will look pretty weird if a face goes dark on the cut. Use the same lighting to insure a consistent image.

☐ If lights must be placed close to ceilings and walls, tape a piece of tin foil or other heat-resistant material to the exposed surface to prevent possible fire or heat damage. And to avoid excessively high temperatures on the set due to overheated lights, keep a door open between takes and turn off lights between shots.

☐ Have two light meters on the set, to occasionally double-check your light readings. Also, if one meter gets dropped during filming, you will have a backup, which is especially useful when you are hundreds of miles away from your equipment rental agency.

☐ It is also a good idea to have several replacement bulbs for your lights with you on location, so that if one blows you can quickly continue with the scene that is being filmed.

☐ Don't lift the Tota kit trunk or other heavy lights by yourself. Ask someone to help. Be careful not to lose all your creative energy by rushing the lifting and setting up of the lights.

USING A LIGHT METER

To take quick, accurate light readings I recommend using a Spectra meter. The advantage of this meter is that if you insert a thin metal plate, one supplied for every kind of ASA, the meter is converted to give you the correct f-stop by simply reading the gauge. Other light meters are more complicated to read and require adjusting dials for each ASA.

When I'm filming I usually take what is called an "incident" light reading when shooting indoors with lights. This reading is taken from the location of the subject to be filmed (actor), toward the lens of the camera. By aiming the white plastic cone cover of the meter's eye toward the camera from where you are holding it in front of the face of your actor, you are able to get an accurate reading for the exposure of the face tones. As long as the exposure of your actor's face is correct, the scene will look correctly exposed. If you want an even light over the entire framing of your shot, you will need to check the corners of the framing with the meter and add light if necessary until you get the same light reading as for the face. But don't worry if parts of your scenes go to black or are overexposed to white because of a great difference in f-stop. As long as your actors' faces are correctly exposed, dark and light areas in a shot can often add to the dramatic punch of the scene.

When shooting outside you will remove the white cone cover and simply aim the light meter at the subject to be filmed from where you stand at the camera. This is called the "reflected" light reading. You'll then double-check the exposure for the actor's face by aiming the meter at the face from a foot or two away. Point the meter slightly down so that the meter doesn't read too much sky and falsify the true reading of the actor. Again, it is always best to expose for the actor. If you are trying to shoot a film in the style of Hollywood, you would probably want to rent some reflectors so that you could add light to an actor's face and body to even up the exposure with that of the background. After you process your first 400' roll of film you will want to pay special attention to your scenes with regard to their exposures. Are the scenes underexposed (too dark) because you closed down your f-stop to a smaller opening (f-11 to f-22), thinking that the scene was brighter than it really was? Your meter may have caught too much bright sky during your reading, causing your actors to look too dark. With a stock such as Color Negative these values can be radically changed by varying timing during printing, so all is not lost if the novice uses this three-f-stop-latitude stock. Each film and filmmaker gets into a rhythm of lighting and taking light readings, and by the end of the shoot this process will be second nature to all concerned. After you see the results of the first roll, you have the option of either making a major style change with regard to lighting or continuing with what you have achieved.

WHAT TO SHOOT? HOW TO SHOOT?

Even though this may be the first time you have ever shot 16-mm film (or even video), it is still very possible to achieve original and carefully designed shots for your movie. The main thing to remember is that all the camera moves and decisions must be in support of the story and mood you are expressing. Don't worry about what other people have done in the past, or what other people think your film should look like. Don't worry if it will be "commercial." Concentrate on really feeling your story and the actors in front of the lens. Use your framing of the shots to convey your special connection to what is happening. Find the spot in each shot that is best, as you feel it, to locate the camera. This camera location may be right because you can see the trees moving in the wind through the window behind your actors. Or it may be right because there is a blank white wall behind them. Go with your feelings and construct the shots using your intuition.

The best advice I can give for choosing which type of shot to use (close-up, medium shot, wide shot) is that your film probably should have a variety of these shots so that the audience isn't put to sleep. If you are doing long takes with stationary camera setups, then have your characters approach the camera (close-up) or walk

NOTE: If you believe you may have a commercial feature on your hands, it is important to compose your shots so that the main action (faces, gestures, vital visual information) does not occur at the top of your frame or at the bottom, where it would be cut off by necessary cropping when your 16-mm original is blown up to 35-mm. It may also be important to frame your action inside the "TV cut-off" lines (the rectangle with rounded corners seen inside the frame line) so that an important part of your film isn't lost when transferring to video or TV. If you have further questions, I recommend you get in touch with the Du Art Film Laboratories in New York City (245 West 55th Street, New York, N.Y. 10019, phone: [212] 757-4580), asking to speak with the director of sales. Ask Du Art to mail you an in-depth brochure called "Shooting 16-mm or Super 16-mm for Blowup to 35-mm." A viable option to the exorbitant cost of a blowup from 16-mm to 35-mm master positive and dupe negative for multiple copies is to make just *one* 35-mm composite print, a single print to be used for the first few film festival premieres. Although you won't be able to make another copy without repeating the cost (under $10,000), your film will at least have a chance to screen in 35MM against the larger-budget features it will probably be in competition with the year of release. Ask Du Art Lab or other high-quality optical houses, such as Expo Opticals (Art Canestro at [212] 840-3222, who did the exquisite blow up for *Brother's Keeper*), or Monaco Video's Interformat (Michael Hinton at [415] 626-1100) for the best "no-budget" figure they can supply for a one-time 35-mm blowup.

away. Anticipate the activity in the scene and allow for any movement that might take place. It's best to avoid using the zoom shot while filming, since this effect usually adds an amateurish feeling to a film, unless it is done very carefully. Vary the level from which you shoot, get up high to shoot down, or shoot from the floor, to create a diversity of shots in support of the mood and concept of your story.

SUPPORTING YOUR STORY WITH IMAGES

The more you can tell your filmmatic story with images, the more impact the material will have on the subconscious mind of the viewer. The highest compliment a film can receive is that "it stayed with me for days after the screening." That's the kind of film you want to make. In his class on directing at the California College of Arts and Crafts in Oakland, Bill Farley handed out notes to his students telling how Italian director Lina Wertmuller (*Swept Away, Seven Beauties*, etc.) takes a completed screenplay and rewrites every scene without any dialogue. She replaces her dialogue with visual storytelling, using images instead of words. Then she does a final draft of the script, a conglomerate of the most successful images she invented for the story (that replace dialogue now no longer necessary) and whatever dialogue must remain for story line. In this way she insures that her films will be first and foremost visual experiences. Farley, a teacher and low-budget feature filmmaker (his *Of Men and Angels* showed in the Dramatic Competition at the Sundance Film Festival, 1989), wants his students to understand the power of imagery before they make their own films.

If you're having a problem thinking visually, it might be helpful to rent some image-oriented films at your neighborhood video store. Check out some films by Godard (*Alphaville, Une Femme Mariée*), or Bergman (*The Seventh Seal, Persona*). Many silent films, from *The Last Laugh* (F. W. Murnau, 1925) to *The Cabinet of Dr. Caligari* (Robert Weine, 1919), can give you a great introduction to the graphic power of black-and-white imagery. Color films with graphic power seem harder to identify so readily, but films like *The Conformist* (Bertolucci, 1970) or *Chinatown* (Roman Polanski, 1974) reveal the power of imagery when a film is in the hands of an extremely talented director.

Another way to immerse yourself in images is to turn on your TV and leave the sound off. What you see are images that apply to your particular lifetime: talk shows, nightly news, movies made for TV. Do any of the electronic images fluttering before your face tell a story or keep your interest? If an old black-and-white movie is on (that has escaped colorization!), you will probably find it has a lot more graphic power than anything else on the tube. Look at the choices of lighting and cuts. Do you understand the story that's being told? Are you being gripped by the images? Certainly it's easy to tell the difference between a film with images at work and a normal TV show. That's the kind of power you want in your feature films.

THE LONG TAKE

One way to shoot a feature film with great economy is to use the low-budget method of the "ten-minute take," honed to perfection by filmmakers like Jon Jost. In Jost's feature *Last Chants for a Slow Dance*, the film has been constructed mostly through beautifully crafted ten-minute takes (full 400' rolls shot in one sequence) that are capable of telling a complex story. Jost has the ability to engineer into his long takes a great deal of narrative energy, so that although each scene is very long and without cuts, the viewer is never bored. To do what he does is very difficult, because *real* magic must be created in each long shot. Every facet of the craft of filmmaking must be used to its maximum capacity: the way the shot is framed and filmed, what is said between the characters (and what is not said), the way the scene is lit, the selection of filmstock (grainy or high-gloss, color), and how the scene functions as part of the story being told. In *Last Chants for a Slow Dance* Jost also uses some spectacular superimpositions (printing two different shots on one roll simultaneously) that are so subtle that the viewer doesn't really notice they are effects, but feels them deeply. To successfully use the long take, the filmmaker must be able to fill the frame of the shot with such a great deal of drama and magic that the audience doesn't ever feel the need for a cut. You must accomplish with this technique what must always be accomplished throughout any film, and that is to cast a spell over the viewer.

"FREEZE" METHOD OF SHOOTING FOR CUTS

If your movie will be constructed of many cuts, one method of shooting is to have the actors freeze their position at the director's command ("Freeze"), while the camera is moved to a new angle. This method designs each cut in a sequence, and the shooting is one-to-one. If the two characters in your movie are having a discussion on a couch and your first shot is wide to include the entire couch, after calling "Freeze" at an appropriate moment in the dialogue, you may want to move the camera into a closer shot of the person talking. Before the camera and sync sound recording have started up again, the actors are fed back the last few lines of dialogue, to be repeated at the next take. This gives the editor several in-points for making the cut work. A continuous sequence can be built with these changes of camera angle, so that the edited film will fit perfectly together. While Hollywood would use two cameras shooting continuously, with many takes, you are able to accomplish the same "look" shooting one-to-one. This process was effectively used in *The Last Roommate* when Jean discusses abortion with Sarah, a nurse at the clinic. Even though the dialogue was improvisational, the use of the "freeze" method structured the filming to create a tightly cut scene.

CUTAWAYS AND PAUSES FOR TRANSITIONS

While shooting your scenes you should protect your ability to successfully edit those scenes together. In some instances a transition can be accomplished by a "cutaway," a short shot that shows either a character's reaction to dialogue said by another, or some action or object that has been part of the previous shot in wide coverage. If one of the characters was reaching for a cigarette, the camera could film a close-up of the hand as it touches the pack. This shot could be used to shorten a sequence that was running too long. Shooting a "reaction shot" of an actor's face is trickier, because without the real scene happening it's very hard for a director to create the energy of the moment, and often the result is wooden and stupid. Sometimes, in a very complicated sequence, it is worth it to shoot the scene twice, making sure that in take #1 you are on the character speaking and that in take #2 you pan over to the character responding. Any of these short little "extra" shots can often save a scene in the editing room.

Also, it is important to run some footage at the beginning and end of each shot while filming, before the actors begin and after they have finished their scene, to film a "pause" that might help achieve a transition during editing. So don't say "action" the second the clap board is pulled away, and don't call "cut" immediately after the last word of dialogue has been spoken. Give your scenes adequate heads and tails for the cut. And after each scene is shot it is important to record at least thirty seconds of "room tone," recorded at the same sound level at which dialogue was recorded. If changes need to be made in the sound track (words deleted or car horns deleted, for example), they can be made during editing by cutting out defects and splicing in your room tone recording (which would be identical to the background sound of your shot if recorded on location directly after the take). When recording room tone you must request that actors remain in position and everyone on the crew stop moving and remain silent.

SHOOTING WITHOUT SOUND

If you are *very* clever, and organized with regard to the structure and storyboarding of your feature, it is possible to shoot scenes without sound sync and piece in the sound later from "wild" recordings. The person off-camera delivers the lines while the camera is on the person listening, and the lines of dialogue or narration are recorded later in the sound studio. During editing, narrations and location sounds—birds, wind, babbling brook—could be added to give the scene a feeling of reality. This process opens up the possibilities of using sound as an effect, much as on radio, where sounds would expand your idea of what was actually happening. Most large-budget productions spend hundreds of thousands of dollars on sound effects that fill up their twenty-four tracks for the mix. And many kung fu movies are shot without sound and are entirely dubbed later. So if the filmmaker has cheap or free access to a high-quality sound studio, this might be an option to consider.

It is also possible to reverse the process and record your sound first, editing the dialogue and effects into a tight cut, and then add the needed length of images. Once again, to use this method of filmmaking and succeed, you must be incredibly well organized in terms of every shot and sound that will make up your story.

The disadvantages of this type of filmmaking can outweigh the results if the method is not perfectly executed. To successfully complete the movie the filmmaker must make a large commitment to the many hours of editing such a feature will require. It will require a lot more editing to piece in the recorded dialogue and sound effects than would usually be needed to edit from the sound sync takes recorded on location. Although the production company that forgoes the cost of an on-location soundperson with gear may initially believe that it is saving money, the added expenses of creating each sound track with recorded "studio" sound, and of editing, may end up being more expensive and bothersome. When I have a soundperson on location, I always record sound sync for each shot, even if it is just a scene of someone sitting at a desk saying nothing. Then, when I sync up each take, I am saved from the aggravation of coming to a scene that has no sound, and from the worry of having to create some sound for that particular image. After the scene is shot, I have the soundperson record any sound effects that might come in handy during editing. If a man is writing a letter in a scene, I record a "wild take" of the sound of the pen moving against the paper. To avoid extra editing expenses, I make sure the soundperson has recorded a long enough take of these sound effects to run concurrently with the sync take for which they are designed. When I finally arrive at the editing room I find it is a great relief to know that, aside from some possible music, I have everything I need to edit my feature. So before you rule out hiring an on-location soundperson, make sure this decision is correct for the style of your film, your story, your editing process, and your budget.

HIGH-BUDGET EFFECTS

By being inventive, the low-budget filmmaker can achieve high-budget effects that will greatly enhance the possible commercial aspect of his or her film. Have you ever seen tree trimmers being hoisted up in a bucket, lifted by a hydraulic lift from the top of a truck? If you are a bit aggressive, you can probably talk someone into loaning you his rig for the film, and use the lift for an inexpensive crane shot. Although the bucket tends to be a bit unsteady, if the camera is hand held while the bucket is raised (one person in the bucket to work the controls, one to film the shot), a beautiful effect can be achieved.

Many filmmakers already know that a wheelchair works splendidly for dolly shots. Just set the cameraperson in the seat and roll backward or forward during the shot. You can either rent a wheelchair or, occasionally, buy one for $20 at a flea market. By the time you complete your first feature, it is quite possible that you will have invented some special apparatus or shots of your own.

DIRECTING ACTORS ON LOCATION

After the camera placement has been set and the lighting properly arranged, the filmmaker/director turns his or her attention to the actors. Turning off the lights to save electricity and bulbs (not to mention lessening the uncomfortable heat), the filmmaker brings the actors onto the set and reviews their dialogue and moves for the shot. Whether dealing with actors who have memorized the lines or with nonactors who will basically be themselves, the filmmaker shouldn't spend so much time practicing the scene that all of the vital energy is expended before the camera is turned on. Although our strict budget requires basically a one-to-one shooting ratio, there is enough filmstock to do the most important shots twice if necessary. The filmmaker needs to get a feeling for the readiness of the actors and be prepared to shoot the scene before the actors have rehearsed and rehashed their performances into a lifeless state.

The most important quality an actor can convey is honesty, and it is the job of the filmmaker to make sure that a phony performance is not in the making. He must get the performance down to earth so that the film rings true to the viewer. Often it seems actors (and nonactors) have pent-up energy just before the shooting, and when the camera rolls they talk too fast and move too fast. To protect against this recurring problem, the filmmaker must slow down the shooting process. Before turning on the camera you should tell your actors that you want them to give a pause before beginning. Ask them to count to five (to themselves) before speaking. It is possible that because of the pressure of the filming they will jump right on their lines the second you say "Action," at which point, camera still running, you will say "Hold it . . . pause and then start again." If the scene is still going too fast, stop the camera and start again.

Shooting one-to-one requires that actors and nonactors must somehow get their performances right on the first try. The direction given by the filmmaker of a low-budget feature is not at all like the cliché of the Hollywood director who browbeats his actors and actresses into submission. You don't have fifty takes to shoot one line from a faltering thespian. If your film has been cast correctly, then as long as your actors believe they are doing a good job, they can maintain good, consistent performances. It may be worth placing prospective actors in front of the camera before the shoot, to see if they will freeze up when you shoot a small, one-minute test. Nonactors operate best with your encouragement, and it's destructive to give them strict criticism for their "performances." Their performances *are* them, and you get who they are. In a low-budget production, the filmmaker has only a few chances to snap the performances into the correct believability he or she is after. Sit down with a faltering performer and explain again that you selected him or her for the part because he or she was absolutely right as the character you envisioned. Tell the person that

On the set for *Emerald Cities* in Death Valley. Photo by Julie Schachter.

if they would just relax things would be great. Have the person break the ice during the next shot by pretending to have a seizure during the scene, falling to the floor and wiggling around. Do something to snap your actor into good functioning order.

DIRECTING FROM BEHIND THE CAMERA

During my last two low-budget feature film productions, *Morgan's Cake* and *American Orpheus*, I developed some new techniques for directing from behind the camera; I hope that you'll find ways to apply them to your own particular situations. In the preface I discussed how my main focus in filmmaking is on real people telling their real truths to the camera within the structure of my fictional story. That means that I've written a full script with dialogue and story development, but don't demand that my actors (usually nonactors) recite all of my written words back to me and the camera. I'm much more interested in filming my characters speaking in their own words, using their own intelligence to complete my scenes. The technique I developed for allowing for this improvisation is to give voice commands to actors from behind the camera, speaking to them while the camera is rolling. If I'm careful and speak to them only at those moments in the scene when no one is talking (no lips moving), then I can remove my voice command from the sound track during editing, replacing the length of mag track that carries my words with other mag track that contains just room tone.

Sometimes, while shooting *American Orpheus*, I would just feed scripted lines to the five-year-old actress who played Eury (Jasmine Carver), telling her one line after another to build a scene which she had partially memorized with the help of her parents. By telling her what to say each time, I could control the timing of when she spoke, and make sure that what she said moved the scene forward as I had envisioned it. Using this technique I was able to shoot a complicated scene with lead actress Jody Esther and Jasmine, where the threat of her becoming a "missing kid" was discussed from the child's point of view, and still maintain my low filming ratio. While I did have to rely on my scripting and the actual repeating of those lines by Jasmine to create this particular scene, Jody (playing her mother) did not have to adhere to the script verbatim, but was able to listen and respond to her daughter's fears naturally, giving the scene a frightening air of reality.

In some instances I have used this "voice command" technique to direct a scene I thought up on the spot. As I've watched a scene develop, and heard the improvisional dialogue spoken, I've been able to interject ideas and needed dialogue to keep the scene heading toward some sort of climax or resolve. This approach allows the filmmaker to complete his or her scenes with a reasonable shooting ratio while trolling the mysterious depths of story and characterizations. This is what "trusting in the flow" is all about. If you're lucky and inquisitive you may suddenly find yourself shooting scenes that aren't simply what you envisioned, but artifacts of the age in which you live. You may perhaps be able to create a movie in which the overall intelligence and message transcends the script from which it was spawned.

FEEDING CAST AND CREW ON A BUDGET

The reason for this section is to remind the filmmaker that he or she has an obligation to help keep alive the people who are aiding in the production of a feature. Regardless of what level of no-budget you operate on, it is important to at least pick up a few meals, lunches and dinners, during the length of time you are shooting. If you are producing on a minuscule budget where every dollar counts then you will probably have to depend on the help of a friend to prepare a few home-cooked meals for your five- or six-person group. Just remember that you don't want to sink your ship by feeding cast and crew such a heavy meal that they can't do their jobs afterward. Keep the food light: heavy on the vegetarian, pasta, perhaps seafood and chicken, light on the roast beef. If you don't have a credit card to take everyone out for some Chinese or Thai food you could always buy a turkey and cook it beforehand, then serve it for a dinner and sandwiches. If the story you are filming is the kind that depends on a growing intensity of emotions you could heighten that intensity by serving everyone turkey day after day. I'm kidding of course, but the point is, buy your group some meals, especially breakfast when the call to the set is super early, dinner when you run late. And always have on hand an array of soft drinks and snacks for breaks.

On my *American Orpheus* shoot I was fortunate to be able to afford a catering service for ten days, supplying my twelve-member cast and crew with three meals a day for around $4,000. This money was the best investment I've ever made in a production. The food was so good that it actually formed smiles on people's faces, including my own. While I was pushing myself and everyone else to do the impossible of shooting a color feature in ten days, I got wonderful meals and well-ordered breaks in shooting three times a day. The good food gave me another burst of energy for the next five-hour segment of work. Contact your local caterers to see if there is a deal that you can afford. It will be the best money you'll ever spend.

CONTINUITY

On the set the filmmaker will want to make absolutely sure that for shots that must cut together the actors filmed are wearing the same clothes and making the same movements for the camera. If the actor is wearing a hat in the first shot, then he must have it on when the filmmaker shoots from a different angle for a scene where those two shots cut together. If the hat has accidentally been removed before the second shot, then the hat will simply disappear at the cut as if by magic. Of course, if it is your intention to use the potential of movie magic in the shot, this is one of the secrets. But for the "normal" film, continuity must be observed. On big-budget productions, where scenes are always shot out of order and only selected takes are printed, the person in charge of continuity must keep a detailed record of each aspect of the filmed scenes ("continuity breakdown") so that a major mistake will not occur. On a low-budget set the filmmaker is responsible for noticing any discrepancy in continuity. He or she must have a sixth sense that "something" isn't right if mistakes are to be caught in time. And the actors must also share responsibility by bringing the same clothes to the set for scenes that are continuous. Since scenes on a low-budget shoot are usually shot in order, it's fairly easy to catch mistakes in mismatched clothing. The real challenge for the filmmaker is noticing hand and facial movements and having actors repeat these movements for the next take so that each shot will successfully edit together in the completed scene. When the small crew of a low-budget feature is totally committed to the film's being made, everyone is constantly on the alert for mistakes in continuity.

SHOOTING TITLES ON LOCATION

A very creative way of saving money on your feature is to shoot your titles while on location. Not only does the creation of titles during the location shoot save you the cost of shooting titles on an optical printer, but usually filming your "title sequence" at the location enhances some aspect of the film's concept.

One method of creating titles on location is by painting them on a wall and panning over to them, one at a time. The credits could be painted with a spray can in the style of New York City subway graffiti. Or the credits could be carefully set up in painted or stick-on letters, white or different colors. There are many interesting ways of creating original titles, and it is up to the filmmaker to choose the typeface and concept of filming titles that best supports the idea of the film.

Another method of shooting titles is setting stick-on letters on clear plastic sheets and filming these credits with the scene showing through behind the acetate as we did in *The Last Roommate*. By using a 9.5–57 wide-angle zoom lens we were able to keep in focus both the letters on the acetate and the scene that showed through. The most difficult problems of shooting credits in this manner are avoiding light flares on the plastic and making sure that the words are level and centered. Our white titles for *The Last Roommate* would have had to have been optically printed by a lab at a cost of many hundreds of dollars. We spent $25 for the white Helvetica stick-on titles and acetate sheets, and $120 for the filmstock and processing/work print.

LOCATION MIRACLES

This is just a reminder not to overlook location miracles that stare you in the face while you shoot your tightly scripted and storyboarded story. Make use of the shadows that fall across a windowsill, real stories of your actors, special sounds, everything that crosses your path during the week or two that you are filming. During the filming of *The Last Roommate* we discovered our actress, Jean Mitchell, had actually lived through the experience of being terrorized by an insanely jealous boyfriend, which was what the story we had selected to film was about! So we took advantage of this irony by filming Jean in vignettes talking directly to the camera, telling her real stories and changing the name of her real boyfriend to our character's name, Greg. And because her fear of her real boyfriend was still very real, she had covered both front and rear doors of her house (where we were filming) with one-inch plywood, adding a wooden plank across the back door for security. We were able to film scenes using these special situations to enhance the story we were telling. Filming at Jean's house also gave us a chance to observe her special touches to the surroundings. She had tied a bunch of dried roses to the end of a curtain string and this shriveled bouquet became a curious image when the curtain was lowered in a shot, the flowers dangling in front of the window with an ominous presence. Keep your eyes open and make use of the special miracles that exist around the creation of a movie.

SAVING FILM ON EACH SYNC TAKE

Now that the big moment has arrived and you are ready to roll the camera and sound recorder to film your actors' performances, on location, you should know the most efficient way to mark sync for your shots. A great deal of film and tape can be saved by marking and notating all information about the coming take on sound tape and slate board *before* the shot is begun. The number of the scene and take is written in chalk on the slate. The description of the coming scene and the scene and take number are recorded on the sound tape by the soundperson. With the actors in place, the lights on, and the camera framed and wrapped with a "barney" to muffle it, the soundperson, who has carefully aimed his or her mikes and set sound levels with the actors' normal voices, waits for the command from the filmmaker to "Roll sound." When the filmmaker feels everyone is ready to begin, he first announces "Quiet on the set." Then, after making sure that the slate is visible in his framing of the shot, he calls out "Roll sound." The soundperson verifies he or she is recording sound by calling back "Sound rolling." The production assistant then reads off the information on the slate, indicating scene number, take number, and some identification of the production (film title or director's name). The filmmaker starts the camera (he or she has already run ten seconds of film at the beginning of the new roll, the required length of head leader the labs usually request) and calls out "Mark it." The assistant closes the slate, making a *clack* for the sound track and a visual sync for the picture, and steps out of the framed scene. Giving the actors a pause to settle down, the filmmaker calls out (softly) "Action" or some appropriate word ("OK, go") and the scene begins. Instead of wasting valuable footage running the camera while the clap board is read for scene and take numbers, this method of reading (and recording) the identification on the slate *before* running the camera, and then shooting film of the slate just for the few seconds it takes to "clack it" for sync mark, saves several feet of footage on each take and several hundred feet of footage by the end of a feature shoot.

BENEFITS OF A TIGHT SHOOTING SCHEDULE

Shooting your feature on a low or no budget most likely means that you'll have to complete the filming within a seven- to ten-day schedule. There just isn't any money to extend the process a moment longer. Since you're probably getting everyone to work for you at much reduced rates, you must release them back to their real lives (real salaries) as soon as possible. The main effect of a tight schedule on a production is that it keeps it moving at a very fast pace. If you can't trust your intuition, can't keep making decisions at breakneck speed, then you won't have a feature film. Your only choice is to jump in headfirst, submerge yourself, and keep striving for the best ideas and shots to back them up. You need to shoot at least twelve 400' rolls to have <u>any</u> choices in the editing. That means you have to run through at least two rolls a day. Even if your budget expands to allow for shooting four rolls a day for ten days (it took Kevin Smith 37 400' rolls to create his indi hit *Clerks*), there will be no time for second guessing. In a sense you have to stop thinking and just *do*. So you have no choice but to believe in yourself. Have you ever done that before? Have you ever just jumped into a project with total faith in yourself? That's pretty hard to do. There are always those nagging doubts. But with a tight budget there is no time for doubt. Your only hope is to produce results. This speed of production will also allow you an element of freshness and spontaneity, the lifeblood of the best and most successful indi features.

MOVIE STILLS/VIDEO OF "WORK IN PROGRESS"

Even on a no-budget film it is vital that you shoot some stills of the production: well-lit, sharply focused photos of the lead actors on the set and shots of scenes from your movie. These stills will be invaluable to you later when it comes time to publicize your finished feature film. Perhaps you know someone who is a photographer with a good camera (Leica, Nikon) who would help you for a small fee, supplied filmstock, and a title in the credits. Remember that one great photo used as a graphic in ads and on posters can make the difference between getting an audience (or distributor!) and not. Have you seen the photo from the movie *Man Bites Dog?* It's memorable for the gun being shown so outstretched from the arm (shot in wide angle, deep focus, right next to the lens) that it's literally "in your face." That photo has become an icon for the film.

You may also find that the use of your carefully taken stills, whether photos or slides, is crucial to telling a part of your filmatic story. Several of my earlier features used montages of images from stills to reveal a side of the stories that weren't shown in scenes during the shoot. My first feature, *A Man, a Woman, and a Killer*, featured an eight-minute sequence of behind-the-scenes narration backing up images shot as slides by one of the lead actors, Ed Nylund. These pictures showed emotional moments between the young leads, Dick Richardson and Carolyn Zaremba, and the development of their real love relationship on the set. So sometimes the stills you take on the set can be invaluable in editing, help you complete your feature, or fill in gaps in the story you are telling.

Once you have shot your film, give yourself a moment to relax and look over the stills, selecting a few of the best ones that you'll want to have reproduced. Quality Photos (5432 Hollywood Blvd., Hollywood, Calif. 90027) gives one of the best deals to the filmmaker, charging approximately $35 per 25 glossy 8"-by-10" copies of an image, with a small one-time fee of around $20 for negative work. Call them at (213) 467-6178.

In this video age you may also want to consider hiring a friend to document your shoot. With the combined high-quality image and portability of new Hi8 video cameras, including every type of accessory from tripods to steadi-cams, you can record the making of your epic on video for just a few hundred dollars. And if your film turns out to be the hit of the year, all that video footage can be transferred over to your laser disc for a behind-the-scenes look at the director at work. Even if your film isn't the one film that succeeds above all others, you may find that in a few years you can produce your own laser disc (the prices keep dropping) and it will be fun to edit the video footage for your own purposes. Maybe some of the footage will find its way to your "electronic pressbook," a videotape used by publicists to sell your film and its ideas.

DEVELOPING AND
WORK PRINTING WITH THE LAB

After your first day of filming you should be anxious to drop off the exposed rolls of 400' film that you ran through the camera to see if your images have been realized. Each can you will turn in to the lab has been carefully wrapped with tape around the edge to make sure that the film inside will not be exposed to the light. The black paper bag that each fresh roll of filmstock was initially wrapped in when you loaded the film into the camera magazine in the changing bag has also been placed around each roll, when the camera was unloaded. On each can you have already applied a label carefully listing the type of stock you have shot, the length of each roll (400' or maybe shorter), your name, address, phone number, and number of roll (in order that you shot). The length of the rolls is an important bit of information for the film handlers inside the developing room and must not be omitted.

Arriving at the lab, you either turn over the rolls to a lab person over the desk, or if it is after work hours you may be able to insert the rolls in a slot called a "night drop" in the side of the building. If you deliver your rolls to the lab at night, make sure that each roll has been pushed into the slot far enough to hear it "clunk" down inside the building. Most labs offer a "daily" processing/work print service, which means that you will be able to pick up a work print of what you shot that day the following morning and be able to screen the footage. You can dream about seeing the results of your filmmaking labors as you drive home and get some sleep before the next full day of shooting.

At this point in the filmmaking process you have already begun to build a relationship with the people at the lab. Someone there, probably the manager, has already helped you to budget your "feature film at used-car prices." And you probably have already met the people who work behind the counter where you picked up your stock for the shoot. All these relationships are important to you; once you have some friends inside the building, dealing with the lab will be much more pleasant. Also, it is important to feel that they are taking special care with your original and giving you the best quality possible in all services. When you call the lab to find out if your work print from your first day of filming is ready, you definitely know that you are involved with the people at the lab. They put you on hold while they check for you and you pray that they know what they are doing and have successfully run your film through the printing machines without any mishap (machines breaking down, original footage scratched, destroyed, or lost somewhere in the lab). At this point, control over your project is in the hands of the lab.

When you hear that your work print is ready for pickup you can heave a sigh of relief. There was something on the film to print, and the lab didn't lose or destroy your film. The lab will ask you if you wish for them to "vault your original," which means they will store the original film you ran through your camera (off which they made your work print), placing the film in a safe, cool location with careful identification to easily locate it later. The worst catastrophe that can occur during a production is for the original film from your shoot, essential to making high-quality prints, to be lost in part or in total. Entrusting this precious original to a lab for storage is a crucial decision. Probably the best solution would be, if a filmmaker could afford it, an expensive fireproof safe, too heavy to steal, in which the original footage would be stored. But since this solution is usually too costly, the filmmaker finds him or herself blindly trusting the lab with the irreplaceable original footage.

PROCESSING WITHOUT A WORK PRINT

The work printing of your footage is one of the largest expenditures on a low-budget feature, and you should give every consideration to determining exactly what your particular film requires. If your feature is simply shot, in sequence order with few cuts, it is possible to skip the expense of using a work print. This method of using the original for (light) editing and assembly is ideal for the "long take" style of filmmaking, since all the filmmaker needs to do is sync up each scene in order with the sound track and then hot splice the picture together, keeping the sound track synced to the picture (see chapter 6). Extreme caution must be used when handling this original film, and each piece of editing equipment that comes in contact with the footage (Moviescope, synchronizer, flatbed editing machine, split reels) must be thoroughly checked to make sure it won't scratch or tear your original footage. To test the equipment, run a piece of clear or white leader through the machine several times and then examine both sides for scratches.

For films with multiple cuts and lengthy editing needs, it will be best to spend the extra money on a work print. And, of course, if you have shot your feature on negative stock, it will be necessary to make a work print to see exactly what you have. But even with negative stock you can save some money by checking the original (very carefully) and omitting the work printing of scenes you know are worthless. And if your project is so expansive that you will need to raise additional money for the last stages of your production, you will probably need a work print to show to prospective investors.

Another option is to get from the lab a "dirty dupe" work print: a low-quality, high-contrast black-and-white copy of your film for editing purposes that usually costs about half of the usual "one light" work print. While this "dupe" is certainly adequate for editing your feature, the lack of quality of the images may not give you the necessary pleasure and excitement needed to maintain the energy you need to edit during the months ahead. It may become depressing to stare at second-rate images every day while you compile your film, even though you can remind yourself that the original is really of fine quality. And if there is any need to interest investors in your film, it will be almost impossible to convince them your film is any good if all they see on the screen is poor-quality images. I think it is much wiser to go through your original and make a good-quality "one light" work print of *only* usable shots, thus saving as much money as possible while still having a work print you will enjoy.

VIDEO VERSUS FILM WORK PRINT

More often than not these days the low-budget feature filmmaker finds him- or herself confronted by the question of whether to go to video for work printing and postproduction. If you can save thousands of dollars editing on video the decision seems to be already made, since money must be saved at every turn. But video is cheaper only in certain cases, usually when you have low-cost or free access to video decks for hourly editing and low-cost facilities for video transfers from your original footage. A film work print is cheaper if you have inexpensive access to flatbed editing machines (FAF in San Francisco and 911 in Seattle both offer single-day and hourly rates as well as weekly rates) that you can pair with your home-built editing bench (see chapter 3 for detailed plans), and basic equipment, including Moviescope, sound reader, sync block, rewinds, and reels, for editing any hour of the day or night without overhead. When I was in production with my 1993 Feature workshop I seriously considered editing in video and came up with the following costs of editing at home for one week:

Video Work Print

Video transfer of 12 400' rolls B&W 16-mm negative $1075.00
    (4,800' = 133 min.) to Betacam SP (stock + $250/hr.)
Transfer ¼" sound tapes/sync up @ $80 × 6 hrs. .... $ 480.00
                                                                     $1555.00

Video Editing
Sony BVW-65 (Player) @ $375/day, and Sony BVW-75 ... $3500.00
(cuts only recorder) @ $500/day, a special weekly rate   _____
   for both machines
                                  TOTAL $5055.00

Film Work Print
Work print 4800' 16-mm B&W film @ .215/ft. $1032.00
Transfer ¼" sound tapes to mag ($45/hr. + stock) .... $ 600.00
                                             $1632.00

Film Editing
Moviola 6-plate flatbed editing machine (1 week) .... $ 200.00
                                  TOTAL $1832.00

While this comparison between 16-mm film and Betacam SP may be somewhat unfair considering that Betacam SP is the ultimate in high-quality video, my idea was to be able to produce a somewhat finished feature on video (if I chose that direction) using broadcast portable "studio" editing machines (Sony BVW-65, and BVW-75) to create a clean final edit. Perhaps a more realistic comparison would be made by detailing prices for a video transfer to ¾", editing in VHS.

Video Work Print/Editing (¾" to VHS) of 75-minute rough cut
Video transfer 4800' to ¾" video (stock + $250/hr.) .... $ 947.00
Transfer ¼" sound tapes/sync up @ 80/hr. .... $ 480.00
Dub ¾" master to VHS (1 VHS per film roll/12 rolls) ..... $ 144.00
Panasonic AG-7650 VHS player and AG-7750 VHS .... $ 787.50
   recorder editing system @ $225/day/special weekly
   rate of $787.50
Miscellaneous costs (3 new master VHS tapes, etc.) ..... $ 100.00
10 VHS dubs (cost of stock) .... $ 50.00
                               TOTAL $2508.50

With this cost a feature filmmaker could produce an assembly edit on VHS and supply each of ten collaborators with a VHS copy of the results, dubbed from the master VHS. To produce a similar quality VHS dub of the 80-minute 16-mm cut would require an extra film-to-video transfer cost, boosting the film editing costs beyond that of video.

Film Work Print/Editing (16-mm to VHS) of 75-minute rough cut

Film work print (16-mm) 4800'	$1032.00
¼" tapes to mag	$ 600.00
Flatbed editing machine (1 week)	$ 200.00
Miscellaneous costs (editing tape, cores, etc.)	$ 100.00
Video transfer 16-mm to ¾" (@ $250/hr + $75 stock)	$ 650.00
10 VHS dubs ($12 ea.)	$ 120.00
TOTAL	$2702.00

As you can see, for the short-term editing (1 week), video editing on VHS is cheaper by a couple of hundred dollars when the filmmaker needs a video copy of the rough cut to show prospective investors or elicit film festival interest. And while editing on video doesn't give the filmmaker an opportunity to screen the cut through a projector as a film, working with a video work print during editing ensures that the cleanest video image will be dubbed to VHS, since the transfer originated from the 16-mm original negative. Perhaps the day will soon arrive when I conduct all my postproduction editing on computers (see AVID Media Composer and D-Vision editing, chapter 11) pushing buttons instead of looping lengths of film and sound track over my arm. But what ultimately matters is that the filmmaker achieve the best cut of his or her material.

MONEY AND THE LAB

A word or two should also be said about your relationship to the lab with regard to money. When I think of my feature filmmaking over the last twenty years, one of the main things that comes to mind is that I was often able to finish my projects because I could

bargain with the lab. Without being able to charge expensive services such as sound mix, answer printing, and occasional titling,
I could not have produced my features without long delays. And
without being able to get special reduced rates in processing and
work printing, I would not on some occasions even have been able
to begin a project. At a crucial moment in each of my feature
productions the lab has let me charge the thousands of dollars
needed to finish. Because of their patience, I have always paid
them off at the earliest possible moment with any money I received from grants, teaching salary, TV sales, or Sheetrocking.
Even the lowest-budget feature film at used-car prices is relatively
expensive, and the filmmaker must be able to complete the project
as soon as possible to avoid having an unfinished film *and* unpaid
bills. It is vital that each feature filmmaker begin to establish credit
with the lab at the earliest opportunity, so that when the editing
is completed he or she will hopefully be able to charge the sound
mix and answer print if money has run out. The pressure on the
feature filmmaker is too great to let his or her film project drag
on for years because of lack of finishing funds. But remember the
obvious fact that your lab bill must be paid off even if it means
selling your other used car, your possessions, or your house.

NOTE: Keep track of all your invoices from the lab (and other film
work) to make sure that you haven't been charged twice for any
services or products.

CHECKING YOUR FIRST FOOTAGE

It is a great feeling to hold that first roll of work print in your
hands in anticipation of what you will soon see projected on the
screen. It's a hundred times more exciting than Christmas. And
probably you will do what most filmmakers do, which is roll some
film out in your hand, just to make sure that there is actually
something on the film. For all the multitude of ideas, decisions,
accidents, last-minute changes, improvisation, and location mira-

cles that went into the first roll . . . the question "Did it work?" now arises. In minutes you will see a part of your film, and you will see on the screen not only the projected images but also all the drama before and after each scene, including your hopes and dreams for the project. For these reasons you will want to screen this first roll several times, first to enjoy the shock of seeing your ideas turned into actual filmatic images, and then, as the excitement wears off a bit, to look at the footage with a more critical eye, checking for the following problems:

☐ If you see scratches on the film during projection of your work print, it is important to check your original to find out if the scratches are also present there. If they are, then you have either been using a faulty camera or a faulty magazine, which must be replaced before continuing the filming. And if the original is not scratched, then thank your lucky stars that only your work print was scratched, probably by the projector, and this will not affect the quality of your final print. Some scratches can be removed during printing by a process called "liquid gate" (see chapter 6 for a description), but deep scratches will probably remain forever on your film, so use great caution when screening original footage. Ask the lab technician if he or she has a special projector used only for original film. If so, you can almost be guaranteed that it doesn't cause scratches, since the lab uses the projector to check jobs that it can't afford to ruin. Even with every guarantee that a projector is "scratch free," the filmmaker must exercise his or her paranoia and still run a bit of leader through the projector to double-check for scratches. Remember that with a used-car-prices budget you can't really afford to waste film, or time, or filmatic moments that will never come again.

☐ Check your lighting. How does the quality of the images you shot feel to you? Is the mood correct for your story? Are the shadows dramatic or clumsy? Now is the time to make a lighting change, so do your best to evaluate the success or failure of your lighting concepts.

☐ Watch out for any foreign objects in the picture plane, such as microphones, extension cords, light stand legs, a hair in the gate of the camera, or anything that might destroy the believability of your movie.

☐ Is everything in focus? Are your actors' faces in focus when they are the center of attention? Soft focus can be effective for certain moods, but if this is not your desired result, it can greatly diminish the quality of your film.

☐ Are your actors giving honest performances?

☐ Is the camera steady, or do you detect shaking, jiggling, bad compositions, poor pans, or uncertain gestures that will detract from your story? If the camera work is sloppy you may want to try again and reshoot your first roll of scenes.

☐ Check for cuts and transitions. Can you string your footage together as you've shot it? This can be further tested once you have synced the picture and the sound track (see chapter 6) and actually edited the scenes and cuts together.

> **NOTE:** One of the most difficult things to achieve in filmmaking is to clearly see footage that you shot yourself. If you worked the camera, almost any footage you screen will seduce you. So, when checking out this first roll of processed film, bring along a friend who may be able to supply you with some critical observations.

CHECKING YOUR RECORDED SYNC SOUND

After the first day's shooting it is also very important to make sure you are recording sound on location that has good quality and levels, and the essential sync pulse to run sync with your picture. Your first step is to transfer the ¼" tapes recorded on your Nagra, or the cassettes recorded on a Sony Walkman Professional, onto mag track.

There are two "schools" of sound transferring. One group says that it is best to equalize the location sound while transferring it to mag track, adjusting treble and bass for each take. The other group believes that the sound from location should be recorded with the widest range of highs and lows (no equalization) and then equalized during the mix. I personally favor the latter method, because I like to select the quality of sound of each scene during the mixing process to tie each edited scene together with appropriate sound values. Also, I believe equalizing during the mix adds up to higher-quality sound on the print. Only if your budget cannot afford a mix of any kind would I recommend equalizing and setting uniform levels during transfer, enabling you to "mix" your tracks by making a straight copy of the spliced-together sound track for your print.

After you have transferred the location sound onto mag track for your first 400' of picture, you will want to listen to the track to make sure the quality is the best that can be achieved. If possible, try to play the mag track on an interlock projector that is in a booth separate from the theater where you will listen to it. Check for the following problems:

- ☐ Hissing or electric static
- ☐ Drastic changes in sound levels
- ☐ Muffled dialogue
- ☐ Street noises (airplanes, cars, buses, people shouting, etc.) that disturb sound quality
- ☐ Sound speeding up or slowing down due to faulty equipment

What you want to hear is "clean sound": distinctive dialogue without overbearing background noise. And by syncing up the mag track with the picture work print and projecting the sync footage, you will be able to determine if the sound track is doing its job of turning your film into a watchable movie. If the dialogue is sync with the picture, and the sound doesn't distract from the experience on the screen, then you have adequate sound.

There is such a thing as "great location sound," but usually the low-budget filmmaker can't afford it, and hasn't ever experienced it. Before I shot *A Man, a Woman, and a Killer*, Wayne Wang and I were working on a short film starring painter Jim Albertson. We had needed a soundperson because our regular sound recordist friend was unavailable. On the wall at a local lab I spotted a card that read NEELON CRAWFORD—SOUNDMAN and hired him by phone for the one-day shoot. After I transferred the ¼" tapes recorded on his Nagra, I played the mag track synced with work print on an interlock projector at the lab. And while I watched the location sync takes I experienced a strange sensation. I actually turned around at one point during the screening, thinking that someone else was in the room. The tracks were so clean and clear that none of the usual electronic imperfections I had grown to expect had accompanied the experience. Even though it cost me one-quarter of my shooting budget for *A Man, a Woman, and a Killer*, I hired Neelon and his assistant, Lee Serie, for $1,500 for the two-week shoot, this price including his Nagra and microphones, with miscellaneous sound gear.

If the recorded sound from your location shoot is poor, then halt the production and be prepared to shoot the first rolls over. Don't skimp on hiring a good soundperson. Poor-quality tracks will haunt and finally destroy your production.

SCREENING FOOTAGE FOR CAST AND CREW

A very important decision during your shoot is when and how you screen the footage ("rushes") for your actors and collaborators. After you have privately screened the footage and checked it out for technical quality, you must decide if showing it to the cast and crew will inspire them—or simply confuse them. If you are working with nonactors, the screening of this first footage could destroy their natural performances. Maybe they have never seen themselves on film (or video) and the shock of the film images will make them too self-conscious to continue with the shooting. If the production is filming for several weeks, there will be a lot of pressure on the director/filmmaker to show the developed footage. Look at the film and decide if a screening would best serve the production's needs. If the footage looks good, is in focus with good camera moves, then my advice is to show the first 400' roll, silent, to the cast and crew if you believe the energy on the set is low, or if you believe that there are doubts regarding your abilities as director.

On *The Last Roommate* production, the collaborators were skeptical about beginning to shoot (and spending their production money) without a completed script. I told them that if they didn't like the first footage we shot, then we would cancel the production. There was no way around a screening of the first roll of film, so this became a make-or-break situation. Luckily, the footage we shot looked great, and everybody was pumped up to continue spending their money, time, and energy to complete the film.

Filmmaker George Csicsery (director of *Where the Heart Roams*, *"N" is a Number*, etc.) told me that he thinks a person can only see his or her film the way the rest of the world sees it once, and that is when the work print and sound track are screened, sync, for the first time. This is probably true. The first screening of your sync footage is very special and important to your production, so it is the filmmaker's responsibility to be ultra-sensitive to all the details surrounding the screening. This screening is the "premiere" of the results of all the effort that went into your film by dedicated and talented people, so ideally the showing should take place in a good screening room with a few bottles of champagne. Usually, not only the participants of the shoot but also members of their immediate families and friends will want to see the results. If this expanded audience is too much for your jangled nerves, then restrict the first showing to just those members of the cast and crew who were on location making the film. Save the families for the first rough-cut screening. Each screening plays an important role in the process of reducing the footage down to the final cut-and-polished gem that is your desired result.

COMPLETING THE FILMING

Whether or not you have decided to screen the first roll of footage for your cast and crew, you have a lot more shooting to do before you have enough film from which to cut your feature. And in the days or weeks of filming ahead you will enter a zone of creativity and energy that only someone who has experienced it will totally understand. At all moments of the day and night you will be striving to do your best, get your best ideas on celluloid. As the days pass and you see one after another of the shot rolls accumulate, your confidence will grow stronger with the realization that you are actually able to make your film. If there are strong emotions on the set, then you will make use of them in your filming. Ideas are coming to you even in your dreams, and you pay attention to them and invent new scenes and shots. By the time you complete the filming, a very special emotional bond will have formed between you and your cast and crew, and you will feel part of this film family for years to come.

Filming does not always go smoothly, and sometimes actors become so emotional that they leave the filming. This and every other problem that occurs on the set is up to you to solve, so that your hard work is not in vain. If you lose an actor or actress you need to quickly find a replacement. If someone leaves two-thirds of the way through the filming, then change the story to accommodate his or her absence. If you somehow run out of filmstock or money, sell something quickly to get you through. Come hell or high water you must complete the job.

After all the film is shot, and you have screened the results for the cast and crew, the production people drift away, leaving you with strands of plastic to weave into gold.

6

POSTPRODUCTION: EDITING YOUR FEATURE

Congratulations! You've looked at all the rolls of film that you shot for your feature and there are literally thousands of images permanently etched in emulsion. You have been surprised, delighted, and at times disappointed by the results of your filming, but nothing can dampen the great relief you feel in knowing that you've successfully completed your task. You are tired, but refreshed and excited, the way an athlete feels after running a hard race. The experiences of directing and filming your feature film have rejuvenated your spirit, and for these feelings alone you know that all the money and effort expended have been worth it. And as you become reacquainted with the normal routines of your life—work, girlfriends/boyfriends, regular meals and sleeping hours—you still seem protected from mundane activities because you know that you've got something "in the can." You also know that your sound recordings are usable because they had a sync pulse, and were clean and clear while being transferred to mag stock. After a couple of weeks of physically recovering from the shoot, you will probably begin to grow restless, a sure sign that you are now ready to edit your film.

MAKING THE FIRST SPLICE

On the next pages you will find diagrams for operating a tape splicer. After spending a few minutes making practice cuts and splices, you are ready to begin syncing up picture and sound track.

SYNCING IT UP

Whether you are editing on a flatbed machine or on an editing bench using a synchronizer, with Moviescope, rewinds, and sound reader, the procedure for syncing up your picture with your sound track is the same. In either case you want to adjust the length of the picture or sound track so that at the beginning of each scene the frame where the clap board closed is in sync with the *clack* on the mag track.

Place your picture roll and sound roll either on the flatbed editing machine spindles or on split reels for your rewinds, sound reel closest to you. Thread the film and sound track through the flatbed machine, or through the synchronizer on your editing bench, taping the ends on the take-up reels. Reeling or rolling the film and sound track ahead, make the "sync mark"—a vertical line with a circle in the middle of it—on a frame about six feet in from the head ends. (See photo 1 on page 147.) (It may be necessary to splice some additional leader to the front of your picture roll to give you the needed length for your leader before the first images appear.) This mark will be used to line up the two rolls when projecting or editing them, and should be made with an indelible marking pen on your picture leader and mag track.

Roll ahead until you come to the first image on the picture roll, and make a vertical mark with a grease pencil on the frame line where the image begins. Directly across and in sync with the mark on the picture roll, mark the mag track with a vertical line using a sharp-tipped felt pen, making sure that you have marked the same frame line for both rolls (photo 2). If necessary, use blank mag track ("slug") to extend your sound sync *clack* past beginning picture sync (for splicing needs). Roll on ahead until you come to the frame on the film where the clap board closes and mark an *X*

MAKING THE FIRST SPLICE
Picture blade makes cut along frame line.

Clear tape pulled across ends of film to be spliced.

Tape pressed tightly across splicing area.

Splicer lowered, handle pressed to cut tape.

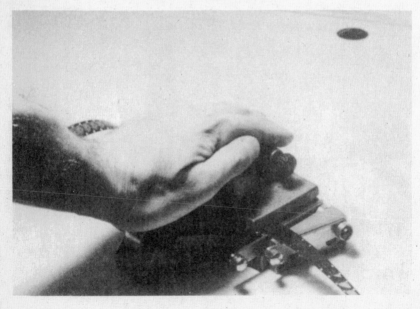

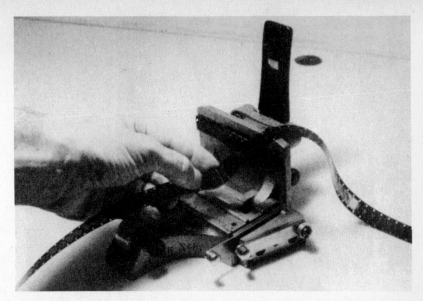

Tape splice checked for punched sprocket holes and cleanly cut edges.

SOUND TRACK SPLICE
Mag track cut by angled (outside) blade.

Sound tape placed on mag, lining up sprocket holes and edges.

Mag track ends brought together for splice.

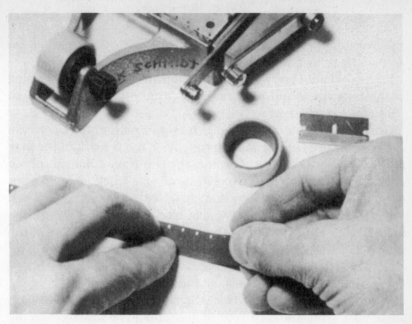

Flip side of mag track showing ends pushed together for splice.

Completed sound tape splice checked for alignment of holes and edges. You can trim tape hanging over the edges with a razor.

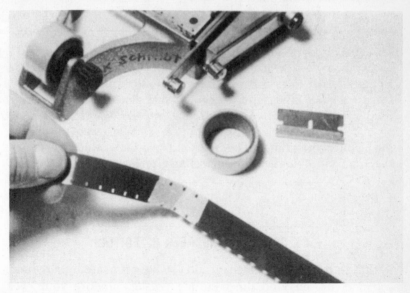

with your grease pencil. Mark a similar *X* with your felt pen on the mag track in sync with the picture *X* (photo 3).

Roll ahead until you come to the sound of the clap board closing on the mag track and mark a circle with your pen at the spot where the *clack* is heard.

Using the *X* mark on your mag track as a pattern for where the clap board closes on the picture roll, place the *O* mark of the mag track *clack* directly on the *X* so that the two frames line up (photo 4 on page 149). Move the two pieces of mag track along in your hand, making sure that they stay together and don't slip. When you come to the mark on the mag track that shows where the scene begins, make a mark with your pen on the frame line of the sandwiched film (photo 5). Cut the sound track at this new mark with your splicer (photo 6) and also at the mark where the scene begins, and roll up the excess cut-out piece on a core.

Tape splice your sound track together and roll up ahead to check your sync. The *X* of your picture should be in sync with the *O* of your sound track (photo 7 on page 150). As you roll your picture and mag track to the beginning of the next scene to sync up, you should notice that words and sounds correspond to the images you are watching.

SYNCING TIPS: When syncing up your film and sound track, it's necessary to have on hand a small roll of blank mag track as well as black leader to extend your rolls when either picture or sound takes are short because of a run-out while filming. You will also need several empty cores for collecting outtakes (see "Filing Your 'Outs,'" on page 150) while syncing up. And you will want to splice the picture work print on both sides to make sure it won't catch in the projector or on the edge-numbering machine.

RICK SCHMIDT'S SECRETS OF EDITING

Now that your rolls are synced up and you have repeatedly screened, flatbedded, or rewound the resulting "rushes" before your eyes

SYNCING IT UP
1. Sync marks on picture and sound track leader, lined up on synchronizer.

2. *X* marks where clap board closes; vertical line marks beginning of scene. Repeated on mag.

3. Circle marked at sound of clap board.

and the appreciative (and at times critical) audiences of cast, crew, friends, relatives, experts, and idiots, it's time to get down to the brass tacks of editing. And although the process isn't such a secret as I'm making out in the title of this section, the information I've amassed during the year and a half of grueling editing on *A Man, a Woman, and a Killer*, the three years of torturous editing on *1988—The Remake*, two and a half years of bringing *Emerald Cities* to completion, and my month's lark of helping Wayne Wang on the final cut of *Chan Is Missing*, plus the enjoyable collaboration with Peter Boza and Mark Yellen while editing *The Last Roommate*, other subsequent features tend to qualify me as something of a sage for surviving such difficult tasks. What I can hopefully impart is a good sense of the best approach to the editing solutions to your project, while keeping you spiritually afloat during the months, and at times years, that lie ahead as you complete your feature. The two main things to remember as you begin are (1) since you created the maze of filmed scenes, you also hold the secret key that will give your footage the life of a cohesive movie; and (2) editing a feature is a long process, and to complete your film you must somehow survive the financial and emotional pressures while still being able to delicately feel the essence of your film. It has been my long-standing belief that the filmmaker must continue to grow as a human being during the span of his or her editing process, so that hopefully at a certain point up the road a revelation can occur that transforms the overwatched footage into a fresh-spirited work of art. Only when the scenes you know by heart jump away from you as bright new moments you've never felt before should you believe that you have completed your task. It is to this end that I reveal my secrets of editing.

EDGE NUMBERING

For complex editing of a feature film, edge numbering of your picture/work print and mag/sound track is a must. By having edge numbers in sync at every foot of your picture and sound track, you can use sound or picture separately without fear of losing sync. If you can't afford edge numbers you will want to put small

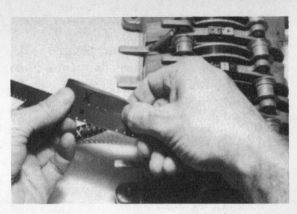

4. Circle and "X"
on mag lined up.

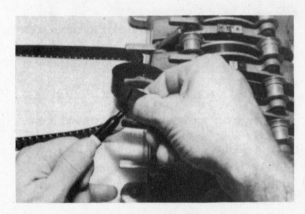

5. Correct beginning
of scene marked on
mag.

6. Mag cut at mark
where scene begins.

7. Picture in sync with mag track.

white paper tabs on picture and sound track, in sync, while editing your feature. Without edge numbers it becomes much more difficult to file the edited "outs" of your picture and sound track so that you can retrieve them later if necessary.

FILING YOUR "OUTS"

As you edit your feature, shifting scenes around, cutting different shots and sounds together, it is important to be able to locate these outs quickly so as not to disrupt the flow of ideas as you work. Before editing begins, each scene on a picture roll should be listed by content and corresponding edge numbers in a logbook. As each piece of film is filed on the picture or sound roll, it is taped on the roll with a consecutive number written on the tape, and then listed by edge number in the logbook under each specific roll. As outs are reused back into your edit, a line is drawn through the number and edge number listing in the logbook. Since all filed pieces of

```
                      ROLL #7

      Scene                          Edgenumbers
      Jean enters clinic (Int.)...........DD0001 - 0031

      J. enters clinic (Int.) short take......0032 - 0040

      J. enters clinic (Int.) short take......0041 - 0071

      J. sits down (clinic)...................0077 - 0103

      J. sits down (wide shot)................0109 - 0127

      View at window of clinic................0130 - 0172

      Bruce and Jean outside..................0173 - 0292

      Jug shop, Bruce enters..................0299 - 0306
```

PICTURE OUTS   SOUND OUTS

① 0045-50 (J. clinic)   ① 0045-50 (J. clinic)
④ 0085-92 (J. sits)   ③ 0052-53 (J. asks question)
⑨ 0093-94   ⑤ 0093-94   J. sits
㉑ 0115-118 (J. looks at   ⑥ 0095-103 "   "
              window)   ⑩ 0152-172 (loud cars)
㉒ 0152-172 (cars)   ⑰ 0241-292 (end J+B
㉔ 0241-292 (end J+B   outside)
       outside)   ㉔ 0301-302 (car reflection)
㉜ 0301-302 (car reflection) ㉗ 0304-305 (good
㉝ 0304-305 (good take)   sound)
㊲ 0093-94   ㉘ 0093-94

Edge number log book—sample page.

picture and sound are taped together in numerical order, an editor
can quickly find the needed footage by watching the numbers on
the roll. Even with hundreds of entries and several filed rolls of
picture and sound, this filing system is a quick and accurate way
of "housekeeping" footage while sustaining creative inspiration.

VIEWING YOUR FOOTAGE AS A "MOVIE"

The first step you want to take to really get an idea of the value
of your scenes is to cut out the clap boards and flashed frames at

the beginning and ends of each take. By removing this footage (and carefully filing it on your picture and sound roll outs) you can begin to see your scenes in a movie context. Scenes still need to be edited "fat," with all beginning and end pauses left on until the order of sequence is determined. These pauses will later be cut down to pace the film and make transitions.

The first screening of your spliced-together scenes can often be disappointing to the filmmaker because without the lighthearted-ness of the "off-camera" moments that clap boards provide, the film becomes much more serious and studied. But remember that the editing process has just now begun. Also, repeated takes and cuts out of order don't give your film a chance to look finished or complete. It is not wise to show this out-of-order assemblage to anyone, especially your investors, unless they are experienced in editing low-budget features. Although this screening may be dis-appointing, it is important to understand that each show is vital to you as an editor, so that when it comes time to make decisive editorial decisions, you will know your footage well enough to make the right choices.

PLACING SCENES IN ORDER OF YOUR STORY

Usually, by this point at the beginning of the editing process, the filmmaker's postfilming depression has bottomed out with thoughts such as "It's all shit!" or some equally profane statement. The anger and frustration of seeing your headless mass of footage must now be changed into the stubborn conviction that you will turn your footage into a film if it's the last thing you ever do. To edit a low-budget feature successfully, the filmmaker often needs to turn a sow's ear into a silk purse. And with determination and creativity it *can* be done.

Before shuffling the scenes of your movie into the order of your story, you must write a list of the scenes as they appear in your assemblage. This list will allow you to locate each desired scene out of the thousands of feet of sync footage. Instead of using a sentence to describe each scene, as you did for your filing logbook, you will want to devise a code word or two that identifies your scenes. This abbreviated list can easily and quickly be reshuffled on paper while you search for the correct scene order of your movie.

Once you have completed your lists of which scenes are in which rolls it's time to write down your scenes in order of the story. Since not all low-budget features are designed or meant to tell traditional "stories," it is assumed that within each body of footage there is a best order of sequence that makes each film as powerful as it can be. For the very abstract feature, an editor may have to write and test hundreds of different-ordered sequences before determining the best one. And even with conventional low-budget feature films it may take many tries to get the order right, since it's often the case that scenes and transitions will be missing and have to be created after the initial filming.

After you have made a list of scenes in what you think is the best order for your story, the assemblage is completed by locating each scene and splicing sync picture and mag track together. If you were smart enough to shoot your titles on location, you will find that once these credits have been edited into the film it will look a lot more like a "real" movie. For scenes that are made up of many short takes, your assemblage will continue to appear rough and unfinished until the pieces of film have been edited tightly together and paced correctly for their order in the sequence. It is best to wait as long as possible before making a "final cut" on multifaceted scenes, because each scene must be cut long or short, fast or slow, in context to the surrounding scenes and the order of the story.

CUTTING FOR STRUCTURE

After viewing the assemblage of your film in the order that seems best suited for your story, it will quickly become apparent that scenes work best when they function properly as part of a filmatic "structure." No piece of film or scene can be correctly cut until the editor knows exactly what job that footage is trying to do within the context of the whole work. For a fairly straightforward feature, the structure may be as simple as identifying introductory scenes, middle scenes that sustain action and plot, and ending scenes that conclude the story.

On the other hand, for an exceedingly complicated film such as *A Man, a Woman, and a Killer*, which needed continually to shift its foundation of "reality," it was impossible to edit two scenes together until the structural "key" was discovered after a year of editing. Shifting scenes around for months and getting nowhere, I returned to the clap board footage in which some very precious and revealing moments had occurred. Discussions with codirector Wayne Wang led me to the idea of recording narrations of each character (the man, the woman, and the killer) telling who he or she was as a person in real life, and talking about the other characters and events of the filming. The final key to the structure came when I realized that the lead character, Dick, could be defined as someone "seeing reality as if it were a foreign film he was watching." I had used the creative device of subtitling English words with English titles in some of my previous short films, so it became obvious that subtitling Dick's words and the words of other characters (much of which he had actually scripted for the movie) added the necessary structural element of the film. In a scene of Dick writing in his journal, which we had filmed on location, subtitles would, at times, silently tell the story. This film was very scary to edit during the year of failed screenings and hopeless editing, but when a structure was discovered that made every action and scene understood, the final editing became exhilarating.

It must be obvious to the reader by now that editing a feature film is more than just sticking scenes together in some kind of order for the story. The highest level of editing requires that the filmmaker rethink his or her original idea in terms of the actual footage being edited. With luck it will be necessary for the filmmaker to put him- or herself through an intense mental exercise in which the filmmaker's knowledge of life is expanded in order to complete the editing of his film. If you wrote and shot your feature in an original way, your way, then what really exists on film is a complex survey of your feelings, emotions, observations, prejudices, beliefs, and personal attitudes about your world. What the editing process then represents is an attempt to unify and make sense out of all these disparate parts of your life. Shuffling scenes around to find the best order for your film must be accompanied by an intense desire to seek out the truth of your footage.

TESTING YOUR EDIT

Whether you are editing on a homemade work bench with rewinds, Moviescope, sound reader, and synchronizer, on a rented flatbed machine, or digitally on computer, in order to fully understand the power of your cuts it will be important occasionally to screen your film before an audience. By seeing your images projected on a screen or monitor, and by hearing your sound track transmitted through different speakers, while a few friends watch with interest, you are able to view your edit within the context of a theatrical presentation. The presence of just one other person in the screening room can help to give you the objective viewpoint needed to see your film clearly. These informal screenings are not intended to show off anything even approaching a finished film and you must always inform your little audience that they are about to see a "work-in-progress," to avoid embarrassment for all concerned. And although there will most certainly be many disruptions and bad edits in the early stages of editing, out of each screening you will emerge with some added insight about various cuts and order of sequence. Sometimes it will be hard not to react defensively when talking to people after your screening, especially if you yourself are disappointed with what you have just seen. Sometimes footage can be so complicated to edit that each screening fails, resulting in uptight silences for audience and filmmaker alike. Nevertheless, because it is your responsibility to make the film the best it can be, it is necessary to withstand these showings.

Since interlock projectors are expensive to rent, and screening rooms (for film or video) cost even more, an editor must constantly search for film schools, labs, or friends who will help him or her screen the film without a fee. Some rental houses, like Adolph Gasser of San Francisco, provide free screenings of works-in-progress (they even advertise the event in conjunction with the Film Arts Foundation). This type of public screening should be used only at the absolute final stage of editing, just before cutting your original for the print. A preview screening can be frightening, but not as frightening as being stuck with an answer print of a poorly edited feature film.

BEGINNING A "ROUGH CUT"

If the structure of your film continues to be evasive, mentally let go of your efforts in this direction and instead focus on improving the edit within particular scenes. If you shot several scenes using the "freeze" technique to create cuts in the action (see chapter 5), it will be enjoyable to edit these pieces of film together. Since this type of editing is straightforward and easy to accomplish, the process will give you the necessary rest from the mental workout of figuring out the whole film. At other times in the editing of your feature it will be a good idea to send yourself on a few days' vacation, just to clear out your head. Making a feature film has often been compared to running a marathon, and any filmmaker who has existed in, and survived, the later stage of editing will attest to this comparison. So it is important to vary the type of editorial job you are performing, making sure that every decision is an intelligent one, not muddled by confusion and fatigue.

By repeated viewing of your assemblage on a flatbed machine or video monitor, you should notice that some combinations of scenes seem to give off more energy than others. By having experienced many different juxtapositions of scenes, you can now begin to edit your favorite combinations tightly together, removing the pauses that have been left on the front and rear of your scenes since initial assembly. Be careful to file accurately the footage cut off of your scenes, since it is very likely you will need to retrieve these pieces when trying other combinations. Once you've made several successful transitions between scenes, your film will seem to spring to life. This is the magic of editing. Because you gave yourself time to learn about your footage, you now have the ability to fuse scenes together in an exciting way. And with each new edit you come much closer to understanding the film's internal structure.

It is now time to return to the opening scenes of the story, to edit together a convincing first-five-minutes sequence. I've learned with each of my features that once the first few minutes of each film were established, once I could get it rolling, the rest would fall into place. These first minutes of editorial structure will teach the audience the "rules" of your storytelling. Your cuts will set the ground rules for the unfolding film. For each feature, the beginning must reflect the heart of the film and introduce the film in a positive and interesting way.

While editing the beginning of *Chan Is Missing* for Wayne Wang, I was able to design a credit sequence that clearly defined the essence of the film. In the cut that Wayne showed me there was a scene in the middle of the film in which a young woman played a loud version of the song "Rock Around the Clock" on a phonograph in her upstairs room. What was interesting was that the song was sung in Chinese. And months before, when I had synced up some of the footage for Wayne, I had noticed a shot of the lead character driving a cab through Chinatown, with alternate reflections of white sky and dark buildings on the windshield. I suggested to Wayne that the Chinese "Rock Around the Clock" song be used with the shot of the cabbie as the beginning of the film. I also thought of superimposing the main titles over the windshield of the cab, titles in white letters when the reflection was dark, titles in black when the reflection was white. The final result perfectly explained the Asian-American theme of the film, introduced the main character and his profession, and presented the credits in an elegant way. By following the lead of this beginning footage, the film seemed to tell us what to cut next, and soon the entire film meshed into place.

DISCARDING YOUR FAVORITE SCENE

It's a classic saying in film editing that often the secret of your cut is hiding behind the seductive beauty of your favorite shot. At the beginning of the editing process, a filmmaker/cameraperson often extols the beauty of one magnificent shot with which he or she is totally in love. In fact, if the filmmaker could not look upon the perfection of this wondrous shot at each screening he or she would have quit editing long ago. This shot is so incredible that the rest of the footage almost looks shoddy in comparison. As the filmmaker continues to edit, suffering through the normal range of disappointments and discoveries, just the knowledge that this great shot exists sustains his or her drive to complete the film. But at every turn in the editing, the film seems to run dry. Except, of course, for the splendor of this gorgeous shot, the film can't seem to keep its momentum. If only all the shots had been as perfect as the unparalleled and utter excellence of . . . THE GREAT SHOT. There is only one solution I know of that can rescue you and your film from this editorial Ferris wheel. With all the will-power you can summon . . . you must remove this exquisite shot from your film . . . (steady now) . . . file it deeply in your outs, and enjoy the rebirth of your project.

SOUND EFFECTS AND MUSIC

As you continue to refine the cut of your scenes, you may want to add sound effects that enhance the original shot. As the camera zoomed out the window slowly in *A Man, a Woman, and a Killer*, I added an eerie, almost imperceptible sound that cut off with the first sound of dialogue. In a scene where Ed Nylund was taking pictures of the two other characters outside in a field, I cut in the sound of a reflex camera shutter being cocked and released. And in another scene where Ed is giving a long monologue in a restaurant, I cut in the sound of low restaurant ambience in order to give the impression of other people milling about. With these small touches the power of a scene increases, and in turn affects all the scenes around it.

The use of music can also boost the morale of a film, giving an injection of warmth, terror, joy—whatever the appropriate emotion requires. Music was added to the beginning images, the title sequence, and the ending shot of *A Man, a Woman, and a Killer*, to give the film a "real" film feeling. It's my puritanical belief that music, as an ingredient in a film, should be used very sparingly and only when necessary.

To add either sound effects or music to your film you need to purchase a roll of mag track "slug" (usually about $20 per 1,200') equal to the length of the roll of edited film in which your effects occur. After syncing up the roll of slug with your edited roll and marking sync at the beginning with a vertical line drawn through a circle, you roll up to where the effect is needed and cut it in. Then splice the slug to the end of your effect and roll ahead, in sync with your edited roll, to the tail end, so that both rolls are exactly the same overall length. Many sound effects are available on records, and you can transfer each needed effect to mag stock for your editing needs. For specialized effects that aren't available you will need to record the sounds yourself with a Nagra or Walkman Professional recorder and then transfer the results onto mag. To use original music in your film you will need to get a written agreement that grants you the use of the tracks (see Appendix G for "Music Rights Agreement."), and probably also pay a fee that can range from around $80 (the cost of music for the main credits of *A Man, a Woman, and a Killer*) up to several thousands of dollars per song.

A better solution for obtaining music for your film would be to purchase an electronic keyboard and make your own (see "Digital Music for Films," chapter 11). Prices range from $70 up to more than $1,000 for keyboards that include built-in speakers, twelve preset rhythms, twenty different instrument voices, four electronic drum pads, and other effects. Some models even include digital synthesizers and internal cassette recording capabilities. If your electronic keyboard can record right onto its own cassettes, as soon as you have composed your musical score you can transfer the sound directly to mag stock and edit it into your movie. And some keyboards now have the capability to store a certain length of music in their minicomputers, so that by projecting your film and playing your composition back with the push of a button, you can finalize the appropriateness and length of your score. Even if you don't consider yourself a musician, you'll find you can enjoy playing with one of these keyboards, and can, surprisingly, create effective sound tracks.

THE "BREAKTHROUGH CUT"

If you continue to spend several hours every day for several months working at editing your rough cut, testing new orders of scenes, reworking the first five minutes, and perfecting the editing of each scene, you are bound to experience many small breakthroughs and maybe even the "breakthrough cut." The major breakthrough of editing a feature-length film occurs only after the structure of your film has finally been revealed and you have edited your scenes together with the stability and intelligence gained from this discovery. How will you know when you have hit upon the "breakthrough cut"? If you have to ask, then it hasn't happened yet! The best way I can describe it is that when the breakthrough cut occurs it's as if the film flies away from you, becomes whole, a living entity that you can't believe you had a role in creating. Everything works.

A breakthrough cut has not occurred unless every scene and piece of film and sound functions better in the cut than ever before. During the months of shifting scenes around to find the best order of your story, you have probably noticed that in each tested edit certain scenes seem more lively and function better than others in the context in which they are presented. And then later, in another cut, the same scenes seem to drag while other previously clumsy scenes look better. This is happening because without knowing the structure of your footage it is impossible to edit in the correct pacing for each scene in your movie. The most difficult thing about editing is that if even one transition between scenes drags or falters in some way, every scene that follows will suffer and seem mistaken. When the structure of the film tells you the purpose of each segment of the film, then and only then can you make the perfect breakthrough cut.

THE MISSING PIECES

Sometimes footage will be unyielding and stiff, as it was for *A Man, a Woman, and a Killer*, and you can never reach a breakthrough cut without the addition of other elements into your film.

Whether you need a narration that ties together your story, a series of still photographs backed by music that fills in the gap in your film, or titles explaining each segment, it is always hard to admit that you failed to supply yourself with all the perfect pieces of film during the shoot. In Hollywood you probably would have been fired and sent back to the bush league for not supplying adequate "coverage." But in the world of independent, low-budget production you have the opportunity to use this "failure" to invent original and distinctive solutions for your film, solutions that may lead you to the "key" of your edit.

ADDING NARRATIONS

Chan Is Missing would still be sitting on a shelf gathering dust if Wayne Wang hadn't realized that the film needed a series of narrations to pull it together. At first he recorded narrations by three characters as I had done for *A Man, a Woman, and a Killer*, but after testing them in the edit he came to realize that only the voice of the older character should be used. By limiting the narration to one character, the film achieved the desired unity, defined the older cab driver as the main character, and revealed its structure. The addition of the narration allowed the main character, a sixty-year-old Asian-American cab driver, to comment on his journey through the heart of Chinatown, giving the film the airiness and humor that made it such a success. Seeing the different aspects of the Asian-American culture through the cynical eyes of an older, "established" member of the community was exactly the right touch, the right concept that knocked the structure of the film into place.

Before recording the narrations for your movie you must first define the concept of these "voice-overs." Will they talk about exterior things such as uncovering a mystery as in *The Maltese Falcon?* Or will they speak for the interior thoughts and dreams of your character (or characters) as in the film *Wild Strawberries?* What is the character's point of view? Will your characters speak in their own voices, making up their own words, or will you script what they say? And, as best you can, each narration should be carefully designed in length and content, so you know where to edit it into your film. Since these narrations are meant to "save" your film and solve structural difficulties, they should be as tightly constructed as possible.

Once you have determined the text or improvisational outline of the narrations, you will need to find a suitable sound studio or situation for the recordings. For $150 an hour plus the cost of recording tape, you could record your narrator(s) in the finest-quality sound studio in your area. If this rate is affordable, nothing beats using a good facility where you are guaranteed crisp, clean recordings. But if you are on a limited budget and know you can only afford one hour to record your narrations, you must be extremely well rehearsed and organized. Another consideration may be that you wish to use the professional setting of a sound studio to intensify the recording session; to make sure your amateur actors perform under pressure similar to that of the shoot.

A cheaper way to record your narrations would be just to sit in a quiet place and speak directly into a cheap audio recorder as I did for my feature *Emerald Cities*. For that recording I used my $100 Panasonic cassette deck, speaking into its built-in mike. Because the speed of the tape was not perfect, my recorded voice sounded a bit strange and distant, but this was fine for its use in the movie. Using a Sony Walkman Professional recorder with an expensive, high-quality mike, and recording in a super-quiet location, you could almost duplicate the recorded sound of a high-quality sound studio. But remember that you will need to pay the cost of the mag stock and a transfer fee for recording audio signals onto mag. And often it is much more difficult in informal situations to elicit satisfactory performances from your actors, because you waste time with repeated takes, and waste money with increased tape and transfer cost. Whichever way you decide to record your narrations, always put the quality of your recording first on your list, charging the costs, if necessary, so that these sound tracks won't haunt the editing of your production with muddled voices and noisy background interference.

PHOTOS AS TRANSITIONS

In almost all of my features I have used a series of photos to tell part of my story. In *A Man, a Woman, and a Killer* I used footage shot from color slides taken by Ed Nylund during the shoot that told a visual story of the off-camera moments. Working with the art department at W. A. Palmer Films (Belmont, California), I devised a concept of the pictures "sliding" in and out from the left side of the frame, in the tradition of the early slide projector. After setting up a rhythm of images sliding in and out of frame at different speeds, I varied the camera moves with pans and dissolves. The few hundred dollars this effect cost created an over-five-minute sequence of the final film.

For my film *1988—The Remake* I used images from a photo album of Ed Nylund's growing up, while he narrated his life story. I also used a long sequence of color slides picturing acts from the *Showboat 1988* audition in my ending titles, around fifty images, each of which showed the performer(s) and information about his or her current activities or status. The printing of the slides and titles cost many hundreds of dollars, but since I could charge the work at the lab, I was able to afford excellent camera work at a time when I was flat broke.

In *Emerald Cities* I once again used photos as part of my film. With the help of videomaker Liz Sher ("Approaching the 14th Moon," etc.) I taped snapshots from my growing up using her ¾"-format JVC video camera. I later transferred these shots to 16-mm as part of a video section that recurs throughout the film. Shooting these photos cost me about $20 for the ¾" tape and another $150 for the transfer to 16-mm film.

SHOOTING ADDITIONAL FOOTAGE

After you have cut in your narrations and maybe even added a sequence of photos to your film, it may become necessary to shoot some extra footage that you now realize must be included in the cut. These "pickup shots" may be as simple as shooting toward the sidewalk from a moving car or filming a close-up of a hand reaching in to change a radio station. A full-scale production team should not be assembled unless it is painfully obvious that many additional sync scenes must be filmed to complete the story. And no additional footage should be shot until you know *exactly* what is missing from your film. Shooting more footage must not be an exercise in avoidance of editing, and should only be done after the maximum pressure has been applied in search of the best cut.

FINAL TIGHTENING AND PACING

Hopefully, by this point in the editing of your feature, you understand completely what your footage is "trying to say." If you don't, and no firm structure can be put into words, it's not worth trying to tighten up the edits. This final editing process must be based on the firm foundation of a film in the correct order by scenes, with a well-defined beginning, middle, and end. An early attempt to "fine edit" will only bring disappointing results and extra work for the editor. If you *have* been able to figure out the structure of your story or filmatic statement, then you will be able to cut out all extraneous frames and footage from each shot.

If you look over your assembled rough cut with an eye toward awkward moments, overstated and elongated scenes, any interruption in the flow, this is the time to correct these problems so that every frame of your movie contributes to the story you are telling. Like Michelangelo, who believed that he was freeing the human figure trapped below the surface of the marble he was carving, you must help the real film emerge, shedding the footage that clearly doesn't belong in your cut. Once you have successfully edited together the first five minutes of your film, every scene and shot that follows will tell you how tightly it should be cut.

As each scene is tailor cut, your film assumes a life you never thought it had. Check the beginning of each scene during your screening. After the tightly edited first five minutes, are there scenes that have an extra few seconds of pause before action or dialogue begins? By knowing the structure of your film, you are aware that certain series of scenes should move fast before cutting to a slow scene. If you cut the fast scenes to the bone, allowing for no extra frames to disrupt the action, when you make your cut to the slow scene the pause of action and sound will eat up the energy. As editor you can count the beats before the dialogue begins: . . . one . . . two . . . three . . . four . . . dialogue. It is your job to select the right amount of pause before the dialogue begins. Will it be four seconds long? Eight seconds? Sometimes the beginning few seconds of a scene have a loud sound that disrupts the feeling of the shot. Just that one sound will disrupt the flow of cuts in your movie, and must be cut out. Now your cut will seem smoother, cleaner, and healthier. And when the first words of dialogue are spoken you will seem to be hearing them for the first time, hearing the ideas and emotions behind the words. Cleaning up your edits can turn a dull scene into a clever one.

After experiencing the enormous difference made by your small corrections, you begin to take charge over every filmatic moment. In some places in your sound track you have listened for months as an actor stumbled over the beginning word in an important stretch of dialogue. Now it is time to locate that three-frame mistake, cut the frames out, and replace them with room tone that you recorded while filming on location. As has happened throughout the editing process on your feature, correcting one cut or transition leads you to other work needed. Every scene and shot, movement and sound, is felt in the context of what exists around it in the movie. A scene that has been adversely affected by a clumsy cut several scenes back now springs to life after the earlier cut has been streamlined.

NOTE: If you have been editing your original picture instead of a work print, this final process of tightening up cuts must be avoided until your rough cut is completed and you cut your original into A and B rolls for printing, because each shot will lose a frame at beginning and end during "hot" splicing.

FINALIZING THE STRUCTURE

Now that your film is close to completion, you will want to borrow some 2,200' reels that will allow you to screen almost sixty minutes of assemblage at a time, (or view your entire digital cut on an extra large "movie screen" monitor). This gives you a chance to get a feeling for the overall movement, so that by designing in some resting places (fade-outs and dissolves) you can insure that the film will continue to flow for its length of seventy to ninety minutes. After screening the first sixty minutes and then the remaining footage, repeat the screening using the 2,200' reel for the last sixty minutes of the film. If you have some extra money, you can screen the full length of your film at a professional facility that switches projectors at reel changes (cost: around $100). What's important is that you get a feeling of where a few fade-outs should occur, and if some footage or scenes should be removed for the sake of the whole film.

For sound mixing and printing of your film, you won't want any one roll to run over 1,100 feet in length (about thirty minutes). This is about the maximum amount of footage that can be supported by the sprocket plate on your flatbed editing machine. It is also the largest amount of mag track that can be loaded onto most mixing machines. Although many labs can print more than 1,100 feet of film at a time, handling rolls of original film over this size is dangerous in terms of footage slipping off the core. Since you will want to assemble your finished film into two large 2,000' reels for ease of shipping to showcases and film festivals, it is necessary to design the best way for rolls 1 and 2 to splice together (reel 1) and the best way rolls 3 and 4 (reel 2) can be combined.

The technical needs of printing dictate that the best way to end reel 1 is with a fade-out, and the best way to begin reel 2 is with a fade-in. This allows for projectionists to splice together your film for showings in black leader where the connection will not be noticed. Also, if footage is lost because of faulty splicers, lost frames in the black leader after the fade-out or before the fade-in will not ruin the transition between the reels. Usually, if a film has only one fade-out and one fade-in during its entire running length, it occurs about halfway through the film in order to break up the time for the audience. If this is appropriate for your filmatic structure, then you have satisfied both the technical needs of printing and the aesthetic needs of your filmwork.

On page 169 are photos of the correct notations for fade-out and fade-in, and dissolve for printing. Although you may not be ready with your final cut for printing, now is a good time to start testing different lengths of fade-outs and dissolves to see which one is correct. If you have edited your film digitally, then you probably have already experimented extensively with these various lab effects, perhaps even utilizing some video moves (spins, page turns, etc.) for your film transitions. Most labs offer effects in lengths of eight frames, sixteen frames, twenty-four frames (one second), thirty-six frames, forty-eight frames (two seconds), seventy-two frames (three seconds), and ninety-six frames (four seconds). By drawing two lines in grease pencil on your work print, from a point at the edge of your frame line, converging twenty-four frames later at a point at the middle of the picture (see photo 1), you have indicated a one-second fade-out. When projecting your film, as these two converging lines wipe from the sides of the frame and meet at the middle in one second, you will be able actually to experience your fade-out and adjust it if it runs too short. Photo 2 shows how to indicate a dissolve by drawing a wavy line in grease pencil from a point where the dissolve begins, through the cut between the shots representing the middle of the effect, to a point on the second shot where the dissolve ends. When marking a dissolve, make sure that there is footage in your shots equal to the length of overlap you've indicated. Once again, during a screening you can feel how the length of the effect functions for your film as you watch the wavy lines moving from side to side on the screen as the scene changes (at the mid-point cut).

NOTE: If you are editing original footage instead of a work print, *don't* mark your picture with grease pencil since this may scratch the emulsion (it will also be very difficult to remove for clean printing).

PREPARING SOUND ROLLS FOR THE MIX

Before you can properly mix your sound onto one unified sound track, you need to split your sound between two or more rolls. Perhaps by now you've noticed that some of your recorded scenes are too loud in volume for where they fit in your edit. And during your screenings you have sometimes kept your fingers on the volume control, turning down the sound when that scene is on the screen. By separating each sound in your scenes you can finally set the volume level for each scene as well as adjust the tone.

To split your tracks you need a blank roll of mag or sound slug, equal in length to the length of your sound track. As you roll through your synchronizer or flatbed, you place a mark on the blank roll in sync with the splice between two sounds. Back up the rolls and undo the tape splice between your sounds. Then cut your blank roll at the mark and switch rolls, splicing the blank roll to the sound track and the remaining sound track to the blank roll in the synchronizer. By alternating each particular sound in your movie, you empower the mixing technician with the ability to adjust volumes and equalize sounds, so that scenes mesh and transitions succeed in turning your pieces of film into a movie.

Before mixing your sound tracks, you will need to write out a cue sheet that indicates each correction and adjustment in sound, and at what footage count it occurs. This cue sheet is a vital guide, absolutely necessary to a technician who must mix a film he or she has never seen. Ask the sound mixer for a cue sheet form.

To make sure there are no imperfections in the splicing tape or dirt on your sound track, you will want to clean your mag tracks with special mag cleaner (available at full-service labs), wiping each side with a moist cotton swab. If the tracks are not thoroughly cleaned, "pops" may occur on your precious and expensive mix. When using toxic cleaning fluids, make sure that you are in a *very* ventilated room, even using a fan, as I do, to make sure that you aren't poisoned by the fumes.

In order for your printed rolls to maintain their sync sound track when spliced together in assembled reels for projection, adjustments must be made before the mix. The sound track on your print will run twenty-six frames ahead of picture, so that it will be

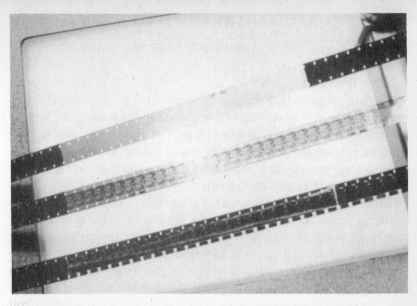

1. Original film and clear leader checked against fade-out, marked on work print.

2. Original A and B rolls checked for dissolve against marked work print. Wavy lines indicate to the lab that you want a dissolve.

broadcast in sync by projectors that read the sound twenty-six frames ahead of where the picture image is projected. If you plan to splice the last image of roll 1 (which has a sync sound track) to the first image of roll 2 (also in sync with a sound track), picture to picture, then you have to account for the sound moving up twenty-six frames in printing or lost part of your sound track. The solution to the problem is cutting out the first twenty-six frames of sound track on roll 2 and adding this piece of sound to the same A or B roll at the end of roll 1.

Photo 1 on page 171 shows the first image of roll 2 in sync with its sound track. The first twenty-six frames of sync sound track have been marked with an ink pen. The first step to correcting your sound track for printing is to cut out the twenty-six-frame length of sound and replace it with an equal-length piece of blank mag track (photo 2). During printing, the first frame of sound track after the blank insert will move up to be even with the beginning of the picture image.

Returning to the tail end of roll 1, mark off a twenty-six-frame length of blank mag track after the last picture image (photo 3 on page 172), cut it out, replacing it with the twenty-six frames of sync sound track from the head of roll 2 (photo 4). When this roll is printed, the sound track will move up twenty-six frames, its end becoming flush with the end of the last image. When prints of roll 1 and 2 are spliced together picture to picture, the sound for the beginning of roll 2 will be supplied by the last twenty-six frames of roll 1.

NOTE: It is important that the twenty-six frames of sound track be switched to the same A or B roll so that during the mix the setting of volume and tone (equalization) will be consistent for both the little twenty-six-frame piece at the end of roll 1 and the continuing sound track on roll 2, to insure no change in sound at the splice. Before the mix, check each splice on the sound tracks to make sure they are tight and haven't stretched from repeated screenings or editing. Replace all faulty splices that threaten to cause mistakes during the mix.

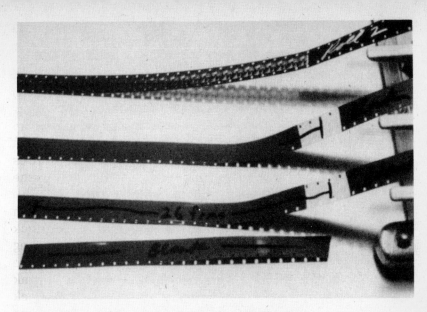

ADJUSTING SOUND TRACK FOR 26 FRAMES
1. First 26 frames of roll 2 sound track marked for removal.

2. First 26 frames of roll 2 sound track replaced by blank mag track.

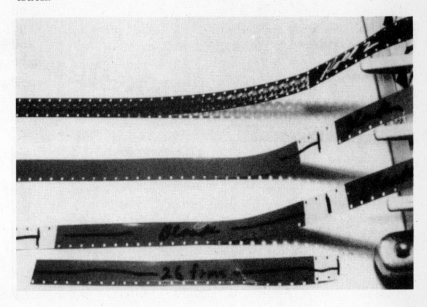

3. Mark off a 26-frame length of blank mag track after the last picture image on the tail end of roll 1.

4. Twenty-six frames of sound track from roll 2 added to tail of roll 1.

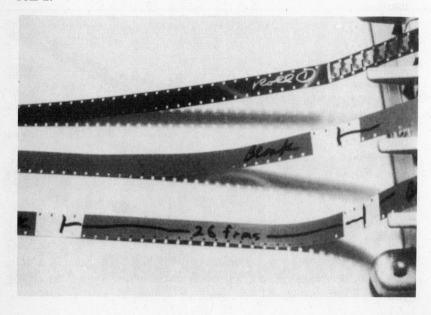

THE SOUND MIX

One of the most important procedures of your editing process is the several hours you spend mixing your sound into one composite track for printing. Not only does the mix fine-tune every sound in your film, but it also immediately tells you if the filmatic structure of your edit is correct. As each sound is adjusted for equalization and volume level, the pace of your film speeds up. If your structure is correct, the mix will feel as if it's tightening up your cuts and energizing your transitions. If you understand how your film "breathes," then in the mix you can properly control the internal movements by keeping some sections quiet, while other sections hit hard. As I've mentioned in an earlier chapter, since a good mix is so vital to the quality of your feature, don't shortchange your effort by settling for a "bargain" mix just to save a few hundred dollars. At a high-quality mixing studio, you should be able to mix a feature with ABC sound rolls in under eight hours. *Chan Is Missing* was mixed at W. A. Palmer Films in seven and a half hours. While it is very scary to sit in a mixing studio that costs $125 an hour (plus the cost of mag stock), the results of your expenditure will usually be well worth it (see "The Digital Sound Mix", chapter 11).

If you come to the end of your editing and have absolutely no possible way of raising another $1,000 for a high-quality mix, you may be able to locate a special "underground" high-quality mixing facility in your area. Begin by checking at your local film school to see if such a low-cost facility is known and available. In each mixing situation, regardless of cost, it is important to follow the advice of your technician, remain calm, and bring some food (sandwich, drink, snack) to keep up your energy.

SCREENING YOUR SOUND MIX

Screening your work print, synced to your sound mix, with all your sound working together on a clean track, you should feel the footage moving twice as fast as ever before. Although there is a definite risk to screening original composite mixed sound, as editor you need to see your film in as close to a final form as possible.

You also must know the exact quality of the mix so that if there is faulty printing or damage to your mixed track, you will be able to give the lab a convincing argument for redoing your print at no added cost.

This may be the time to have the courage for a semipublic showing of your feature, possibly at a screening room, or friend's apartment. It is very important to submit your film (and yourself) to a final test with an audience, because it is necessary to be completely satisfied with your edit before cutting apart your original footage for printing. Since you lose a frame at every splice of your original A and B rolls, make sure that the film you see being projected with your mix is the film you can live with for years to come. If there are major mistakes . . . (this may be hard to accept) . . . return to the editing room and, with careful consideration, keep editing.

If you make careful splices, you can cut out a section of mixed sound track, in sync with a shot or scene you have removed, and not hear any sound disruption or *pop* on the sound track of the print. If you do cut your mixed track, be very careful to make sure that your picture and sound track are in sync when you mark your mixed mag track with ink pen before lowering the blade of your splicer. And after removing the sync footage from your film, do a final check by holding up the mixed sound track together with your picture work print to make sure each piece measures the exact same length in frames.

CONFORMING ORIGINAL FOR PRINTING

Just as you have checkerboarded your sound into AB (and possibly C) rolls for your composite mix, you will now need to checkerboard your picture rolls of original footage into AB rolls, in preparation for making your print. If you have been editing your original rolls all along, you will want to place them in a final checkerboard position for printing, at the same time editing out the few frames you left at the front and rear of each scene during your rough cut, which you knew would be lost to splicing. While the process of "matching" original footage to work print and/or AB rolling the original in checkerboard rolls is basically the same, in concept, for all different filmstocks, there is enough difference between conforming Reversal stock and Negative stock to require separate discussions. And AB rolling original that has been edited instead of work print also has unique problems that must be separately addressed.

AB ROLLING FROM A WORK PRINT

The first step for conforming Reversal or Negative stock is to obtain a clean, dust-free editing bench. Your home-built, Formica-topped editing bench would be perfect for AB rolling, although when AB rolling Negative stock you may want to rent a special editing table with a built-in fan that blows all dust out of the enclosed shell of the table. On rewinds you need three 1,200' split reels (reels that split apart to hold film on cores), one for your original roll, one for an equal length of black leader, and another for your work print. And you need four take-up 1,200' reels, two for your original checkerboarding rolls, one to take up your work print, and one to roll up the original outs as you cut. If you plan to conform your AB rolls at home, you will need to rent a hot splicer with which to glue the film together. If you rent an editing room in which to AB roll, this facility should come with the reels and splicer you need to complete your job. It is also wise to wear white cotton gloves while handling your original film, since sweat and oil from your fingers will help dust to collect on the film. Once you have gathered together all the implements necessary for conforming, you are ready for the next step of listing edge numbers and pulling out original in order of the film's scenes.

For AB rolling of Reversal stock, an editor would first begin listing shots of the edited work print by first and last "latent edge numbers." Along the edge of your work print you will notice small numbers that are printed into the film. These "latent" numbers, existing in duplicate on your original footage, are not to be confused with the edge numbers that you may have had printed onto your film at one-foot intervals for keeping sync. Once you have written down this list of latent edge numbers for each shot in your edited work print, your next step is to locate each segment of original film holding corresponding numbers. After rolling once through your original rolls (labeling the top of each can with the edge prefixes enclosed), your next job is to locate each piece of original in order of your edit and roll it up on a reel. When you find the correct shot in your original footage that corresponds to your work print, cut out the entire take, including the clap board and the flash frames at the end of the shot, and tape it onto your reel. Once you have pulled your original footage, carefully roll back to the beginning ("heads out"), so that the first scene of your movie is first on the roll.

NOTE: When reeling original footage, always keep a steady tension on the film to insure that you won't form creases in the emulsion ("glitch marks") because of uneven pressure. And when filing outs, use *only* special tape for original film that pulls off easily and leaves no gum residue.

The next step is to measure out ample black leaders for your A and B rolls and work print. Since you probably haven't used a long leader in editing, it will be necessary to add several feet of leader between sync mark and first image of the work print. Most labs require 12' leaders, but since lab needs vary you should call the lab that will print your film and ask them what they prefer. All rolls are then placed in the synchronizer and rolled up to a sync mark on the work print. Place sync marks, drawn on white stick-on tabs for better visibility, on each of the black leader AB rolls, and roll up to your first work print image for matching.

AB rolling of original Negative or Reversal filmstock follows the same basic procedures, but in every instance great caution must be used in order not to scratch the emulsion with rough handling. Since even repeated reeling of Negative film is risky, each stage of handling the original must be completed as carefully as possible. For this reason, "pulling the original" takes the most time to complete. After the latent edge numbers are listed in order of scenes off the work print, each roll of original is checked at the first scene for edge number identification and is appropriately tagged. Please note that instead of rolling through the rolls of original in search of edge numbers as we did with Reversal stock, the original Negative rolls still haven't been reeled. Now, instead of "pulling" each scene and shot in order of the work print scenes and rolling them up on a reel, we slowly roll from one end of the Negative to the other end, as each shot is identified by edge number, cut off at the beginning and end of each take, and rolled up carefully on a separate core with identification label.

Splicing of Negative original also requires special care and handling of the film. The first thing to know is that Negative original must be glued with a splicer that has been specially adjusted for Negative film, to insure that no frame lines are seen on the print. When renting a splicer you must remember to specify that you will be AB rolling *Negative* film and need their *Negative hot splicer*. Before beginning to splice once again clean your editing bench of dust and clear all unnecessary equipment and items from the tabletop. Aside from your rolls of black leader that match the length of your feature, you will need a few hundred feet of Negative "clear" leader. When your editing space and your head are organized, you are ready to begin the assembly of your original into AB rolls.

For both Reversal and Negative film, the basic AB rolling procedure is the same. To best illustrate the process, the following plates will show how each new scene is matched at each cut on the work print. Rolling to the end of your first matched scene, make a mark on both the original and black leader with your grease pencil, *one frame longer* than where your scene ends on your work print (photo 1 on page 179). That extra frame of black leader and original will be cut off during hot splicing. After you've cut off both rolls at the marks, match the latent edge number of the original for the next scene with the edge number of the work print, and cut off the original *one frame longer* than the beginning frame of the new scene (photo 2). You are now ready to splice your original and black leader together in a "checkerboard" of A and B rolls.

The first hot splice you will want to make will be the black leader of the preceding scene to the original of the next scene.

Place the black leader on the splicer, *one frame past* the center line, holding the film tightly between the top pin and guide (photo 3). Lock down the splicer on the black leader and lift up that half of the splicing bar. On the other half of the splicer repeat the procedure with the original for the next scene, holding the film tightly between the pin and upper guide while locking it down, making sure that it sticks out *one frame longer* than the center line edge (photo 4 on page 180). With your finger, press down the excess frame of original (photo 5) and scrape off the emulsion with the retractable scraper, pulling it across your film end a few times. Brush on liquid film cement in one movement across the scraped end (photo 6) and immediately close down the top bar of the splicer, locking that side to the base, at the same time closing your cement bottle (photo 7 on page 181).

To hot-splice the original from your previous scene to black leader, the same procedure is followed, but this time the film and black leader must be looped around the splicer to make the splice (photo 8). Again, you must remember to set the black leader and original in the splicer *one frame longer* than the center line. After both splices have been completed, check your A and B roll to make sure the splices are in sync and that the latent edge numbers of your original line up with those of the work print (photo 9). Photos 1 and 2 on page 171 show examples of Negative AB rolls set up for fade-out and dissolve. Notice that a length of clear leader must be added to the black leader equal and in sync with the fade-out effect.

Once again you can benefit from making test splices before actually beginning to AB roll your feature. To test the strength of your splices, gently make a slight twist at the cut and see if the two ends separate at the edges. Only test your splices on the AB rolls with the greatest sense of caution, making sure you don't rip your original. If splices you've made on test pieces of film, using outs from your original and some of the same black leader, hold up after being tested, you should have the same dependable splices throughout your AB rolls.

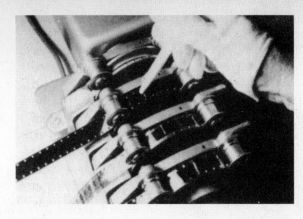

AB ROLLING
1. Original picture and black leader marked in sync, one frame past work print splice.

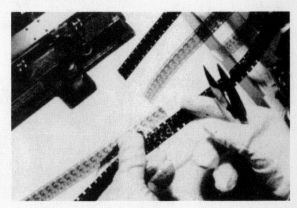

2. Original scene to be added, cut one frame longer for splice.

3. Black leader inserted in hot splicer, one frame longer than cutting edge.

4. Black leader and original clamped in splicer for cut.

Retractable scraper

5. Extra frame of original bent down before removing emulsion with retractable scraper.

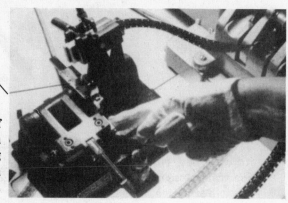

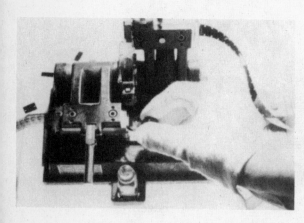

6. Applying fast-drying glue to emulsion-scraped edge of original film.

7. Clamping original film and black leader together in a hot splice.

8. Ready to hot-splice black leader onto original from previous scene.

9. Examining "checkerboard" AB rolls, checking splices and edge numbers against work print.

NOTE: The utmost care must once again be taken to make sure that a Negative original doesn't get damaged by running it along the editing table or coming in contact with equipment. Fortunately, most labs now offer a service called "liquid gate" during printing, which fills in most imperfections and scratches and removes dust by printing your film through a liquid coating. Liquid gate is essential for printing a clean, high-quality image in Negative or Reversal film.

AB ROLLING WITHOUT A WORK PRINT

If you have not been able to afford a work print for editing, having instead edited your original into a final rough cut, and also mixed your sound in sync to your original picture, AB rolling your film is much less of an effort. Since your film is already in order of assemblage, it will obviously not be necessary to spend hours locating original film. After you have cut and synced up proper-length leaders for printing, also sync up your mixed sound track. If you haven't anticipated the loss of a frame at the beginning and end of each shot in your original, then you will have to cut out and resplice your sound track to keep sync. If this sounds incredibly messy, then either AB roll on a flatbed editing machine, correcting your sound track as you cut (mixing the tracks *after* AB rolling the original), or somehow dig up additional funds for a work print. Of course, if your film is made up of only seven or eight long takes, it won't be much of a problem to sync up your mix at these few cuts.

CUE SHEET FOR PRINTING

For each AB roll of your film, whether Reversal or Negative, you will need to supply the lab with a cue sheet for printing instructions. Since each lab has its own particular needs so far as the form of cue sheet they require, ask them for guidelines. After splic-

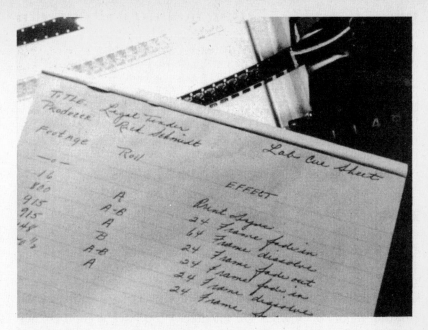

Lab cue sheet with footage count, roll, and effect identified for printing. Ask your lab technicians what they require.

ing your AB rolls together and carefully reeling them back to "head out," set the original rolls back in the synchronizer, at the sync marks, and set the counter at "0" feet. As you roll through your completed rolls, fill in your cue sheet, while at the same time checking that splices are in sync. This final checkout is vital to insuring that your printing will be correct. Also, check each dissolve and fade-out against your marked work print to make sure that it is correctly placed and spliced. Once you have reached the last frame of your images and marked down the final footage count on your cue sheet, carefully and firmly roll up each AB roll, one at a time. Finally, place each set of AB rolls in a can or protective box, including its cue sheet, and your film is ready to be given to the lab for printing.

NOTE: It's best to let the lab mark your sound mix mag track for the correct "print sync," twenty-six frames behind your "dead sync" (the sync mark of your AB rolls and mix). In this way you will be assured that this procedure is done correctly and that your sound track will be in sync with the picture on the finished answer print. And if the lab does this incorrectly, then they will be responsible for supplying you with another print free of cost.

LAB PROCEDURES FOR PRINTING

I've always spiritually approached the lab with the idea that if they make a mistake on my film because of some confused decision, it's *my* fault because I didn't make it absolutely clear what I wanted. By taking total responsibility for the outcome of your printing (short of obvious lab mistakes) you have a good chance of getting a perfect answer print on the first try. Since most labs consider the answer print a "trial" print, with the attitude that they will produce a good print after a few tries, the filmmaker with a budget for *one* print must be exceedingly precise at every stage of communication to get this first print correct on the first try.

Since a feature-length film is a major printing project for most labs, you should ideally be granted the opportunity to review the footage, roll by roll, with a "timer." The timer is a person who adjusts the exposure of your scenes (if necessary) and works with filters to balance the color of each shot. Although most labs now use a machine such as a Rank Cintel to electronically balance color and exposure, it's still important to communicate with the individual who will be responsible for the overall look of your finished print. Ask him or her to explain what changes he or she would recommend in the areas of exposure and color correction. If you've shot your film in black-and-white stock and purposely underexposed for richer blacks, you definitely don't want an uninformed timer to "correct" those exposures. If you don't speak up, you can be guaranteed that the timer at the lab will work feverishly to pump light into dark scenes, unless you communicate that the dark quality is what you desire. And if you don't want any changes of exposures on your film, write at the top of your cue sheets "NO LIGHT CHANGES" and underline the words. A rule of thumb when dealing with the lab is that if you have done anything at all "creative" or unusual, make sure you tell the lab how to handle that footage.

After you roll through your original AB rolls with a timer, checking fade-ins and fade-outs, dissolves, and cuts between scenes as logged on your cue sheet, your months, maybe years, of work . . . your film . . . is in the hands of the lab. As I've mentioned earlier in the book, if you reach the printing stage of your film and don't have enough cash to complete the film, most labs will extend you credit if you make some amount of "good faith" payment (usually half down) when ordering the print. By arranging to pay off the remainder of your lab bill at so much per month, you are then able to complete your project, using your film to earn money with rentals and video sales, and to enter film festivals and grant contests.

NOTE: The final control you should exert over your feature is in ordering that the lab *make your answer print on Estar-based 16-mm stock*, and that the print be sent out for *protective plastic coating by AFD Photogard* (1015 North Cahuenga Blvd., Hollywood, Calif. 90038, [213] 469-8141) to insure against projector damage. The Estar-base printing stock is so strong that almost no projector can break your print, and the AFD Photogard coating insures that the wonderfully clean and clear images that you've worked so hard to create won't become obliterated with new scratches from each additional screening. My prints are unbroken and still look as new as when they left the lab, even after numerous film festival and theatrical showings. Be very clear with the lab that you won't accept your print unless it has been protected as ordered, with Estar base and AFD Photogard.

All you can do then is wait, hoping that you have been specific enough about all aspects of your film to deserve a perfect trial answer print. If you have let the timer know that you have enough money for only this one print, maybe he or she will be sympathetic to your cause and work extra hard to get it right. At any rate, you now have a few weeks' vacation while the lab prints each roll with the changes and corrections you have detailed. While you try to remain calm, awaiting word that the first reel is "up" and ready for viewing, you can daydream about how all the pieces of picture and sound, fades and dissolves, effects, music, and credits are merging into a real movie.

SCREENING YOUR ANSWER PRINT

As soon as the rolls that make up your feature have been printed, you will want to screen them at the lab's best screening room, to check for mistakes in picture and sound. This screening should include only you and your major collaborators (codirector, cinematographer, producer), with whom you created the film, and the lab technician. Because of the shock of seeing your print for the first time, it may take several viewings to actually see mistakes. Of course, major errors in color balance, missing fades or dissolves, loss of sync, garbled sound, or poor print quality will be easy to recognize. Although each lab has its own set of standards with which to gauge the necessity to reprint "lab errors," below is a list of mistakes that should warrant a second trial print at the lab's expense.

- [ ] *Improperly timed main titles.* If your titles are white on a black background, or superimposed over a scene, they should be a solid white and not look grayish or uneven.
- [ ] *Missed cues for fade-in, fade-out, dissolve.* If you have clearly stated on your cue sheet the footage count for beginning and end of your effects, plus the length in frames, the lab is responsible for delivering a print to these specifications.
- [ ] *Overall incorrect exposure.* If you've been a customer at a lab for several years (and several feature-length projects), they may be willing to completely reprint your feature because it was printed either too light and washed out, or too dark and muddy. Because an answer print is regarded as a trial print you will

have to forcefully (but calmly) argue your point. It will help a great deal if your timer is dedicated to helping you create a perfect print because he believes in your film.

☐ *Imperfect frame line registration.* Only after I received my second *Emerald Cities* print, mailed back to me from the Australian Film Institute seven-city tour, was I able to screen the film and catch the frame line registration mistake on the fourth reel. I had been under so much pressure to get the film printed and air-expressed to the tour that I hadn't been able to screen the results. Even though I brought the mistake to the lab's attention five months after the printing, they stood behind their work and supplied me with a newly printed roll. On the screen, this mistake was visually obvious because at every other cut between shots, a white line appeared at the bottom of the frame. Examining the print over a light table, it was easy to see that the frame line was not centered exactly at the middle of the sprocket hole.

☐ *Obviously poor color balance.* If the faces of your characters are reddish-purple instead of flesh tone, you deserve a new print.

☐ *Excessive scratches.* If you are printing from Negative or Reversed AB rolls, and have ordered "liquid gate," the images of your film should not be covered with white dust marks and scratches. If this is what you see, first check your invoice to make sure the words *liquid gate* are written on your print order, then request a new print.

☐ *Picture and sound out of sync.* If you projected your film's work print with the mixed sound track and they were in sync, and you rolled through your AB rolls and they were in sync with your work print, then the lab is at fault for slipping sync during their printing process, and they owe you a new print.

☐ *One missed light change, or one lost fade-out or dissolve.* Usually your lab will reprint just the part of your film where the mistake has occurred, and your print will now have a splice in the middle. Although this acceptable lab practice will anger the perfectionist filmmaker, the splice will be virtually unnoticeable during projection. If there is more than one mistake, calmly pressure the lab to print over the whole roll.

☐ *Bad sound.* How bad does your sound have to be to get the roll reprinted? If there is hissing that sounds like electronic disruption, and this sound definitely isn't on your mix, you must firmly make a stand with the lab, if necessary, to get a new print. Also, if there are noticeable sound-level differences between the rolls of your feature, ask the lab to please reprint whichever roll is in error. You must be firm in declaring to the lab that varying sound levels are unacceptable. If you hear *pops* or other imperfections on your sound track that were not heard when you screened your mix, insist (in a polite way) that these faulty rolls be reprinted at the lab's expense.

ASSEMBLING YOUR PRINT

After you happily are holding the several perfectly printed rolls that make up your feature, it is time to splice them together onto two large reels, to simplify projection and future mailing and handling.

All that's left to do on the production of your feature is to make a few splices connecting rolls 1 and 2 (reel 1), and rolls 3 and 4 (reel 2), and to roll them up on large 2,000' reels. You will also want to splice on protective head and tail leaders on which you will identify the name of your film, your name as director/producer, and a return address and phone number. Most labs will give you an editing bench for an hour, with hot splicer, for this purpose.

If you printed your film on Estar base from Negative, you will need to tape splice your print together, carefully taping both sides of the picture, since it is impossible to hot splice on Estar-base stock. In any case, assemble your film in order, first rolling your head leader for roll 1 onto a 2,000' reel. Then splice roll 1 to the leader and reel up to the end. Splice roll 2 to the end of roll 1 and reel that roll to the end, filling up your first reel. Splice on your tail leader and then, taping the end of the leader to an empty 2,000' reel, roll the assembled rolls 1 and 2 back until you are at the head end. Securely tape the end of the head leader to the roll, and repeat the procedure with rolls 3 and 4. For reduced expenses during mailing, I recommend assembling your film on plastic reels and packing it in a double 2,000' plastic case. This reduced weight of your print is doubly important when you become a touring filmmaker and have to carry your heavy print(s) from airport to airport. Once your print is assembled and securely packed into its carrying case, take it and walk out into the sunshine . . . *you've done it*! Now it's time to show the finished results to your cast and crew.

SCREENING YOUR PRINT FOR CAST AND CREW

Showing filmatic results to cast and crew is a thrilling moment for any filmmaker. In a way, you have served their talents by laboring many months to edit your film to completion. And, of course, without all their help and belief, there wouldn't even be a film. Along with the thrill of showing the new feature, there also comes the pressure of wondering how it will be received. So to give your feature the opportunity to look its best, try to obtain the highest-quality screening room possible. Maybe your lab will let you use its screening room to show the film to a few of your friends. If your timer wants to see the results of all his or her work, this also might help you to arrange an in-house screening at your lab (for free). Even if your screening costs you some money, make absolutely sure that the technical aspects of projected picture (sharp, bright image) and sound (clear, good acoustics) are at their best, since this showing represents such an important moment for everyone involved. For my first showing of *A Man, a Woman, and a Killer*, I rented the main theater at the Pacific Film Archive in Berkeley for $60 for the two-hour Sunday afternoon show. For that small amount of money I was able to screen my feature in one of the finest theaters on the West Coast.

After you have exposed your friends and colleagues to the special "underground" preview screening, packed up your print, and brought it home, you may feel a bit of the emotional letdown common to completion of such an extensive project. You have survived a filmatic trial by fire, and now it's over. You've seen the wonders and the secrets of your film (and life) revealed, and now you wonder "What next?" You're impatient to do something, but at the same time too tired to really do anything. And you may be scared because you owe several thousand dollars to the lab and are not sure how you can raise this amount of money to pay them back. But you do have a feature film, and after a few days of rest it's time once again to get to work—work that can be done by writing letters, phoning, and filling out forms—the work of *promotion*.

7

PROMOTION OF A
NO-BUDGET FEATURE

After each part of the process of making a feature-length film, it seems that the last round of difficulties to overcome has been the worst and taken the most amount of time out of your life. After shooting is completed—two weeks of directing, lighting, designing sets, composing shots for your cuts, loading and unloading your camera, spending your money—it's easy to feel that the hardest part is over. Then comes editing, and as the months run by while you search for the structure of the film, you come to realize that the editing process is even more demanding. It may take years to complete this careful task in order to make every scene and cut work to build the pieces of film into a unified whole. And when you project your first print of the film, you experience a real sense of exaltation. Against all odds, you have created a feature film, almost by willing it into existence. Surely the worst is over now.

Well, the worst *is* over once the film is finished, but now it's time to enter the next phase of your film and your life—promotion. In the world of high-budget, commercial film production, the film-maker's responsibility ends when he or she turns over the film to a distributor, who handles all the promotion and marketing from that point on. Since a film produced at used-car prices is, to put it mildly, quite unlikely to attract a commercial distributor, it's up to you to promote your own film.

Fortunately, many avenues are open to the talented and persistent low-budget feature filmmaker—film festivals, New York and regional showcases, even television. With each showing you can arrange, you will gain more exposure and, if you're lucky, a little more money as well. Once your film has been seen—and admired—by the "right" people, you may be approached by a distributor who wants to handle your now-successful feature. By that point, ironically, you may even conclude that you're doing as good a job on your own as an agent could do for you.

Although each phase of the filmmaking process takes a good-size bite out of your life, it's promotion that actually lasts the longest. Promoting your low-budget film will require a relatively small amount of money and a great deal of time, energy, and determination. Here are the various steps you can—and should—take to insure that your film will receive the attention it deserves.

PREPARING YOUR PROMOTIONAL PACKAGE

Commercial distributors today still employ the same basic mechanisms they used during the silent era: press releases, posters, newspaper advertisements, and the occasional well-timed scandal. The low-budget feature filmmaker can also use any and all of these methods to make sure his or her film is seen by as many people as possible. While a major distributor may spend as much as $10,000—almost twice our total used-car-price film production budget—just designing and printing a full-color poster, you can finance a successful promotional campaign with an expenditure of $500 to $1,000—and a lot of creative and practical ingenuity.

VIDEO COPIES FOR PROMOTION

Since the filmmaker who creates an ultra-low-budget feature out of economic necessity doesn't usually have the ability to rent a commercial theater and advertise for a "world premiere" as a distributor would do, the first step is to secure some showings for the newly completed film. And because you only have one 16-mm print of your feature, and that print probably cost you every cent you could scrape together (including some charging at the lab), it is essential that you use that print *only* for actual showings—rentals, film festivals, and the like. For promotion, you should use inexpensive video copies. Prices vary quite a bit, but in 1995 you can make a high-quality copy of your film on ½" Betacam SP for approximately $600, a master copy from which to make inexpensive VHS copies. Many labs now have video departments with machines such as the Bosch and Rank Cintel that specialize in high-resolution, high-density color transfers to video from film.

You can easily pay more than $1,000 to transfer a film to video if you have to pay a technician $250 an hour to balance the color and exposure for each individual scene. But if your print is correctly balanced for color and exposure, you should be able to have a high-quality video copy made more cheaply, by running the print through the video transfer machine only once, without stopping. This low-cost method of transferring your film to video falls into the category of "video dailies"—the video work prints that high-budget production companies use to review each day's shooting.

Since each city will probably have several labs available for video transfers, it is important to shop around to locate the best deal. You could save hundreds of dollars with a few phone calls. Monaco Video in San Francisco ([415] 431-2760, ask for Anne O'Toole) first offered to transfer my features at its video daily rate of ten cents a foot (now thirteen cents a foot), then lowered its rate to eight cents a foot for all Film Arts Foundation members after I explained how much new business this price break would probably bring them.

You can also save some money by supplying your own videotape stock for the transfer. For a feature-length film running seventy minutes, you will need a ninety-minute cassette of ½" Betacam SP videotape, which costs around $95 per cassette. The lab or video facility that transfers your film to video will charge you perhaps $135 for the tape, costing you an extra $40. If you buy your own tape, make sure that you have purchased the exact same type, number, and brand used at the transfer facility. But beware! There is a risk factor involved in trying to save on stock. If the tape you supply causes any problems, the lab will not be responsible for redoing the job.

To begin your search for a film festival that will present your feature, you will need at least two video copies in ¾" and about twenty-five VHS, these copies dubbed from your ½" Betacam SP master. You will want to save your ¾" copies for some European festivals, using VHS wherever you can in the United States. Twenty-five VHS copies should be enough to enter all the major film festivals that are interested in American independent (and low-budget) features, assuming that as soon as each video copy is returned to you, you mail it out again.

Once you have your ½" Betacam SP "master copy" of your feature, you can make inexpensive video copies of high quality at a "dubbing service." Again, it is worth your while to shop around for the best price you can find for your ¾" and VHS dubs. And to insure that your master ½" Betacam SP copy is not damaged by continued copying, I strongly recommend first dubbing a "sub-master," also in ½" Betacam SP, that can then be used to strike additional copies for promotion. It has cost me about $30 to dub a ¾" video copy from a ½" sub-master (price doesn't include tape). (Be sure to store your master copy in a cool place, away from motors, magnets, metal shelves, and electricity.)

The cheapest price I've run into in the Seattle area for high-quality VHS video copies in multiples of ten of a feature-length film has been around $10 per copy at Video Presentation (2326 6th Avenue, Suite 230, Seattle, Wash. 98121, [206] 728-9241). For copies of 100 or more you should find prices for dubs in your area comparable to those of Film Craft Lab (66 Sibley, Detroit, Mich. 48201, [313] 962-2611, ask for Dominic T. Troia), which offers the incredibly low price of $3.50 per tape, with an extra charge of sixty cents per box with full window album cover (you supply graphics).

PROMOTIONAL GRAPHICS

Even before your film is completed, you can begin to create the graphics (poster, letterhead, pressbook, etc.) that will help publicize your product. It's the graphics of your feature that will make the film seem *real* to others. Film festival organizers usually require a pressbook and poster (if one is available) when you enter the competition. And they usually request a photograph from the production of the film (a "still") for their catalog and newspaper coverage. These materials are equally useful for submitting your film to showcases, television stations, and other screenings.

THE PRESSBOOK

A pressbook is exactly what the name implies—a book for the press. Some film companies spend many thousands of dollars printing up a slick cover with high-tech graphics to better sell their film to the critics (and thus to the public). Critics are handed these pressbooks as they enter the screening room to view the film, and they help start the film off on the right note.

Usually the independent filmmaker doesn't have the money or the ability to package such an elaborate graphic presentation as a full-fledged pressbook, but with a little imagination he or she can create an appropriate pressbook that does the job. The pressbook should contain a page with a synopsis of the story and a list of credits, along with any reviews that help promote the film. Some stills from the film that have a strong graphic/image power should also be included.

For the covers of the pressbooks for my features, I have used the word *pressbook* in large Helvetica type, repeated over the full length of the page. For our synopsis of *The Last Roommate*, we created our graphics by using a still from the film that was given a "bullet screen" effect, available at many typesetters, in which concentric circles form the image we are seeing.

If you shop around, you should be able to find a talented typesetter who can help you create similarly striking special effects for very little money. Total typesetting costs for our synopsis of *The Last Roommate*, including the bullet screen effect, were only $30. But typesetting charges vary greatly, so you should talk to several shops before you decide what you can do for the money you can afford to pay.

THE STILL

You can shoot stills from your 16-mm film by using a special adapter lens that fits on most 35-mm cameras. The adapter has no f-stop control. If you aim the lens holding the 16-mm film at the sun and "bracket" the shots by adjusting the speed of the shutter (1/60, 1/100, 1/250, 1/500, etc.) you should be able to shoot a well-exposed still. You can rent this 16-mm adapter lens from some film equipment rental houses. An easier alternative will be simply to take 35-mm photographs on location during the filming.

It is fairly expensive to print 8"-by-10" prints in black and white if you order each print separately, but there are special photo services that will make you twenty-five prints for about $50 (see "Movie Stills," chapter 5). To find this deal, call around to the photo services in your town.

THE POSTER

Posters are the most radical way to advertise your film showings, by taking your graphics to the street. With posters you can spend a few hours pasting them up, stapling them on bulletin boards at a university, and create an audience for your film. The several hundred posters put on the street to advertise the showing of rushes from *1988—The Remake* brought over a thousand people to the screening.

The expenses for this type of advertising are the initial cost of the typesetting, halftones from photos, and the printing costs. By keeping the graphics black and white and using cheap paper, you can create inexpensive posters that you can use to advertise your film as well as to fill out your pressbook. As long as you don't print the date of a particular show on the poster, you can always use it for future shows by adding a sticker with show times and locations. I have even reused part of the graphics of my posters as covers for my films on cassette in the home video market.

FILM FESTIVALS

Film festivals can revive the comatose filmmaker who is deeply stuck in his or her rut of trying to survive. Festivals can help sell your film and make you a star. At a film festival it is possible that a film may be graced with one of those unbelievable showings where the right audience and the right theater on the right night turns a good film into a great one.

The lucky low-budget feature filmmaker may get a chance to see his or her film, scorned by a local showcase, acclaimed a "work of genius" by a European film festival. (It has often been proved that the farther away from home an artist travels the better chance he or she has of recognition, so don't get discouraged by negative reactions to your film in your hometown.) A film festival also offers the chance to see one's filmwork in relation to other films being done around the world, and this is important to every artist.

Because a low-budget feature filmmaker does not have the large amount of money required to travel the "festival circuit" to promote a recently completed feature, and even the money spent on video copies and mailing can be quite a hardship, you must very carefully select the festivals that are worth entering. If you subscribe to *Variety* (which is available only in certain magazine stores) for a year, you will at some point see a film festival calendar listing. This calendar, which shows about six months of film festival dates and locations around the world, is valuable because it gives you an idea of how to time the mailing of your video copies to the festivals. Film magazines such as the *Independent Film and Video Monthly, Filmmaker Magazine,* and *Release Print* (published by the Film Arts Foundation in San Francisco) also carry extensive listings and descriptions of domestic and foreign film festivals, including requirements and deadlines. Study these listings carefully and try to determine which festivals have presented your type of low-budget features so that you don't waste your money and time sending out your few ¾" and VHS video copies, along with high entrance fees, to festivals that only select and appreciate Hollywood-type films. Early on, I naively entered a print of *A Man, a Woman, and a Killer* in the Cannes Film Festival by

Bullet screen effect.

Promotional graphic for *1988—The Remake*.

**Los Angeles premiere of *1988—The Remake*. It can happen.
Photo by Julie Schachter.**

mailing my 16-mm film with an entry form (no fee seemed to be required). About three months later I received a notice from a postal service that my print was ready to pick up at the San Francisco airport, and the postage and agent fee was $190! Don't let this happen to you. Ask around about festivals, inquire at AIVF or FAF, read about the festivals, and then enter the appropriate ones for your American independent low-budget feature.

Perhaps the first American film festival to approach for your "U.S. premiere" would be the Telluride Film Festival in Colorado. Although a tremendous long shot for the first-time feature filmmaker, a premiere at Telluride guarantees the most intense media focus for your feature (a favorite "discovery" festival for Roger Ebert and other critics) in probably the most relaxed and humanized setting. But be cautioned that they will only accept films that have had *no* screenings or festival exposure. Their small selection committee begins screening films usually in June, for the early September festival. Contact the National Film Preserve at (603)

643-1255, Box B1156, 53 South Main Street, Hanover, N.H. 03755 for information and application. While it's certainly worth taking a shot at getting your film into Telluride, don't tie up your entire festival effort waiting for their response to your film. You must enter several festivals to give your feature a chance for success.

Although more major film festivals than ever are now interested in low-budget American features, the list is still very small. Below are the eight festivals that are most intensely interested in and supportive of this type of feature film, and if your film is presented at any one of these festivals, it will probably be seen by representatives of at least ten other festivals. As soon as you have a good idea of when your feature will be completed, you should write to these festivals to request applications.

LONDON FILM FESTIVAL
(November–December)
Attn: Sheila Whitaker
British Film Institute
127 Charing Cross Road
London WC1, England

SUNDANCE FILM FESTIVAL
(January)
Attn: Indi Competition
225 Santa Monica Blvd.,
   8th Fl.
Santa Monica, CA 90401

ROTTERDAM FILM FESTIVAL
(January–February)
Attn: Director
P.O. Box 21696
Rotterdam 3001 AR
The Netherlands

BERLIN FILM FESTIVAL
(February–March)
Attn: Lynda Hansen/AIFA
New York Foundation for the
   Arts
155 Avenue of the Americas,
   14th Floor
New York, NY 10013

AFI/LA FEST
(June)
Attn: Program Director
2021 N. Western Ave.
Los Angeles, Calif. 90027
(213) 856-7774

ROME/FLORENCE FILM FEST
(August or November)
Attn: Fabrizio or Eugenia
   Fiumi
Italian Cultural Institute
686 Park Avenue
New York, N.Y. 10021
(212) 744-2278

CINEQUEST
(November)
Attn: Halfdan Hussie
P.O. Box 720040
San Jose, Calif. 95172
(408) 995-6305

SEATTLE INTERNATIONAL
(March)
Egyptian Theater
801 East Pine Street
Seattle, Wash. 98122
(206) 323-4978

THE NEW YORK PREMIERE

While you await word of which foreign film festival will select your film for the "world premiere," your next step is to promote your film in New York City and try to get it a "New York premiere." If you show your film at a high-quality showcase or museum and you get good press, then word of your fabulous film will instantly spread to all other parts of the country because of the wide distribution of the *Village Voice*, *The New York Times*, and other publications. The best-quality premiere, the one that gives you the brightest spotlight and the most important press coverage—a review in *The New York Times*—is guaranteed if you have the good fortune to be selected by the New Directors/New Films showcase run by the Museum of Modern Art. For information, write: Museum of Modern Art, Film Department, 11 West 53rd Street, New York, N.Y. 10014, or call (212) 708-9612.

The Cineprobe program, also administrated by MOMA, presents the filmmaker in person with his or her film. But this exposure does not guarantee a review, so other showcases should also be considered. The Whitney Museum and the Film Forum also sponsor independent film programs that guarantee a *New York Times* review.

WHITNEY MUSEUM
Attn: John Hanhardt
945 Madison Avenue
New York, N.Y. 10021
(212) 570-0537

FILM FORUM
Attn: Karen Cooper
209 W. Houston St.
New York, N.Y. 10014
(212) 627-2035

If all these showcases see your independent feature and turn you down, don't be discouraged. It usually takes a few tries to be selected. I was turned down by all these showcases in New York when I tried to get a show for my first feature, *A Man, a Woman, and a Killer*, before I was selected by the Bleecker Street Cinema. From that showing I received press coverage in both *The New York Times* and the New York *Daily News*. Here are two other showcases in New York City that are worth trying:

MILLENNIUM
Attn: Howard Guttenplan
66 East 4th Street
New York, N.Y. 10003
(212) 673-0090

PUBLIC THEATRE
Attn: Fabiano Canosa
425 Lafayette St.
New York, N.Y. 10003
(212) 598-7167

PROMOTION BY LETTERS AND PHONE

If you can't afford to travel to New York and promote your film in person, write (or FAX) letters to the various showcases, telling them about yourself and your feature. After a few weeks, call person-to-person and ask for the director of programming. This will cost you some money, but at least you will be able to talk to the person who can make decisions regarding your film.

Yes, it is like gambling—spending money in hopes that you will get something in return. You are betting on yourself and your good work. My attitude is that you should try *all possibilities* to give yourself a chance to survive the first feature (and get rolling on the next). And if no one in New York City will touch your feature with a ten-foot pole, it is time to try the rest of the country.

AMERICAN SHOWCASES

While you are waiting for responses from New York, or after you have actually been turned down by these showcases, it's time to begin working on an "in-person" tour of the United States. Although it works best when you have some New York press to show the directors of other showcases, it is possible to build your tour from scratch. Below I've listed some of my favorite showcases and favorite people who may help you launch your film. Call them for information or for a complete mailing address.

MUSEUM OF FINE ARTS
Attn: Bo Smith
Boston, Mass.
(617) 267-9300

WEBSTER UNIVERSITY
Attn: David Kinder
St. Louis, Mo.
(314) 968-7487

SHELDON FILM THEATER
Attn: Dan Ladley
Lincoln, Neb.
(402) 472-2461

WALKER ART CENTER
Attn: Bruce Jenkins
Minneapolis, Minn.
(612) 375-7619

S. F. CINEMATHEQUE
Attn: Program Director
San Francisco, Calif.
(415) 558-8129

CHICAGO FILMMAKERS
Attn: Brenda Webb
Chicago, Ill.
(312) 384-5533

CINEMA ARTS CENTRE
Attn: Vic Skolnick/Charlotte
  Sky
Huntington, N.Y.
(516) 423-7610

NEIGHBORHOOD FILM
  PROJECT
Attn: Linda Blackaby
Philadelphia, Penn.
(215) 387-5125

UNIVERSITY OF WISCONSIN
Attn: Don Skoller
Milwaukee, Wis.
(414) 229-3907

911 MEDIA ARTS
Attn: Robin Reidy
Seattle, Wash.
(206) 682-6552

CHICAGO ART INSTITUTE
Attn: Barbara Scharres
Chicago, Ill.
(312) 443-3733

PACIFIC FILM ARCHIVE
Attn: Program Director
Berkeley, Calif.
(510) 642-1413

ROXIE CINEMA   PITTSBURGH FILMMAKERS
Attn: Bill Banning   Attn: Gary Kaboly
San Francisco, Calif.   Pittsburgh, Penn.
(415) 431-3611   (412) 681-5449

These showcases are my favorites (along with the Whitney Museum and the Museum of Modern Art in New York) because their programmers are, first of all, interested in low-budget features. And the programmers know how to do everything right: They advertise to fill the theater for your show(s), often get the newspapers to review your film, have excellent screening facilities, and pay a good film rental and in-person fee. Lists of other showcases may be available at such foundations as AIVF in New York, FAF in San Francisco, or at local filmmakers' co-ops such as Canyon Cinema (San Francisco), which will sell you their mailing list of 250 showcases that most often rent independent films. But since many showcases operate on such a low budget that they can't afford the higher price for feature-film rentals ($150 to $200), think twice before spending your postage reaching all the listings. For the filmmaker touring with a feature, it's best to focus your energy on just the showcases known to present low-budget movies. Remember that the showcases nearest your hometown will probably be the most difficult shows for you to get . . . so don't get discouraged. Once you are booked for a show on the other side of the country, contact your local showcase and give them another chance to be part of your national tour.

After you and your film are selected to appear at your first in-person show, the next step is to try to book more shows in that region of the country. A filmmaker needs several shows in each area to make a profit. Ask the programmer who selected your film to help you find other shows.

It is also important to schedule your shows tightly together so that they occur every other day, if possible, with time to visit with the programmer and see his or her city and then make your flight connections to the next city. The programmers I have listed are very skilled at helping the filmmaker successfully make his or her connections to the next tour stop.

The most important tip I can give you before your initiation into the world of the touring filmmaker is this: Try to get an airline credit card. For many years I scrambled to raise the necessary $500 plane fare to get to the shows to earn the money to pay for the flights. The most I've ever earned on one tour was $3,300 for eight shows. Subtracting the $700 for airfares, my actual earnings were around $2,600, and I was on tour for three weeks. By now you must realize that this is a hard way to make a living.

Still, the benefits of showing your film at in-person shows greatly outweigh the difficulties. First, you are able to show your film to an interested audience and then hear their feedback during the in-person discussion following the screening. There's no better way of finding out if you have touched your audience, reached them with your ideas and images. Audio record each in-person show, creating a taped record of a filmmaker (you) doing his or her best in the year 19— showing a film called _____. If your film is very provocative, it may infuriate your audience, as my film *Emerald Cities* did when I showed it at Cinema Arts Centre in Huntington, New York, in 1983. The programmer, Vic Skolnick, had told me on the phone that he thought it was "a hard film," but that he wanted to show it in his theater. During the in-person portion of the screening the audience seemed to break in half. One half loved the film and thanked me for bringing up the important issues in it, while the other half hated me for putting them on such a big "bummer." One guy, a professional-looking man of about forty, seemed to be approaching the stage with the intent of harming me in some way. Quite a show! In St. Louis I had another hot response from a member of the audience at Webster University (1984), where programmer David Kinder screened *Emerald Cities*. At this show I was pushed hard enough by the irritating feedback to actually become articulate about my film and its relationship to the world.

Another benefit of these in-person shows is that the reviews you receive may help convince other showcases and film festivals that your film is valuable and should be seen. So make sure to keep copies of all press your film receives.

Although the money from the shows will not make you rich, it

does help to get an extra $1,000 to $2,000, visit strange and exciting cities, and occasionally be treated like a celebrity. And who
knows—one of your reviews might catch the eye of a distributor.

TELEVISION PREMIERE

Since the video revolution has opened up many doors to sales in
television, you should try to show your feature to some cable, PBS,
even network people. Here are the most accessible national television outlets for low-budget feature films.

BRAVO CABLE
150 Crossways Park West
Woodbury, N.Y. 11797

NEW CULTURE NETWORK
2909 Stanton Avenue
Silver Spring, Md. 20910

AMERICAN PLAYHOUSE
1776 Broadway
9th Floor
New York, N.Y. 10019

LEARNING CHANNEL
7700 Wisconsin Ave.
Suite 700
Bethesda, Md. 20814

POV
220 West 19th St., 11th floor
New York, N.Y. 10011

PBS
475 L'Enfant Plaza, S.W.
Washington, D.C. 20024

It is still a long shot that one of these outlets will purchase your
movie, since your low-budget feature probably has a number of
qualities that make it "unbroadcastable." Your film probably has
no recognizable stars, unconventional editing and structure, and
perhaps even some profanity. But occasionally the door cracks
open and a "weird" film will be purchased. I was lucky to get such
a "bail out" when the Learning Channel purchased my *Morgan's
Cake* feature for over $16,000 ($1000 beyond its total cost) because it fit well into their current series entitled "Growing Up." To
get a financial break like this you first have to hear about programming needs, and then apply with VHS copy and written
materials. So watch your filmmaking magazines for these timely
announcements. Many cities also have a local independent PBS

channel and arts-oriented cable channel that might be more open to including your independent feature in their programming.

Although you might get paid as little as $300 for a TV showing on PBS in your hometown, you would have the satisfaction of reaching many thousands of people with your film. And this television exposure won't really wreck your chances for future showings at film showcases, which play to very specialized audiences. You should bear in mind, however, that New York showcases, such as the Whitney Museum and Film Forum, insist on "premiering" films they present. If you decide to accept an offer to show your film on PBS in New York, you would most likely be forfeiting the chance for an important New York film premiere and the reviews in *The New York Times* and the *Village Voice* that would follow. So make sure the amount of money you will be paid is enough to make it a wise decision. If the Whitney Museum will pay you $1,200 for a two-week run of your feature and PBS offers you $4,000 for one showing at 10 P.M., which "premiere" would you select?

In Europe, several countries have well-funded television stations that produce and purchase low-budget feature films. For $30 you can purchase the most up-to-date listing of European buyers from the Independent Feature Project (see "The Film Market" for more information). In Germany alone, there are three channels that pay from around $10,000 to $50,000 for each film they show. And in England, Channel Four has purchased many independent features, including my second feature, *1988—The Remake*, for which I was paid £7,000 (around $13,000). Write a personal letter with a short synopsis of your film's contents. With luck, you may receive a request to send a ¾" or VHS videotape for preview.

ZDF-STRASSE 1
Postfach 4040
55100 Mainz, Germany

ARD
Am Steinernen Stock 1
Frankfurt, Germany 60320

WDR
Attn: Werner Duetsch
Appelhofplatz 1
50600 Koln, Germany

CHANNEL FOUR
Alan Fountain
60 Charlotte Street
London W1P 2AX, England

THE FILM MARKET

While feature films are sold every day at various film markets around the world, the average independent filmmaker doesn't have enough financial resources to afford the travel, hotel rooms, and PR materials necessary to participate. The one event I can recommend is the Independent Feature Film Market (IFFM) held each year in New York City, run by the Independent Feature Project (IFP). Begun in 1979 as a support group to aid the independent feature filmmaker, IFP provides the format of its film market at reasonable rates while maintaining a low-key and congenial atmosphere for both film buyers and filmmakers alike. If your feature has failed to attract attention at either film festivals or showcases, the Independent Feature Film Market offers you one more crack at selling your work to buyers from American and European TV, including representatives from Germany, England, and other progressive countries that buy original films. You may even be surprised to find your feature invited to several European and American festivals by week's end.

> THE INDEPENDENT FEATURE PROJECT (IFP)
> 104 W. 29th St., 12th Floor
> New York, N.Y. 10001
> (212) 465-8200

Once your feature is accepted for presentation at the market, you will be required to pay a fee of $425 ($375 for early registration), which covers the costs of your screening at a high-quality theater and the printing of a catalog containing a photo, short synopsis, and contact address and phone number for your film. If you don't have friends to stay with in New York City, the film market will help you find affordable housing. Like any good festival, the IFFM offers many opportunities for socializing, chances to meet buyers as well as other filmmakers who may become lifelong friends. To take advantage of the Independent Feature Project's continuing programs, screenings of features, seminars, and monthly newsletters, you may want to join as a member, yearly dues costing $85 for individuals, $50 for students. For information on the East Coast, call the Independent Feature Project in New York; to inquire about IFP/West, call (310) 392-8832. For IFP/Midwest call (312) 467-4437.

DISTRIBUTORS

I have the urge to make this section of the book the shortest one of all. Just two words—STEER CLEAR! Does this mean don't distribute? But how can a film be seen by the general public if it doesn't get distribution?

One of the dreams of most independent filmmakers is that a distributor will pick up his or her feature film, blow it up to 35-mm from 16-mm, and present it in the best theater in New York to rave reviews. And for some, such as Wayne Wang (*Chan Is Missing*), Jim Jarmusch (*Stranger Than Paradise*), and Spike Lee (*She's Gotta Have It*), this dream has become a reality. But no distributor will pick up a low-budget feature unless that film first proves it has the potential for pulling in an audience. This proof must be in the form of a very positive review by a leading critic. And a low-budget feature film will only be reviewed by a critic such as Vincent Canby of *The New York Times* if it is presented at the New York Film Festival, the Film Forum, the New Directors/ New Films Showcase at the Museum of Modern Art, or at some equally prestigious showcase.

If you manage to beat the odds and your film is chosen by one of these important showcases, and you receive rave reviews, you must be *very* savvy in selecting the right distributor. Only a few distributors are skilled at making money with an "offbeat" independent feature. New Yorker Films in New York has been regarded as a top distributor for several years. It specializes in award-winning foreign films, "art" films such as Godard's, and occasionally American films that review well such as *Chan Is Missing* and *Atomic Cafe*. New Line Cinema of New York has successfully distributed the low-budget features of John Waters (*Pink Flamingos*) and for a while handled my feature *1988—The Remake*. Several large distributors, including Miramax, Sony, and Samuel Goldwyn, are now distributing smaller films under the

Hunter Mann pursues his alternative method of 16-mm film distribution, bicycling around the country with his "Highway Cinema" trailer filled with film prints (Harrod Blank's *Wild Wheels* documentary among others), EIKI projector, even plug-in audiocassette and mike for background "theater music" and announcements. Photo by Rick Aubert.

"Classics" banner, in an attempt to handle less-mainstream (but equally profitable) feature films.

The one thing all these distributors have in common is their expectation that, since they are taking such a big risk in handling an independent feature, they should be well paid if the venture succeeds. If you sign the wrong contract, you can be giving one of these distributors up to 90 percent of the earnings of your film.

If you want to earn any money under a distribution agreement, you must first understand the difference between "gross" and "net." If you sign a contract that promises you 50 percent of the net earnings of your feature, you will receive half of the money left over from the ticket sales after the distributor pays off all the office help, his or her salary, advertising costs, printing and promotion, travel expenses for the distribution rep to foreign film festivals, cab fares, business lunches, and expensive dinners. In other words, you will receive about 10 percent of the money your feature earns, if you're lucky, after doing 100 percent of the writing, producing, directing, shooting, editing, casting, and financing. Does this seem fair? Does it seem right that the person who sells your film should get almost the total financial benefit from your good work? Perhaps, if the distributor (Miramax, Sony) has the clout to distribute widely enough that your 10 percent equals several hundred thousand dollars.

A far better deal would be a contract offering you 50 percent of the gross, stipulating that of every dollar returned to the distributor from the theater you receive fifty cents, period. This is the deal that you want, but it is almost impossible to get. Another way to alter the contract in your favor is to agree to a net deal but limit and detail (in the contract) exactly which expenses may be paid for out of the net proceeds. In my contract with New Line Cinema for *1988—The Remake*, I limited their net expenses to $3,000, so that I would receive a true 50 percent of the earnings from our 50–50 deal after these initial expenses.

In practical terms, very few independent filmmakers receive any money from their distributors beyond the "advance," the initial payment for purchase of distribution rights. And usually the distributor offers *no* money up front for a "risky" independent film. If you want to make any money on your distribution deal, you should be prepared for a tough negotiating session. Ask for an advance, insist on either a gross deal or a detailed limited net deal, and be sure to add a clause stipulating that the distributor does *not* have any legal rights to edit your film under any conditions. **And don't sign any contract with a distributor until you first review its contents with the best entertainment lawyer in your area**. Even if it costs you $1000 (which you may be able to arrange to pay from rentals or out of the advance), hire a good lawyer who will check every word in the contract and change the particularly offensive clauses so that you will have at least a glimmer of hope of receiving some money. Don't be so overcome by the dream of distribution that you give away all the earnings of your "breakthrough" feature.

AGENTS

For the most part, no quirky, no-budget independent feature can make it in the marketplace and get major distribution without a certain groundswell of success. That success might begin with being selected for Sundance Film Festival's Dramatic or Documentary Competition or New Directors/New Films in New York. These extremely prestigious festivals guarantee that a film will be solidly in the spotlight and have the potential for substantial success. Usually by this point the film will have attracted enough attention for film agents, who position themselves to have pre-existing deals with certain films that they think will emerge as the success stories of the year. Certain agents, like John Pierson (ISLET, 44 Market Street, Cold Spring, N.Y. 10516, [914] 265-2241), who have strong track records for launching small films, can actually add to the fire of interest in a feature by signing it on for representation. Pierson's involvement was one of the crucial steps that led to the success of Kevin Smith's *Clerks* being sold to Miramax in 1994 out of the Sundance Dramatic Competition. Look for Pierson to have an even stronger influence in the sales of indi features now that he and his new venture, Grainy Pictures, have been given their own distribution pipeline through Disney-owned Miramax. An earlier contributor to the *Clerks* success story was Bob Hawk, a consultant with ICI (Independent Consultation for Independents, 1870 North Vermont Avenue, Suite 507, Los Angeles, Calif. 90027, [213] 856-6205) who "discovered" the no-budget feature at a sparsely attended screening at the IFFM in New York. ICI can help some features find a home with festivals and honest agents, as well as assist the filmmaker in earlier stages of production, scripting, and final cut.

Those many filmmakers whose "undiscovered" low-budget features won't be the hit of the year must decide between self-agenting their features or turning the films over to lesser known agents and distributors, gambling that the expenses incurred by the agents won't outrun any actual funds earned in the marketplace. For some filmmakers, like Jerry Barrish, whose career began by having his first feature, *Dan's Motel* (80 minutes, 1981) selected by New Directors/New Films in New York, with strong interest generated by New Yorker Films for distribution, it has been an uphill battle to get the financial return his films deserve. Although Barrish has amassed an impressive record of festival screenings (including Berlin Film Festival's Forum, Edinburgh, Rotterdam, etc.) and sold repeatedly to German TV, it has often been the agents who have received the money from TV sales, as they have recouped their unchecked expenses for hotel room, food, and air travel fees to festivals and film markets. For example, Barrish's third feature, *Shuttlecock* (87 minutes, Color, 1989) earned $14,000 at the Roxie Cinema in San Francisco, all of which was owed his agent for costs already incurred from sales trips to Cannes and the IFFM. Even though the film, which won a top prize at Rotterdam, is now distributed in Europe, Barrish has not, as yet, seen either statements or earnings beyond his advance. His one consolation is that the European distributor fronted the money to blow his film up from 16-mm to 35-mm (saving him more than $20,000). Because there are so few real possibilities for sales and distribution of low-budget features, the filmmaker may be better off acting as his or her own agent, sending out well-targeted VHS cassette copies with personally written cover letters, and using an experienced film attorney (instead of an agent) to negotiate sales, review contracts, finalize payment. Perhaps then it will be you and your significant other who will enjoy a well-earned working vacation in Cannes, meeting those few distributors who have expressed genuine interest in your unique product.

OTHER FORMS OF DISTRIBUTION

Whether or not your film receives the kind of review attention that will attract distributors, you will want to consider some alternatives. Instead of signing away most of your future earnings to a commercial distributor, why couldn't you rent a theater, do modest advertising, hire ticket takers, and earn the most possible money from your successful run? One major obstacle to this simple alternative is that the best theaters in New York are locked up, "owned" by certain distributors who make payments to insure that the theaters are available only to their companies. But in other areas of the country, a filmmaker can rent his or her own theater (this is called "four walling") and earn a much higher percentage from a film's showings. The largest drawback to four walling your feature is that it takes a great deal of time away from what you probably should be doing—making films.

Aside from running your own shows at various locations, there are many other opportunities for showings that you can pursue on your own—at regional showcases, on college campuses, and in independent theaters. For some feature filmmakers, like Joe Berlinger and Bruce Sinofsky (*Brother's Keeper*, 1992) who have turned self-distribution into an art form, the rewards are high, their earnings now topping the million-dollar mark for their prizewinning documentary. The essence of self-distribution is simple: People who want to rent or buy your film get in touch with you by phone or letter. You tell them your price and then, if they agree, you arrange to send them your print after receiving their down payment. If you trust them, you might allow them to pay you after their use of your film. All the details of this process vary with each situation. Usually, you will pay for the shipping to the showcase and they pay for return postage when they mail it back. For my first few rentals, I was incredibly excited that *anyone* wanted to show my film and would actually pay me for its use. But after the initiation of renting the film and having it returned damaged or waiting in vain for the "check in the mail" to arrive, I began wondering if there wasn't a better way to handle distribution. Fortunately, there are some practical low-cost alternatives to doing it entirely on your own.

For a small annual fee of around $40 a co-op distributor, such as Filmmaker's Co-op in New York or Canyon Cinema in San Francisco, will handle all rentals, mailing, and invoicing for you. In return, they receive a reasonable percentage of the rental charge—usually 35 to 40 percent. Most co-ops are very honest, considerate of the filmmakers, and careful with stored prints and rentals. And although this type of service will generate few rentals unless the filmmaker commits to spending some money advertising his films, occasionally you will be surprised with an extra $50 when you really need it.

ADVERTISING FOR ALTERNATIVE DISTRIBUTION

For a very reasonable rate of $450 you can place a ⅓-page ad in *Film Comment* magazine. Tony Impavido, who is in charge of advertising at *Film Comment*, has been known to give low-budget filmmakers even lower rates. For a *very* targeted audience of indi film lovers, Seattle-based *Movie Maker Magazine* [(206) 860-3831] offers highly competitive ad rates. If you hunt around you may find other good advertising rates with film or television magazines, but most are very expensive. A ⅓-page ad in *Entertainment Weekly* magazine costs around $16,000! Sometimes if you let the advertising manager know that you are a "feature filmmaker at used-car prices," you may get a reduction in your rate, but I doubt that there is a much better deal than the advertising rate of *Film Comment*, which reaches between 30,000 and 50,000 interested filmphiles.

Because of the ads I've run for my three features in *Film Comment*, my films have been selected for showings at several commercial theaters in the United States. In 1983 the St. Marks Theater (now defunct) in the East Village section of New York City ran *Emerald Cities* for two Friday/Saturday midnight shows for which I had been given a $150 advance guarantee (check sent to me before the show) versus a 35 percent cut of the gross receipts. I earned about $650 for the four shows. The ads also helped me get three in-person shows, each of which paid me $600 to appear with *Emerald Cities*. Subtracting my $510 travel expenses ($1,800 – $510 = $1,290), I was still well paid for two weeks on the road. And after subtracting the cost of my ads in *Film Comment* ($1,290 – $600 = $690), and adding my earnings from the St. Marks show ($690 + $650 = $1,340), I at least made a small overall profit that I wouldn't have made if I hadn't advertised.

Advertising can pay off in other ways as well. When I went around to the video stores to sell my features on cassette, one store buyer in San Francisco immediately ordered all my tapes (in VHS and Beta), saying that he had heard of my films. This sale was due to my constant advertising in *Film Comment*.

And don't overlook the possibility of getting your features reviewed in magazines, which could be free advertising worth hundreds of dollars. Mail your VHS copy and pressbook to the current critics you admire, offering them the chance to discover you and your work.

SETTING PRICES

When you set your prices for film rentals, print purchases, or videotapes in VHS, make sure that you don't price yourself right out of the market. I've tried to keep my prices reasonable: $150 for seventy-minute features, $175 for ninety-minute features for rentals in 16-mm to small theaters and showcases. And for the purchase of a print, I charge an extra $500 over cost. I have sold several hundred videotapes of my features to stores in the San Francisco Bay Area by charging the reasonable price of $35 wholesale. Since it costs me $10 to produce each tape, I'm basically tripling my money with each sale. Some of the buyers in the stores have told me that other independent filmmakers want $49.95 for their tapes, and the stores refuse to pay that much for something that isn't mainstream.

For your in-person shows, the prices vary quite a bit, but you should try to keep your minimum price around $200 to $250. On your first time out as an unknown filmmaker, it might help to be looser with this minimum and take what you can get, since many showcases have disappeared in the last few years and many others have been forced to cut their budgets. Don't price yourself out of the market, but don't sell yourself too cheap, either. Overcome your shyness and ask if any travel allowance can be made available. Perhaps several showcases can share the expense of your round-trip airfare. If a showcase wants you and your film, it will certainly try to meet your financial needs.

THE LONG HAUL

It is not unusual for a foreign film festival or showcase to call you up two years after you began promoting your feature to tell you they want to show your film. If you've made an entertaining, thoughtful, and original feature, you will continue to get a sprinkling of rentals for years to come. Be patient. My feature *1988— The Remake* was chosen for showing at the London Film Festival in 1980, two years after it premiered at the Whitney Museum in New York.

And the video market will continue to demand new films, so while you conceive and begin to script your new feature, some time each month should be spent promoting your completed feature to the video stores. You may even want to purchase a mailing list of video stores and do a major mailing.

While you continue to search for feedback and shows for your recently completed feature, using the video copies to apply for grants, film festivals, and purchases by video stores, you must also pause for reflection. Of course, it's important not to fool yourself into thinking that you are making a living with your feature if in fact you are not. Be realistic about your expenses, keep a running list of the money you spend for typesetting, postage, travel fares, so that you can honestly evaluate your "business of filmmaking."

But no matter how much or how little money you make with your first feature, you should enjoy the recognition that you have succeeded, that you have actually fulfilled your goal of creating a feature film. Regardless of what anyone thinks of your film, the completion of it is a great accomplishment, and you should celebrate this achievement. Remember that some artists, such as Van Gogh, were never appreciated in their lifetimes, hardly sold a painting . . . so try to appreciate any rentals and enjoy every sign of success. And while you wait for responses from festivals and showcases, use the glow of your accomplishment to begin thinking of your next film. If you are thorough in your promotion, you should have a chance to try again—with Feature Film at Used-Car Prices #2.

8

REALITY CHECK

et's say that you somehow, against all odds, pulled off the no-budget production of a feature film. And when you finished the film and showed it to all interested parties (friends, parents, investors, cast and crew) everyone raved about your accomplishment. You were flying high. You had done it. Look out, Spike Lee and Jim Jarmusch! A star was born. The sky was the limit. Easy street was around the corner. You were made to feel extremely confident in your film by everyone concerned, and with that optimistic feeling you began the process of promotion. You made VHS dubs of your feature and started submitting to the most obvious film festivals; Sundance, New Directors, Rome/Florence, Seattle, Berlin, Rotterdam, London, New York, Chicago, Denver, AFI/LA, even Cannes. You checked your calendar, wondered if you'd be in France in May, perhaps Park City for Sundance in January, New York in September. You had fantasies that you expected to be realized, and you awaited the call. But when the letters showed up, enclosing variously worded rejections, a sense of defeat, maybe even betrayal, began to emerge. How could a film a good as yours continue to be overlooked at the (dumb) festivals? What the hell was happening?

You soon learned that one major mistake you had made was

trumpeting to all your friends and associates which festivals you had entered. Now all they did was drive you crazy asking you about Sundance. You had been so sure. . . . And at the IFFM (Independent Feature Film Market) in New York City your film had shown to a full and enthusiastic house and received compliments, but the festivals in Europe hadn't bitten. Berlin had sent you a curt letter, spelling the doom, erasing the promise of German TV sales in two sentences (I got much too used to those form letters before I finally got in with *Morgan's Cake*). Somehow you'd been set up to expect a lot more positive response from the festivals. You had at least expected to get in one. But no go. A total bust.

If your low-budget feature was so good then why didn't any festival (art museum, showcase, theater) want to show it? Let's say for now that the fault lies entirely with *them*. It is possible that the film you created was so artistic that no one was prepared to understand it, much less accept it (see Ray Carney's interview in the Foreword). If you hit the cutting edge it might take a few more years for your "ahead-of-its-time" film to find a home. Or maybe you hit upon such strong issues, dug so deep into the psyche of America, that no one can stand the results of your folly. Your film may have pushed too many buttons in the panel of experts at Sundance and built up a distaste for it that resulted in its dismissal (I like to think that is why my *American Orpheus* failed to make the final cut in 1991 when it was among the final sixteen dramatic features from which they selected the final few features for competition). So your feature *is* good, it's just that no one wants to show it or have anything to do with it. Can you really believe that? Is your ego sufficient to handle all that rejection, downcast looks from friends, a bit too much sympathy from family members? If your film is that good then don't give up. Try some of the smaller festivals that can offer you a great show, good attendance, even press coverage (Cinequest/San Jose, Ann Arbor Film Festival, Wine Country Film Festival/Napa, Aspen, etc.), while continuing occasionally to tempt the majors (San Francisco, Seattle, Boston, Venice, Locarno). Have you tried Telluride? How about Munich in Germany? How can you be sure that you haven't been lax in your job, sunk your film because you couldn't maintain a positive mood. You need to get the proof from *all* festivals (that nice big pile of rejection letters) before you can say for certain that no one wanted your film.

On the other hand, what if your film is as unworthy as your (well-hidden) doubts might say? How can you deal with such an artistic failure? The only way I know to make use of an artistic disaster is to give it another shot—try again. If you honestly made your own brand of mistakes, entered into the making of a feature film with your own ideas about content and form, then the true nature of your accomplishment can only be realized up the road, a couple of features later, when the new ground you are intuitively carving out for yourself will finally accomplish its goals for all to see. Until then you must not get discouraged. Your work is too valuable. And the temptations to forget your individual path will be immense. Pressures from all sides will seem to be forcing you toward making a more mainstream second feature, one that will try to more closely resemble Hollywood's product. You may find yourself actually writing a script that runs exactly 118 pages, has strong story lines, plot points, even characters with known actors in mind. You want to do it "right" this time, never have to feel like a failure again. Right? Is that how it is?

What happened to your personal vision? How ornery and crazy does a filmmaker have to be to try it his or her way for a second time in a row? How about for a tenth time in a row? Most great art that you've seen didn't just materialize from the artist's hand on the first try. It took years of hard work, probably decades, for that artist to finally swoop in on the nugget of perception that was his or her gift to the world. And it took an equally long time for that artist to master the particular technical expertise in his or her field to make such a convincing statement, whether it was in oil paint, carved marble, or film. Great art takes a lifetime of hard, relentless work. Are you up for that? Did you forget that a first feature film is just the bare beginning of your career? You barely got your toes wet and you're ready to quit? That's ridiculous. Won't it be enjoyable to tell your friends that you're making another feature film? Won't it be worth it just to see the look on their faces? When they ask you "why?" you can tell them that you're an artist, and all artists are crazy. They'll probably nod knowingly and end up helping you again.

9

COLLABORATIVE
FEATURES

For most readers who have reviewed the first eight chapters of this book, the idea of directing and producing a feature may seem as distant a dream as when they first picked up the book, since raising even $6,000 is quite difficult to do in an age when often half of all earnings goes just to rent. Other practical-minded individuals who shun credit cards and believe in the axiom, "A penny saved is a penny earned" (but can't save nearly enough to make a feature film) may be stuck in their self-imposed rut of deciding that the sacrifice of economic stability is too high a price to pay for even such a major aspiration as feature filmmaking. And then there are those veterans of filmmaking wars who have somehow scraped up the necessary funds to grind out a first feature, often at a cost of $20,000 to $30,000, and then had difficulty recouping their investment. Psychically weakened from their failure to get invited to major film festivals, and worn out from explaining to relatives and other investors that no money has, as yet, been earned, they may think that the idea of making a second feature seems ridiculously farfetched. Yet for both the first-time dreamer and the veteran with one or more features under his or her belt, there may still exist a flicker of hope that lack of money won't put an end to their promising careers. In the following pages I describe a method of making features by collaboration in which filmmakers can band together and produce a super no-budget feature by sharing costs and workload.

FEATURE WORKSHOPS

In 1993 I committed $700 to ads in two national magazines, *Film Comment* and *Film Threat*, announcing that Light Video was conducting something called Feature Workshops. The ad stated that for the cost of $2,250 each, "10 people will collaborate with Rick Schmidt to write, direct, film, edit & complete a co-operatively owned 70 minute feature." From the fifty or so serious inquiries five people were chosen to enact their dream.

The three men and two women who committed to the project came from diverse backgrounds, were of different ages, ranging from early twenties to over fifty, and brought with them substantial experiences in education and the school of hard knocks. The youngest man was twenty-four, a self-published poet and an actor of his own one-man-shows who had written such a strong essay in high school about an alienated teen who commits suicide that he turned the whole school and community upside down. So he had discovered early on how "the power of art" could change social structure and help people see their lives differently and make meaningful changes.

Another participant, a man in his mid-thirties, had given up an $88,000-per-year job in advertising to work for CNN and pursue his love of media. Before his move to Atlanta he had conceived, produced, and sold an alternative music show, entitled "Cross Currents," that has since become a model for current cutting edge radio. Now he was ready to make his own feature films.

The third man in our group was in his late twenties. Somehow he was able to break away from his seventy-hour-a-week job as an executive creative director at an ad agency (he'd produced more than 100 thirty- and sixty-second commercials) to join us. He said he had planned to go to NYU film school, but couldn't get the twelve weeks off. After reading my book he decided to use my workshop to get the ten-day experience of working on a 16-mm no-budget feature.

The younger of the two women had learned to fly at age fifteen and later attempted solo flights across the country. Along with her aviation experience she brought an education consisting of a BA in Communications, and a strong will to make feature films.

The oldest member of our collaborative team had worked in social services. She told a story in her application about trying to help a Hispanic family of ten children: all six of the boys had ended up in prison and later died, while the girls survived. With her short story she had posed a major question about what role environment plays in a person's life.

To the initial list of collaborators I added on the needed technicians for the shoot. Fortunately I was able to locate a sound-person who gave me a good rate ($500) for recording sync with his own Nagra tape recorder, and a cinematographer who dropped his usual rate to $1,500 for the four days and supplied his own Arri SR camera and lights. With our small budget of $11,250 we needed all the breaks we could get.

Before the five collaborators arrived in Port Townsend, Washington, for the shoot, we exchanged ideas and scripting to come up with a workable premise for our breakneck production. The story was finally hung on two locations in town, one a weird "pilot house" cabin (part of a boat that had been dumped on dry land), and the other a "gypsy wagon" on a farm that looked like it was right out of Fellini's *La Strada*. Each location would have an unwanted guest as its inhabitant. At the pilot house a young woman would be temporarily housed while waiting for her husband to show up, while across town a man temporarily housed in the gypsy wagon would be given two weeks to vacate the property, having been ordered away after a horrendous breakup with his girlfriend, who owned the place.

When the participants met me for dinner on July 7 I brought out our contract (see "Collaborative Feature Agreement," Appendix J) that explained how we would all equally share in whatever profits were generated from our collaborative venture. For the next four days we all wrote scenes, directed actors, made use of all the miracles swirling around the set, then spent the next five days editing footage, finally traveling to Seattle to have a video transfer to VHS made. Perhaps you and your friends can follow our example, end up at the Independent Feature Film Market in New York City as we did with our seventy-eight-minute "work in progress" entitled *Blues for the Avatar*. For a few thousand dollars this goal is now within your reach.

TEN-WAY COLLABORATIVE FEATURES

If you could round up ten people like yourself, men and women who share your dream, who could afford to pay in a total of $2,500 each over the period of a year, then with that total budget of $25,000 you could become a producer/director. And it is possible that not everyone would want to be a director like yourself. They may not want to write and direct scenes, but be content with recording sound or shooting camera for an equal share of revenues earned up the road. Perhaps you'll find that you end up with an ideal collaborative group. Out of the people you meet and explain to about making a collaborative feature, you might find a (1) cinematographer, (2) soundperson, (3) lead actor, (4) lead actress, (5) writer, (6) expert at lighting/dolly/electrical, (7) camera assistant approved of by the cinematographer, (8) set designer/costumer, (9) line producer/production manager, with yourself (10) as director/producer. Each of your ten experts would pay their $2,500 share to work with you on your premise, and each would receive in return an equal percentage of ownership in the film. If you could successfully and accurately budget your feature in 16-mm so that all costs could be covered within the $25,000 total budget, then each person working with you for the common goal would receive (like you) 10 percent ownership. This would all be spelled out in a contract similar to the one I used for my Feature Workshops (see appendix). Each person would, in fact, also be considered an executive producer in the project.

This (ideal) arrangement in which you are the only person who wants to attain the status of a *film director* may exist only as a pie in the sky, but it's worth spending a bit of time seeing if it is feasible. What you must be most cautious of is the cinematographer who actually wants to direct and other unsatisfied people who will eventually get into an ego war with you on the set. You have to be sure that each person (actor, technician, writer) is well grounded in his or her expertise and has no aspirations for rocking your boat. Can you be sure that nine intelligent people working *with* you, not *for* you (remember they are equal shareholders), will blindly follow your each and every command as you direct the feature film? A strange thing happens when friends suddenly watch their best buddy play god, talk in an authoritative tone, order people about. After a few days resentment starts to build up, maybe subconsciously, but it's still there. A simple request by you might blow the lid off. They've watched you be totally "full of yourself" for three days and they just can't take it anymore. In the normal professional world of big-budget filmmaking you would be expected to be such a firm leader. But with your friends you will be held accountable for being something more than an equal buddy. Maybe the solution is to work entirely with strangers, so there's no baggage that can drag down the production.

What if the only people interested in making feature films are your filmmaking friends or fellow film students? Can you all rise above petty concerns to pull off a collaborative feature? Is there enough glory for everyone? What if each person is a graduate student in filmmaking, fully capable of doing any job, from shooting and recording sound to writing scenes and directing actors? Could this highly skilled group get together to make a collaborative film? I would like to think so. But the overall concept of collaboration would have to be designed to accommodate the situation. Since each person probably wants to direct his or her own films, there is no way you can relegate them to other jobs (even for an equal share of the pie). Each person must be able to direct or they certainly won't join the project. What if the feature film is made up of ten segments of equal length, seven and a half minutes each, for a total of seventy-five minutes? Given the fact that each 400' roll of filmstock equals about eleven minutes of screen time, if each person directs two 400' rolls, shoots their part of the story with a 2:1 accuracy, and edits their portion to the prescribed length (270' of 16-mm), each will be a proud owner in a collaborative feature-length film. As each filmmaker (film student, knowledgeable professional) directs his or her particular portion of the film, all the other directors-in-waiting fill in with the needed technical duties. Most filmmakers will want to shoot the film themselves, but their collaborators using all the skills that they learned in film school, can cover the work of loading magazines, helping to take light readings, doing on-location sound recording, etc.

How is a ten-way collaborative feature written? If each participant wants to direct (ten directors!) then an agreement has to be reached among the interested parties regarding the basic premise. Everyone must search for, and finally vote on, one overall concept for the film. Whoever comes up with the best idea gets an additional title in the credits ("Story by _____"). From there each writer/director either picks a part of the story or draws straws to see what his or her contribution will be to the project. The entire group must agree on not only the basic premise but also the ideas behind each of the ten segments, so that a kind of overarching confidence can be infused into the filmmaking process. Each person has to be turned on to the entire concept in order for it to be allowed to move forward.

At every stage in the project there must be checks and balances, ways of determining that for the good of all, the film is getting done to the satisfaction of professional standards. After the premises are discussed and one unanimously selected for production, then an outline must be written, each of ten story sections derived from the outline, and each section written as a separate treatment by each director. Again the group should read all treatments, suggest improvements in some, approve others, until everyone is solidly behind the scripting. In these meetings it helps if one person is elected as spokesperson, but the authority remains equally divided among the members (fellow investors all!).

COLLABORATIVE BUDGET

A vital first step of your ten-way collaboration is to assure yourself and all other participants that the money for the completed feature is actually secured and available for production. Without this power to get the film done none of the meetings of the filmmakers-

Cinematographer Kyle Bergersen shoots camera for 1993 Feature Workshop film *Blues for the Avatar* as filmmakers view framing on monitor connected to video tap. Photo by Julie Schachter.

to-be will have the necessary edge. The money must be in place, deposited in a bank account. Probably the most practical thing to do is to open a business account either in the title of the film you are about to make, or in a company name all ten participants agree to. If you trust that no one person in your group will write a check for the entire amount and head for the South Seas, then list all ten names on the signature card of the account, so that anyone can write a check. If you want more control over the total budget, and want to make sure no one can back out of the feature film production after committing to the project, select a parent or accounting firm to write checks. Or pick two members of the group who must cosign checks. Whatever you decide, make absolutely sure that the budget for the feature is available before you even start conceptualizing your film.

If you and your compatriots have access to film equipment (cameras, Nagras, editing gear) and can each fulfill the changing roles of technicians (soundperson, cinematographer) then a small budget can accommodate either a decision to shoot color, or more black and white filmstock, additional locations, more actors, better all-around services. If your fellow filmmakers are skilled enough to cover (with you) the jobs of cinematographer, soundperson, and conforming of original footage into AB rolls for printing, then you can drastically reduce the budget of a "used-car" shoot, thus requiring much less than $2,500 per person for the production of a collaborative feature. Your budget for a black-and-white feature listed backward from hard costs of lab work, would look something like this:

FILM SCHOOL BUDGET (16MM)

1 80-minute liquid gate Answer print (2,880')	$1,396.80
Final sound mix (film school) mag stock only	$ 150.00
Sound transfer (¼" to mag) mag stock only	$ 250.00
Negative cutting (done by collaborator)	$ 0
Black leader (3,000') for conforming	$ 300.00
Work print ($.215/ft.) 5,600' 16-mm B&W	$1,204.00
Processing original footage ($.15/ft.) 5,600'	$ 840.00
14 400' rolls Kodak 7222 B&W neg ($56.80 ea.)	$ 795.20
Soundperson (only need 14 rolls of ¼" tape)	$ 64.26
Salaries, 2 lead actors (fellow students)	$ 0
Titles (typesetting/negs/filmstock)	$ 300.00
Flatbed editing (free school equipment) + tape	$ 30.00
Edge number 5,600', picture & mag	$ 168.00
TOTAL	$5,498.26

Dividing this budget up among the ten collaborators it's apparent that for considerably less than $1,000 per person, a group of earnest filmmakers can produce a feature film at "used-car" prices if free equipment can be obtained. The project can either be divided up into a ten-way collaboration at $549.82 each, or reduced in size to a five-way collaboration at $1,099.65 per person to limit the possibilities of personality clash. And if this five-way production consisted of a committed cinematographer, producer, soundperson, writer, and director, then the people responsible for production of the film would finally follow a normal configuration. The bottom line is knowing that you can make a feature film with very little money if you have friends who share your dream.

TEN SHORT STORIES
VERSUS TEN SEGMENTS

To create a ten-way collaborative feature that allows everyone a chance to direct, there are basically two different ways to approach the scripting. In one case each of the ten writer/directors is responsible for producing a separate part of a central story. Either through choice or luck of the draw, each collaborator is given a particular part of the script to work on, writing approximately twelve pages that will ultimately be part of a 120-page script. This might become a difficult proposition given the multitude of writing styles and differences in attitudes toward directing, but remember that this actually happens in Hollywood! Numerous writers are hired by big-budget productions to fix an important script for which directors are hired and fired seemingly at will. I personally favor a second approach, in which each writer/director is responsible for coming up with an original short story, that will either play off of the other nine stories by virtue of using the same actors or theme, or be completely different. Even if different actors are used for entirely different stories, a certain totality will, in fact, be conveyed in the viewing experience (see *New York Stories* by Coppola, Scorsese, and Woody Allen). And the more quirky each person's writing and directing, the more refreshing the overall result.

No matter what direction is chosen for the story or stories that make up the collaborative feature, what's important is that each participant feels a certain freedom of expression and is able to write and direct his or her segment without an overabundance of scrutiny and criticism from others. It is important to the project as a whole that the potential for spontaneous fun and creation is maintained. And why even bother if it won't be an enjoyable experience? The production can't be allowed to turn into a argumentative free-for-all. Each collaborator must have the ability to make a contribution without the experience becoming too much of an ordeal.

Of course, the group may find that one or two segments of the total ten are just not up to par, and this is something that must be dealt with by the group as a whole. Will there be an allowance for some reshooting? In a worst-case scenario, when the writer/director of a particular segment thinks his or her work is great while everyone else thinks it stinks, does the group impose their value systems on the individual? Before the shoot, which is that part of the process where real money starts getting spent, there must be some sort of document, signed by all participants, that states the parameters for freedom of expression versus acceptable quality.

QUALITY CONTROL AGREEMENT

If ten different people are going to try and collaborate on producing one feature film, then there must be some control over the finished product in order to protect everyone's investment of time and money. But this control must still give leeway for unhindered creative work and expression. While the following provisos may not cover any and all collaborative circumstances, I hope that they will offer a direction for agreement.

(1) If an entire segment, or substantial part of one, is out of focus by mistake (as opposed to "soft-focus" for conceptual creative reasons), then those faulty areas must be reshot.

(2) If sound recorded on-location is poor quality (garbled, fuzzy, out of sync, etc.) then the scenes that depend on those recordings must be reshot.

Have we stepped on any creative toes yet? Has this agreement reasonably "encouraged" the collaborator to reshoot his or her precious work? Have we in any way ignited an ego, offended one of our fellow writer/directors? Is there a way for each collaborator to take responsibility for his or her own quality control, so others don't have to shove rules down his or her throat? The mine field of hurt feelings and bruised egos must be avoided at all costs. Somehow the collaboration must keep all of its members empowered with high expectations and the ability to deliver good works.

Look again at the first two items of our agreement. Try to imagine the absolute craziest problem that could arise in the areas of either out-of-focus images or bad sound. Maybe one of the collaborators is into a type of pinhole imagery, where every shot in the segment is slightly blurry, all straight lines a bit curved with distortion. Let's also say that the collaborator has purposely recorded the dialogue in and out of sync, so that sometimes the words are in the mouths of the actors, sometimes not. The end result of this dynamic filmmaking is an eight-minute film that looks to be of poor quality, but actually delivers a strange point of view. Will all the other participants see the brilliance? The answer is yes, *if* in the early stages of writing and preproduction the filmmaker lets the other collaborators in on the filmatic goals he or she is trying to achieve.

What if the poor-quality images and sound are real mistakes? What if the low quality of a particular eight-minute segment stands to pull the entire feature-length experience down with it? How will the filmmaker be informed of his or her failure? And what will be the procedure for the reshoot? Where will the extra money come from for purchasing additional filmstock, rehiring the sound recordist and cinematographer if necessary, and processing the footage? If each film school collaborator pitched in $54.98 that would equal the $549.80 needed to budget a redo of one segment. Each collaborator must be made aware in the contract that he or she will be responsible for doing a reshoot if his or her work does not attain professional standards as outlined. It should be a privilege, not a punishment, to be able to have a second chance at producing a segment of the feature.

Of course if a professional soundperson and cinematographer are hired to work on all the segments, with each of ten writer/ directors, it should be obvious from the quality of images and sound on the first eight-minute production whether the level of quality is suitable. All collaborators must see the first dailies, screen the synced-up footage, and then vote unanimously either to continue with the technicians or to hire new ones.

The key to quality control is *communication*. While the contract will state in plain language the agreed-upon rules for the group ordering up a reshoot, the best protection against future problems is if at every stage of production every member of the group is familiarized with everyone else's work. These "checkpoints" should occur at the obvious intervals of (1) story concept, (2) treatment, (3) script, (4) shooting schedule. If each of the ten collaborators reads all the other existing story lines—treatments running a couple of pages of description—and later, eight-to-ten pages of scripting, then not only will they all have confidence in the abilities of their fellow collaborators, but each collaborator's own contribution will be positively affected by all the other projects. Some small kernal of consciousness from each person's segment will have a way of influencing the total work, somehow making it speak with a more unified voice.

WRITING/DIRECTING EN MASSE

If your particular Feature Workshop uses the simplest structure for creating a ten-way collaborative film, that probably means that the same actors will be used in each eight-minute segment. It also means that the same technicians will shoot and record sound for all the separate parts of the film. And if the technicians are recruited from the group of ten collaborators, that means that not only will the cinematographer and soundperson help shoot and record sound on everyone else's segment, but he or she will also shoot and record sound on his or her own part. The stablizing influence of using the same people for these jobs throughout the production is probably the most desirable control of quality. And, of course, each filmmaker could elect to operate the camera, leaving the worries of f-stop and magazine loading with the fellow collaborator who already gives his or her energies so generously as cinematographer.

The shoot should also be organized in the simplest and most direct fashion. If the ten stories have been designed to build into an overarching structure with a beginning, middle, and end, then it will probably be to the advantage of the project to shoot the segments in order, giving the actors a chance to develop their characters naturally. Shooting in order will also help to protect the performances from the intervention of ten different directors. The actors will be better able to have a hand in navigating themselves along, instead of depending solely on the input of each director.

If the shoot is scheduled to take place over a ten-day period, then each writer/director is expected to accomplish his or her work in just one day. A list should be drawn up showing which director is responsible for which day. Once the shoot begins, the process of group effort will in a way resemble the handing off of the baton in a marathon relay race. Goodwill and best wishes will accompany each new director as he or she takes up the cause and leaps into the fray. It will be all for one and one for all. Because everyone depends on the good work of each of the other participants, petty jealousy and envy will be put aside. Any competitiveness, usually harmful in such situations, can only help in this case as each person tries to outdo the other collaborators in creating the best segment that he or she possibly can. Think of the wonderful energy you saw on TV when Carreras, Domingo, and Pavarotti, the three greatest tenors in the world, appeared together for the first time at the Baths of Caracalla in Rome in 1990. After each singer completed a song he would return to the dressing room at the rear of the huge stage, giving a hearty "high-five" hand slap to the next fellow tenor. These three tenors put aside their normal competitive feelings and worked hard to give what is perhaps the greatest single operatic concert of our time. That's how you want it to be for your collaborative feature film.

AUTEUR THEORY DEBRIS

There are people who will say that to make a good or great film with such a ten-way collaboration (ten voices!) is impossible. They will throw the "auteur theory" in your face, stating precepts and postulates about how only one singular vision can enact a work of high art. Of course they are right to a certain extent. A film will certainly be much better if the ideas of the writer/director are not diluted by factors of annoyance and interference, the kind of power plays that occur on almost every Hollywood set. An artist must be able to express himself or herself in an intuitive way, with the freedom to make creative choices without compromising.

These decisions must be made with joy, introspection, and acute observations. To be an "author" of an artwork is an honor and a privilege, something almost sacred. Aren't you just a bit curious about what a feature film made by ten committed artists with a common story thread or theme to hold it together would be like? Does this in any way dilute the "auteur theory"? In a grand way this kind of true collaboration, where each person delivers a personal vision to the screen, only reinforces what the auteur concept is all about. Ideally a collaboration of several personal visions can deliver an experience of earthshaking proportions (see *Hoop Dreams* by Steve James, Peter Gilbert, and Fred Marx). It can certainly be a celebration of the power of art. How could that much humanity be denied?

EDITING BY SEGMENTS/CINEMATIC JAZZ

Probably the biggest threat to a cohesive, unified film made by a Feature Workshop group would be having ten different cuts from ten different directors. Of course, if the collaborative feature is made up of short stories, each different in concept and execution, different editing styles won't distract the viewer. In fact the audience for that film would relish the various cinematic approaches to the segments. The main threat to the quality of a feature-length film constructed of different short stories would be a lack of precision in some cuts. If one of the ten directors failed to come up with the tightest cut for the material, allowed extra beats in the pacing, and killed the performances with clumsy intercutting (basically was inept as an editor), then once again the entire project would suffer.

A film is nothing until it's cut. Only editing can infuse magic into a loose collection of celluloid strips. Even the worst film you've ever seen probably contained at least some of this editorial magic. On a basic level, most films can convince the viewer that when the two main characters are talking together, and one is seen on the screen at a time, they are in the same room. This, of course, is rarely the case, since often each actor's lines are delivered to a point off-camera, without the second actor present. But the magic of cutting, first to one speaker, then another, allows the audience to put the conversation together. And in that most simplistic task of editing a two-way conversation there is almost an endless number of variables for the cut. The director may decide to have each speaker complete his or her statement each time before cutting over to the other person (as in *My Dinner with Andre*, where long monologues are allowed time to exist without a lot of back-and-forth cutting, giving the audience ample time to get to know each personality). Or maybe the director will enact a more "modern" cut, hardly ever letting a character finish a complete sentence without clipping the last few words with a cut to the listener. This type of "distractive" editing tries to convince the viewer that what is being said is, in some way, important, even though usually it just isn't. In fact many films depend totally on convincing the audience that what they happen to be watching is entertaining, a sleight of hand accomplished by the frenetic pace of the cuts. Hopefully none of the ten directors in your collaboration will have to resort to such contrived editorial manipulations.

If a filmmaker gets in touch with his or her creative powers, then something called "cinematic jazz" can occur. In that state of creative grace, every intuitive decision is correct, all the elements of the film are somehow able to manifest a unity of images and sounds, ideas and emotions, that result in a profound experience for an audience. It is as if the "hand of God" has intervened; some supernatural, omnipresent force has guided the filmmaker to accomplish a feat of creation beyond the powers of mortal human beings. How could a person conceive, write, shoot, and edit such a diverse body of ideas and emotions into a perfect whole? How could he or she achieve the perfect cut?

CONSENSUS (OR NOT)/FINAL CUT

Each person is born with tastes and attitudes. Somehow we just know when something is right and when it's not. In film editing you may have a hunch that more energy and clarity can be derived from "the cut," while your best friend thinks it's great as is. When someone else would have stopped editing and gotten the film printed, you continue on in the editing room, spending perhaps another year in search of the cut that helps transform the material. How can an eager group of collaborators tolerate your additional editing time? How can they wait the extra year your sensibilities require? And how difficult will it be to try and ferret out the best cut possible when your fellow collaborators insist upon completing the film?

So how does a Feature Workshop consisting of ten directors (ten different stories) control the mine field of editing the final cut? One simple solution is to make up a document for signing that states that the film can't be released without all ten directors in agreement that the feature is completed. Only a full ten signatures will count. This type of document can, of course, be very dangerous, since one obstinate director can hold up the entire show. If one director refused to sign the document, then all the time, effort, and cash investments of the others would be for naught. In essence, though, this is a fair approach, since each person connected with the project will be associated with its ultimate success or failure. Each collaborator's film career will be affected by the film for years to come. Each person has the right not only to feel good about his or her own contribution, but to be proud of the entire feature. If the other nine collaborators you invited into the project are reasonable men and women, equally talented and eager for success, then any dispute over editorial quality should be able to be resolved in a thoughtful way. If your group has been assembled in a haphazard way, allowing anyone in for the $2,500 price of admission (or for $549.82 on the "Film School" budget), then you probably deserve the excruciating editorial problems suddenly in your face.

A "Completion Agreement" can also include a deadline date by which the film must be completed. If that date is reasonable, giving the directors six months after the shoot to complete editing on each segment of the film, with leeway for a six-month extension if absolutely necessary, then major fisticuffs should be avoided. And since many participants of a Feature Workshop are probably trying to make a first feature, it is imperative to the success of the venture that everyone understands that the creative process can't be kept neatly in a bottle. There needs to be ample time to work out the problems associated with attempting a ten-way collaboration. Certainly each participant must possess a good degree of patience and kindness toward the creative antics of others. If all goes well, one and a half years from the inaugural meeting with your collaborators you will be sitting in a theater watching all your and their good work hit the screen.

PROMOTION POWER/PULLING STRINGS

As soon as your collaborative film is completed and all your partners are delighted with the results, thoughts will quickly turn to promotion. Which festivals must be entered before what upcoming deadlines? Will you submit your completed feature to the Independent Feature Film Market in New York (September/October)? Of course a good-quality video copy will be essential to get your film seen; the cost usually comes in around $1,000 for transfer of 16-mm film to Beta SP and ten dubs to VHS. Even if your filmmaking group is broke, having spent every dime on the production, it will still be necessary to come up with this transfer cost. And following that will be the costs of packaging and mailing VHS cassettes to festivals, TV buyers, and showcases for future shows and sales. Most likely members of your collaborative production will be able to pull a couple of hundred more dollars from someplace (piggy bank, MasterCard, etc.) to back up a feature film they are proud to have created.

Also it's likely that a few of your filmmaking partners will have connections you only hear about now that the film is looking good and being praised by others. Maybe someone in your group has an uncle who owns a movie theater. Another person's father works in TV. Maybe someone's dad is in advertising. From ten collaborators may come some very surprising leads. Hopefully the cooperative power of the group will get your film out into the world, maybe even earning back all the investments!

Whatever money does come back from film showings, film festival prizes, TV sales, etc., must be divided up among all the members as soon as the check(s) clear. You will not want to conduct business the way it's done in the real world of distribution, where payments are made to the filmmakers on a quarterly basis, after large deductions have been taken for "operating expenses." All members of the collaborative team (along with any actors and technicians promised profit points in the production) must be paid fairly out of the gross profits, quickly and efficiently.

If you want to know the complete score on your feature film you will enter it in every festival in which you may have a chance of acceptance. Only when you have in your hand a fistful of rejection letters, along with several acceptance notices, can you be absolutely sure that you haven't sunk your own chances for success by faulty promotional thinking. Dub 100 VHS tapes at a time, considerably lowering your per unit cost (see "Video Copies for Promotion," chapter 7). Get those tapes into the mail (UPS, Fed Ex when appropriate), along with film festival fees (certain festivals will require fees to help with their operating costs, so just pay the small amounts with a minimum of grumbling—try to remain positive!), and wait for the results. Don't let the first few rejections throw you and your collaborators into a funk. Keep trying. Your film will only be a current feature for the first year after it comes out. Most festivals *only* want current, cutting-edge films completed in the last twelve months, so make sure you don't let yourself down. Don't become your own worst enemy. Be thorough. Follow through. Explain to your fellow collaborators that it can sometimes take as long as four years after a film is released before it sells to TV (U.S. or Europe) even when there is initial interest.

As you tread the dangerous waters of promotion and distribution, keep in mind that you and your fellow collaborators have done the impossible: turned the mysterious, expensive process of writing and directing a feature-length film into an affordable experience. No rejection letter from a narrow-minded film festival can take that accomplishment away. If you are as persistent as you probably needed to be just to complete your collaborative feature, you will surely enjoy the benefits of your promotional efforts.

10

SHOOTING IN VIDEO

A s the seduction of video moves into full swing, with prices dropping on home video units such as the Hi8 camcorder, while the picture resolution approaches broadcast quality, video continues to gain momentum as a viable option for producing low-budget features. Ironically, to rent a broadcast Betacam SP camera that would produce images equal in sharpness and definition to an Eclair 16-mm camera, it would now cost you around $500 per day (if you got a good deal). And for that amount of money you could rent a high-quality 16-mm camera along with lights, light meter, tripod, Nagra sound recorder, and mikes—full production package—for two days of shooting. And although the initial costs of videotape are much cheaper than even most out-of-date 16-mm filmstock, postproduction editing prices in Betacam SP, or ¾" video formats easily outrun 16-mm editing costs. So is video really a cheaper way to produce a feature "film" at used-car prices in the 1990s? The best way to answer this question is to first review the selection of possible video formats (Betacam SP, ¾", VHS, Hi8) comparable to 16-mm quality, and then budget the cheapest, high-quality video feature production.

SELECTING THE RIGHT VIDEO FORMAT

Just as there are several different film formats, ranging from 35-mm to 16-mm, and 8-mm, video also offers a wide range of choices, from professional to amateur formats. Although 16-mm film has basically been regarded as more of an amateur format than 35-mm, it continues to be possible to optically blow up a 16-mm image to the 35-mm format for theatrical showings, such as has been done recently for *Slacker*, *Clerks*, *Go Fish*, and Franci Slak's sumptuous Slovenian feature *When I Close My Eyes*, which was selected in 1994 as his country's official entry into the Academy Award competition for best foreign language film of the year. Many of the TV shows you've watched for years have been shot in 35-mm film and then transferred to 2" videotape for broadcast. In the last few years the quality of video cameras and recorders has greatly improved, to the point where TV shows are often shot by "broadcast quality" video equipment. The new Betacam SP ½" Sony camera/recorder is light enough to shoot from the shoulder and produces excellent, broadcast-quality images and sound. This format in video would be the equivalent to a 16-mm Color Negative production. Also, the ¾" video format would equal 16-mm for definition of image if you used one of the higher quality cameras and recording decks (cost: around $50,000) defined as broadcast quality. Shooting in either VHS or regular Beta, the quality of the image would not be suitable for broadcast, but several of the new video Hi8 camcorders like the Cannon L-2, can supply 400 lines of resolution for a cost of under $5000 (broadcast resolution on most home TV's is around 250–300 lines). To protect the investment of money and man-hours put into your feature project, you will want to shoot your video feature with either Betacam SP, professional Hi8, or broadcast-quality ¾" equipment, to insure that if there is critical success you will be able to enlarge your format for commercial television or theatrical release.

The possible exception to this advice would be that with an expensive video-to-film transfer, VHS, and even Hi8 format could be blown up to 16-mm or 35-mm with fairly good results. Of course, the cost of transferring your low-quality-format video to film at feature length would almost double our used-car budget.

Even using a less expensive kinescope process of video-to-film transfer such as the one developed by Bill Palmer at W. A. Palmer Films of Belmont, California, the cost of $50 per minute would add at least $3,500 to the cost of a seventy-minute video feature. The video sections that appear in my film *Emerald Cities* were transferred from broadcast-quality ¾" video to 16-mm Color Negative stock at Palmer Films, still retaining some TV scan lines. The color sections of my *Morgan's Cake* feature were shot on regular 8-mm video, the 16-mm film transfer, with scan lines showing, adding a certain grittiness to the subject matter. Although with an expensive transfer the video scan lines disappear, this cleaning of the image may not be appropriate for your video film. *Signal 7*, a feature-length video/film by Rob Nilsson, was shot in video for the reported price of $2,500 and expensively transferred to 35-mm film for theatrical release (final cost for transfer, prints, advertising: around $200,000). By shooting with broadcast-quality equipment, Rob insured that his feature had the necessary degree of excellence to become a theatrical success, the image on the screen hardly revealing that it was originally filmed in video. For information on high quality video-to-film transfers contact either Four Media Company (formerly Image Transform) at (818) 985-7566, or Film Craft at (313) 962-2611. While Four Media is known for making the best video-to-35-mm film transfers, Film Craft tends to be exceedingly competitive in its excellent video-to-16-mm transfers, as it was for Marc Huestis's award-winning *Sex Is* documentary.

BUDGETING A HIGH-QUALITY VIDEO FEATURE (AT USED-CAR PRICES)

BETACAM SP

The basic price for renting one Betacam SP video camera, with included recorder, playback unit with monitor, AC charger, and batteries, would be around $375 a day. Many rental facilities, such as Adolph Gasser of San Francisco, offer the excellent savings of a weekly rental for the price of four days, $1,500. Lights (Lowel

"D" kit) would rent for approximately $40 a day ($160 per week), and special Beta videotape for Betacam SP would cost around $30 per twenty-minute cassette ($300 for two hundred minutes).

Editing our Betacam SP feature would be accomplished by making VHS dubs from our SP videotape originals, and then conforming the original Betacam SP tapes after the edit was finalized. If you had a home video cassette recorder (VCR), you could review the VHS tapes without cost until you were able to design the structure of your feature. By purchasing (or renting) a second VCR you could edit at home, assembling your shots onto the second recorder. The last major expense would then be editing the original Betacam SP cassettes into final form, with a technician and the necessary high-quality videotape recorders equivalent to Betacam SP quality ($1,000 a day).

Within the framework of the basic used-car-prices budget for our seventy-minute feature film, our Betacam SP feature video budget is as follows:

BUDGET (SHOOTING IN BETACAM SP)

10 cassettes (Betacam SP) for 200 minutes	$ 300.00
Betacam SP camera (monitor, playback, etc.), 1 week	$1,500.00
Lights (Lowel "D" kit) @ $40/day	$ 160.00
Dubbing (4 hrs. @ $50/hr.)	$ 200.00
10 VHS tape cassettes for dubs	$ 50.00
2 actors' fees	$ 160.00
Camera assistant's fee	$ 80.00
Food (4 dinners for 5 people)	$ 140.00
Transportation	$ 30.00
Purchase of VHS VCR for assembly	$ 300.00
Final Betacam SP assembly on high-quality recorders	$1,000.00
	$3920.00

This Betacam SP budget has not really included sufficient fees for extensive editing of a complex feature video. But if your concept only requires a simple assembly, then this budget would approximate your expenditure. If your feature did not require a great number of titles, they would be added to your video during the final assembly by means of a "character generator." Under some conditions, the videomaker would dub Betacam SP tapes to ¾" video for editing purposes, adding the cost of ¾" tape ($10 per twenty-minute cassette) and the editing room rental cost of $50 per hour (with operator). This price would be lowered to $35 an hour once the videomaker was able to operate the equipment him- or herself without operator assistance. I should mention that these editing room rental quotes are quite low in relationship to the general video costs, and only represent the special rates of Video Free America in San Francisco. Within the approximate limits of our $6,000 budget for a seventy-minute video feature at used-car prices, we could afford to rent an editing room in ¾" format for around forty hours, at $50 per hour with operator ($2000), plus the cost of dubbing our Betacam SP tapes to ¾" ($200 for recording decks and operator plus $100 for ten 20-minute ¾" tapes at $10 each, would total $300).

> $3920.00 (video production)
> $2000.00 (¾" editing)
> $ 300.00 (¾" tape and dubbing cost)
> $6220.00

NOTE: Although shooting with video cameras with built-in microphones tends to obscure the need for a sound recordist on location, I strongly recommend hiring a soundperson for your video shoot to guarantee a high-quality sound track. While this cost may cut into your editing budget, it's worth remembering that poor sound can ruin your entire production. If this is impossible to afford, then at least spend the $100 or so that it costs to buy a Sony microphone and bracket, lifting the microphone above the camera body to insure that your sound recording will not be ruined by camera noise.

Morgan Schmidt-Feng of *Morgan's Cake* holds staff supporting 8-mm video camera, a handmade apparatus for crane shots featured in video portions of the 16-mm feature. Photo by Julie Schachter.

BROADCAST-QUALITY 3/4"

Renting the much heavier and more bulky 3/4" video cameras should definitely be your second choice, and only be used if the Betacam SP is unavailable. The rental price for a broadcast 3/4" Ikegami camera and recording deck is $400 to $450 a day, almost $100 more than a Betacam SP. And keep in mind that if you use a cheap 3/4" video camera, the quality will be quite inferior to the 1/2" Betacam SP image.

VHS, HI8, AND U-MATIC 3/4"

As I've said earlier in this chapter, shooting your video feature on formats that are not of broadcast quality tends to limit the level of success your product may achieve. But if you pick an appropriate subject for "grainier" video images, and transfer the final video to 16-mm film, you may beat the odds and create a salable product. For two years filmmaker Brad Vanderburg lived on the road with a struggling band called Popdefect, shooting their private moments and performances in Hi8 video. Although much of the taping was done in extremely low-light situations, causing a fairly grainy 16-mm print from video transfer, the end result seemed perfectly in tune with the material, leading to a successful world premiere of *Live with This* (*Adrift in America*) at the Rome/Florence Film Festival. So don't forsake your feature film-making dream just because you can't afford high-end gear.

The prices for rental of these "amateur" formats is much less than for broadcast outfits. A camera in VHS rents for $60 a day ($240 a week), Hi8 rents for $50 a day ($200 a week), and ¾" U-matic rents for $75 a day ($300 a week). Shooting in any of these formats saves you hundreds of dollars on the initial camera rental, money which you might consider using to transfer your video to film as a final result. Adding together the $1,700 you would save on the camera rental, plus the $1,800 budgeted for the video ed-iting, you would have $3,500 for the video-to-film transfers.

I began my feature *Morgan's Cake* by borrowing an 8-mm cam-era and cheaply shooting some on-the-street interviews and scripted scenes with my son Morgan (age seventeen at the time). Because I was still in debt to the lab for *Emerald Cities* print costs, the only way that I could at least get my mind on a new project was by scraping up $15 for an 8-mm cassette and just beginning. For my first shot I convinced three high school guys to sit in a Chinese restaurant and talk to the camera lens as if it were Morgan, giving him their advice about registering for the draft. Even though I shot in a very-low-light situation (neon lights on the restaurant's ceiling), the one-minute test I ran at W. A. Palmer Films showed that 8-mm transferred to 16-mm film with excellent picture and sound quality. I also shot several interviews with street people (a stoned hippie, a hustler) talking to Morgan (the camera's eye) about the draft, and I was very impressed by the fine-grain resolution and clean sound track. I had borrowed a microphone extension arm that held the mike off the camera body, insuring that I wouldn't pick up extra camera noise from a squeaky cas-sette.

At most high-quality video-to-film transfer facilities you can choose between either transferring your video directly to a fin-ished 16-mm print with optical sound or transferring it to a "double system" that provides you with an original picture roll, work print, and sync mag track for editing. The most economical transfer you could make would be going directly to the 16-mm answer print from your final cut on video, but this process would not supply you with an original needed to make additional prints from your AB rolls. At this point you would have to ask yourself why you didn't just shoot it in film in the first place.

LIGHTING FOR VIDEO

Whether you are producing a feature-length video as an end product, or shooting "amateur format" video that will be transferred to 16-mm film, it is important that you use enough lights to insure that your video camera will record the strongest image possible. Video cameras "like" light, and even with the best broadcast cameras such as the Ikegami and Betacam, which can successfully film in very-low-light situations, lights are a production necessity for giving your images commercial "snap." Since what you see on your video monitor during taping is "what you get," examine your image for a well-defined sharpness and bright quality. It may be helpful to have a technician with you on the set for a few hours, to give you a sense of the best image quality you can achieve. For shoots that require more than one camera, technicians adjust each Betacam SP camera for white balance as well as setting color balance so that separate shots will edit together perfectly. For your one-camera shoot (you can only afford one camera on a used-car budget), it is still essential to take a "white balance" before shooting. If you are not completely positive that you can prepare your video camera for filming after instruction at the rental facility, spend the extra $250 to hire additional technical assistance on the set. Ask the people at your rental agency which lights they would recommend, and ask any other questions that will help to insure a successful videotaping.

I must add that when I shot my first few video movies I used only available lighting sources, taping with only the natural light flooding into a room, or the illumination of one light bulb. And although the videotape-to-16-mm transfer appeared drab and dark at times on the final black-and-white film product, for the most part the mood created by the low-light situations actually enhanced the concept of my work. The important thing is to decide what "look" you are trying to achieve and then use all means necessary, within the used-car budget, to achieve this end.

SHOOTING AND DIRECTING IN VIDEO

One of the most tragic mistakes made in shooting video is that with the knowledge that shots can be forever retaped, all the intense focus that accompanied the requirement of one-to-one 16-mm shooting is forgotten. Shots that should have been recorded in one minute are taped over and over in ten. Everything seems worth taping, piling up a maze of loosely constructed video that will be exceedingly difficult to edit when the time comes. My major recommendation in this section is to shoot your video one-to-one, only repeating a take when a major problem has been identified. The pressure of this frugal attitude will hopefully force you to tighten your grip on the concept of your production.

Directing actors for your video feature is basically no different than for a 16-mm film production. And once you have impressed upon the actors that you don't plan to tape constant retakes just because video is reusable, you should be able to encourage the same dynamic performances as you would have for 16-mm film. The one advantage with shooting in video is that you can tape a performance for twenty minutes or longer instead of the eleven minutes offered by a 400' roll of film. To direct a quality video feature it's really necessary to apply the same sharpness of purpose, the same intensity, as would be needed for a similar film production.

SAVING COSTS ON VIDEO EDITING

If you have shot a complex video feature that requires hundreds of hours of editing to complete, it is obvious that you must find an alternative to paying $20 or $30 an hour. Fortunately, in most large cities there are now numerous nonprofit video facilities offered at discounted rates that will help you finish your project. In the San Francisco/Oakland area the Film Arts Foundation ([415] 552-6350) offers VHS editing at $25 for a half day, and $50 for the fifteen-hour night shift or 9 A.M.-to-6 P.M. dayshift. If you look hard in your area you may find even cheaper facilities. In New York City, the Young Filmmaker's Foundation offers VHS editing at $10 an hour and ¾" editing at $12 an hour for straight cutting, and $40 an hour for dissolves, credits, and other special effects. If you know you will be editing for over fifty hours, video facilities such as Video Free America in San Francisco may offer a special package rate that should save considerable editing cost.

As I've mentioned earlier in this chapter, a good solution for editing ¾" or VHS may be to make VHS dubs off your original video and assemble the scenes at home on a two-VCR system. You should be able to buy two used VHS VCRs for around $200. By hooking into your TV as a monitor (if proper connections exist) you could watch your footage, assembling and reassembling the scenes until the rough cut was complete. If you had originally shot your video feature with Betacam SP, then your videotapes would have time code numbers that would allow a technician to match your original taped scenes to the order of your edited "window" dubs, just as we matched our original 16-mm footage to the edited work print using latent edge numbers. The remainder of the editing budget could then be spent working with a video technician to add special effects (dissolves, fades, other fancy moves), credits, and a final assembly to your video (at around $150 an hour).

PROMOTING AND SELLING
YOUR VIDEO FEATURE

Once you have completed your video feature, and have made high-quality dubs in several video formats, you will want to enter video festivals and contests in the United States and Europe. In the last few years there has been a great increase of interest in independent video, with many major film festivals offering special programs celebrating video art. And many major museums, such as the Whitney Museum in New York City, now present ongoing video programs featuring in-person shows. With the recent improvement of video projectors, there are now many more avenues for video presentations, including many video clubs in Europe and the United States. Videomaker Joe Rees, of Target Video in San Francisco, was one of the first video artists to take his show on the road, traveling with his punk-music tapes and high-quality video projection system to numerous video clubs in Europe for sold-out performances. While many major film festivals accept video works for consideration as part of their programming, the best way for a videomaker to secure a current listing of appropriate festivals and contests for his or her work is to get in touch with either the Film Arts Foundation in San Francisco, 911 Media Arts in Seattle, or the Association of Independent Video and Filmmakers in New York City.

If you have transferred your video feature to 16-mm film, then you have the opportunity to follow the promotional steps outlined for filmmakers in chapter seven.

VIDEO VERSUS FILM

With the current explosion of attention being given to new video products invading American stores from the Japanese markets, and with prices continuing to drop as quality improves, it's easy to be seduced by the video revolution. And with the ease of shooting in video and the low initial cost of videotape that can hold hours of filming for under $10, it takes a stretch of the imagination to believe that 16-mm filmmaking has much of a chance for survival in the marketplace. And yet, for the media artist who can somehow manage to overcome his technical fears, 16-mm film still offers the sharpest image and highest-quality print for a feature-length product—and the cheapest price. I have no doubt that in a few years the lowered cost of sophisticated home-video-editing equipment, plus video systems such as Hi8 Video, offering broadcast-quality picture and sound, will make the idea of shooting in 16-mm film seem archaic. But for those diehards who enjoy the all-or-nothing aspect of exposing film to images, and for those magicians who yearn to hold strips of time etched on plastic, film will continue to offer the best means for telling a story.

11

DIGITAL TECHNOLOGY
AND THE FUTURE

If you blink your eyes you may soon find yourself creating your no-budget feature films through the use of digital technology. To some old salts (like myself) it has, for the last few years, seemed like a preposterous idea to switch from the usual practice of editing film work print and mag track on flatbed editing machines to pushing buttons on a computer. But as filmstock and lab costs for processing and work printing have risen in price, in some cases doubled, and the prices of powerful computers have dropped to less than half price, I have found myself paying much more attention to every development of the digital age. I guess it is inevitable that I will soon be editing my films with the help of digital electronics, forsaking the transport of a Moviola flatbed to my house, where I coax that old circuitry to behave, spin my rolls of work print and mag in a sync tandem that keeps slipping, worrying about a burned-out motor as I use up most of my time waiting for the rolls to rewind before I can view the latest cut. It is apparent that times have changed and it is now up to the filmmaker to figure out ways of using these latest advances in technology to cut costs, solve problems, and speed up production of a no-budget feature.

THE DIGITAL SOUND MIX

A recent example of my film work being helped by new technology was the sound mix I did for my 1993 Feature Workshop film *Blues for the Avatar* with Scot Charles at Alpha Cine Lab in Seattle ([206] 682-8230). I scheduled a $135/hr. "cleanup" mix to prepare for a work-in-progress screening at the IFP Feature Film Market, but dreaded one long stretch of sound track that was, I thought, permanently ruined by camera noise. This flaw in the recording was all too evident since the accompanying close-up visual was a ten-minute static shot of actor J. Cheyenne Wilbur's face as he delivered a monologue about falling in love while on a trip through London. And the poor sound quality was even more obvious when the picture cut to actress Tasha Roth McCormick as she listened intently to how Cheyenne and her mother (in the film) first got together. As an audience we listened with her not only to his words, but to the constant camera noise as well. It wasn't until Scot and I got to the monologue portion of the mix that I had any idea that a computer could cleanly erase the disturbance while leaving the quality of the spoken voice intact. Although it did take a couple of extra hours to remove camera noise, at the slightly higher rate of $185/hr., it was a very small price to pay for the resurrection of a crucial ten-minute chunk of a feature film.

The digital workstation Scot built at Alpha Cine Lab is powered by the Mac II FX computer paired with Hewlett Packard hard drive, and uses a modular plug-in system incorporating software called Digital Intelligent Noise System by DigiDesign to remove camera noise and other sound manipulations. The client's mag track rolls are first transferred to ¼" tape, then sync-locked to a ¾" video copy of the film to be mixed, thus supplying an image and sound track that can be controlled by computer. After the sound is mixed to the satisfaction of the filmmaker, the mix can either be off-loaded to mag or recorded directly to video for cassette duplication or broadcast.

For filmmakers who wish to mix their sound tracks the old-fashioned way, recording directly from edited mag track onto a master mixed mag track, Will Harvey of Music Annex in San Francisco ([415] 421-6622) is able to make use of digital technology for noise reduction and patching while helping the filmmaker to avoid the added costs of transferring sound to ¼" multitrack and work print to video. Because the sound is patched through a computer, he can control every aspect of sound quality as he did when mixing my *American Orpheus* feature (cost is $185/hr., less 10 percent with FAF discount).

DIGITAL MUSIC FOR FILMS

With his Korg M-1 8-track sequencer and tone generator keyboard, musician Paul Baker was able to compose and record the musical score for my *American Orpheus* feature with only $1,000 worth of equipment. The keyboard gave him 100 different sounds with which to create his compositions, layering eight different recordings over one another and electronically storing the results for mixing and mastering. The digital revolution has made it possible for young musicians like Paul (then age twenty-four) to professionalize their dream and create an inexpensive recording studio at home to produce their works. In his studio in Emeryville, California, he has partitioned off a small sound booth, building a wall with 2" × 4" lumber and Sheetrock that includes a window and door leading out to the recording area. To the Korg M-1 keyboard he has added several new pieces of equipment that allow him not only to create music electronically, but also to mix in live performances by guest musicians. His new equipment includes a 16-channel Mackie mixer ($1,000), an 8-track Tascam recorder ($1,500), AMR power amp and Toa 312 ME speakers ($600), a Mac II computer ($1,000), and Performer software ($400). Using Sony "studio monitor" headphones ($100) he can maintain the quality of recordings, select takes for overlay, and build up unique sounds for output on DAT.

For a musician to be portable enough to record his or her sound track while visiting the set of a shoot and absorbing the mood of the story (Paul was on location during the *American Orpheus* shoot, working as "boom man" for sound recording), it would be necessary to bring not only a keyboard like the Korg M-1, but also a mixer with at least two channels ($400–$500), a DAT recorder (under $1,000), and of course earphones.

Musicians focused on composing for the screen may wonder how Paul wrote and performed songs for my film without using a lock-in system or video recorder playback to time his compositions to correspond exactly to the length of scenes. Reminding the reader about believing in "the flow" (see "Fifteen Rules for No-Budget Feature Filmmaking," chapter 5), it may seem less surprising when I mention that several songs created by Paul were completed months before the shoot. Somehow these songs fit magically into several of the scenes Paul was on hand to help record in sync while holding the boom. Another song that Paul had written for my daughter Heather (they grew up together in Berkeley) that he played for me on an available piano during a break from shooting was so beautiful that I asked to use it in the film. After soundman Neelon Crawford strategically placed his microphones on and around the piano (he had once recorded music for jazz great Benny Goodman at Goodman's residence) Paul again played the song, entitled "Witness of a Birth," for recording on the Nagra. In the film this song was used to convey the craziness of falling in love, as lead actress Jody Esther flirted with the male lead Curtis Imrie while entangled in a patch of hydrangea flowers.

Because I used music in *American Orpheus* that was originally written by a musician for himself, rather than asking a musician to work at composing songs just for my movie, I was able to avoid the horrendous costs of scoring and orchestration, and could instead obtain Paul's music for a few hundred dollars (not thousands!) after he signed a Music Rights Agreement (see Appendix G). This agreement protected his ownership of the music aside from its use in my film. For a fee of less than a thousand dollars I was also able to obtain the enchanting song "Thanking You" by Diane Witherspoon, produced by Tonal Gravity Records of Berkeley, which was recently listed in the Top 20 of jazz hits! So thanks to digital technology, music like Paul's and Diane's that was produced in small independent music studios can be made available to the low-budget feature filmmaker, for fees that won't break the postproduction budget.

DIGITAL SYNC SOUND ON LOCATION

When soundman Neelon Crawford showed up to do location sync recordings for *American Orpheus*, he carried with him a Nagra and a small secondary "digital audio tape" (DAT) recorder. While he stuck to the reliable Nagra for all sync work on the film, he used the digital recorder for wild sounds, collecting ambiences that he thought I might need later in editing. It was impossible not to admire the small size of the DAT recorder, and Neelon spoke of its quality with a sense of awe in his voice. There's no doubt that digital technology will play a major role in sync recording on location for big- and small-budget feature films in the future. The affordability of digital equipment means that even the no-budget feature filmmaker will soon be able to purchase his or her own sound gear, saving thousands of dollars on the shoot by bypassing normal sync sound costs.

For soundmen like Bob Israel of Seattle ([206] 557-2202), whose reputation as an on-location sync recording expert rests on his ability to deliver top quality sound every time, the current low-end ($1,000 or under) DAT recorders aren't dependable enough to use for sync recording without a backup unit. Since the machines don't like heat, cold, or rough handling, he says you may find an entire day's worth of field recordings locked into a machine that suddenly stops working, requiring that you disassemble the unit in order to extract the sync tape for transfer. Since the DAT recorder may die just because it is moved from a cold room to a hot one, Israel sometimes carries along a portable hair dryer to revive a stubborn recorder. Even for recording effects, Israel will bring along a second unit, but he feels that this non-sync recording of ambience on location is an excellent application of digital technology because of the machine's quick access to recorded information.

When using a cheap portable DAT machine for recording on-location non-sync ambience, Israel recommends first rolling the digital tape at fast-forward through the machine to make sure that there are no imperfections. Then he rewinds to zero and resets the "real-time" counter. As he records different effects—bird sounds, wind, ocean, footsteps, etc.—he creates an index on the tape and corresponding written log. Each time he hits the Pause button the recorder moves the index number to the next numeral. This internal DAT filing system allows Israel and a producer to have instant access to effects and ambient sounds during post-production, by simply typing in a command on the playback unit. Since it only takes thirty-five seconds to wind from one end of the DAT to the other, instead of two minutes of rewind time with a Nagra, the digital recorder is a wonderful time-saver during editing.

For the fearless filmmaker who must attempt his or her sync on-location recordings with a low-end DAT recorder (bring a backup!), sync will be achieved by renting a time-code generator that can lay down a "30 frame non-drop time code" on one of the stereo tracks. When transferring the DAT to video work print at the lab, the sync sound mono recordings on your second track will play back at a desired sync rate because the time code controls the telecine machines. The internal control track built into the DAT is what guarantees that the tape has been recorded at a constant rate.

Although I'm hesitant to recommend even a top-of-the-line DAT recorder such as the Fostex PD-2 with its internal time code and multiple sampling rates for on-location sync sound recordings without a backup unit, I look to the future for DAT recorders with higher sampling rates to improve sound quality, and units that will perform reliably on location. In fact even Nagra has entered the field of digital recording with its Nagra T, which uses its standard ¼" tape format. It's not a stretch of the imagination to think of recording sync sound for features directly onto computer hard disk, and handing a 3½" floppy to an editor who then syncs up the sound and digital images on a laptop Mac PowerBook.

DIGITAL PRINTING AT THE LAB

Another way my films have recently been aided by the digital revolution is through access to the computer-controlled printing machines now used in some high-quality film laboratories to produce answer and release prints. I realized my good fortune at selecting Forde Lab of Seattle ([206] 682-2510) for printing work on my *American Orpheus* film during the question-and-answer session at its world premiere showing in Rotterdam. Film producer Will Watkins, of the award-winning short *The Room*, asked me where, how, and at what cost I had produced the beautiful matte effects of the "little Indian girl" character magically materializing into existing scenes. When I told him the effect was accomplished simply by the standard "lab dissolve" he couldn't believe it. What had thrown off his perception was the fact that there was no obvious shift in the level of density of the surrounding frame, none of the obvious darkening and then lightening that usually accompanies a dissolve of two matching images. While the image was printed over itself (both shots that dissolved were exactly the same except for the inclusion of actress Katrina Eggert, who was placed into the shot while the camera kept its precise framing), the registration was so accurate in the printing machines that the two shots didn't set up the usual double-image blurriness that would have betrayed the source of the effect.

Speaking with Forde Lab manager Rich Vedvick upon my return I learned that he had recently outfitted the lab with state-of-the-art electronically controlled 16-mm and 35-mm printing machines, whose on-board computers were responsible for adjusting the density by invisible increments during dissolves. And, of course, the newer machines had better registration than the overworked older models currently in use around the country. It was wonderfully reassuring to me in an era in which many 16-mm labs have either folded or drastically cut back their volume of business, that a lab would actually be upgrading its equipment, acquiring new technology to help me produce my work. Perhaps all the activity of new features being made at used-car prices will contribute to the resurrection of the neighborhood film lab and encourage older established labs to take 16-mm film production more seriously in the future.

For the best in 16-mm printing results (magical dissolves and dead-on registration) search out a lab that uses the BHP Modular Printer or its equivalent. The BHP Modular Printer at Forde Lab can choose from eight different fade curves, each setting offering a different quality of light exchange. It was this precision and flex-ibility that helped me achieve such a strong effect with the dis-solve of my fictional Indian character. The printer also has an option for selecting "liquid gate," which insures that your original is perfectly free of dust while being duplicated. Liquid-gate printing is essential for top-quality printing from negative original (see note, p. 182). Since every function of the printer, from the me-chanical drive to the programmable fader, is controlled by com-puter, the lab should be able to supply the filmmaker with a usable first print (answer print) more easily than older machines allowed. And your precious original footage used for printing is handled more delicately by the printing machine since the computer dic-tates that the main drive more slowly begins and ends the move-ment of your film through its printing cycle, avoiding harsh stops and starts. In this way less stress is placed on the thin plastic strips of 16-mm and 35-mm film that carry your images.

So when it's time to select a film lab, make sure that you inquire into exactly what kind of machines they use for printing, insuring that you can get the best possible results currently offered in this digital age.

FILMLOOK: VIDEO
THAT LOOKS LIKE FILM

Some video producers who are trying to shoot high-quality video with feature-film techniques, with an eye toward distribution on videocassette, will want to consider using a recent digital process called Filmlook that gives video the appearance of motion picture film. By offering a choice of either twenty-four or thirty simulated film frames per second, and rendering film texture, film gray scale, and color, Filmlook gives the video producer the choice of adding the element of filmlike sophistication to the feel of the images, elevating the appeal of the project. Certainly the biggest benefit offered by this product is the immense savings of eliminating film-stock, lab developing, and printing costs. But he cautioned that Filmlook recommends that only the top broadcast-quality video can be expected to get top results with their system.

Filmlook advises that video destined for their award-winning process (they received an award for Outstanding Achievement in Engineering from the Academy of Television Arts and Sciences) be produced on broadcast cameras such as the Sony BVP701S Series or equivalent, and recorded on a broadcast tape format such as Betacam SP, 1", D2, or D3. The video camera's high-speed electronic shutter must *not* be used, and detail enhancement should be minimal. Any optical filters that would be used for a film shoot should be retained for the video camera. "Film-style" lighting with normal video levels and the obvious correct exposure control should be exercised during the shoot. Modification in gamma and overexposures/white clipping should be avoided. Filmlook asks the producer of videos to consult with them first before planning on using any D.V.E.–type moves, flips, spins, manipulations, computer animation, moving C.G.'s, fast or slow motion.

If you are a skeptic and can't believe that any digital process can change your video magically into film, then get in touch with Filmlook at 3500 W. Olive Avenue, Suite 1050, Burbank, CA 91505 ([818] 841-3211), to request supportive literature and an example of their effect on VHS cassette. They charge $75 per minute for the first thirty minutes, $60 per minute thereafter, with a ten-minute minimum charge of $750. For $300 you can make a test of your video footage up to three minutes in length. If you've spent your life examining the difference between video and film as I have you're definitely in for a shock. Filmlook really works!

DIGITAL EDITING

For several years I've been aware of filmmakers editing their 16-mm film by transferring from their film negative to video and then feeding the electronic visual and audio signals into a computer for editing, but the cost of such systems seemed out of reach for a no-budget feature filmmaker who had a lot of time but very little money. But as the cost of computers like the Macintosh Quadra have plummeted toward the $1,000 mark, the hardware to run advanced editing systems has suddenly become affordable.

With the advent of new players joining the field of digital editing, AVID competing with D-Vision, and labs like Alpha Cine of Seattle initiating in-house digital editing systems like Lightworks, this competition to win the hearts and minds of the no-budget feature filmmakers of the future will continue to bring the cost of digitizing boards and software packages to more affordable levels. Considering the speed at which the computer and software industries are moving ahead in developing new technology, it shouldn't be long before the rising tide of new filmmakers (applications to film schools have doubled in the last five years) will be able to edit their movies on computers that fit in their briefcases. In fact an entire collection of video production equipment, Hi-8 video camera and Mac PowerBook, will be able to fit inside a bowling bag! But until video technology can produce an image with as high a resolution as 16-mm or 35-mm film (a system of lasers developed by David DiFrancesco of PIXAR can now reproduce a film image electronically pixel by pixel, but cost is prohibitive) this discussion must center on transferring a film image and audio with time code to video, transferring from that medium to computer hard disk for storage and output, and editing on a nonlinear software system that can produce an edit decision list (EDL) for conforming the film original to match the precise electronic final cut.

AVID MEDIA COMPOSER

Certainly anyone who has ever watched an AVID Media Composer editing workstation ([800] 949-AVID for information) can't fail to understand that the future of film editing rests with computer systems like this one. In seconds you can call up a selection of shots that AVID presents like still photos checkerboarding the entire face of a computer monitor (the "bin"), and with the click of a mouse send that frame and the footage that follows to a second monitor for editing. As easily as operating a Macintosh at home, the editor can rapidly put the AVID through the paces of inserting the shot, adding or subtracting its length, changing order with other shots, even adding effects like fade-in and -out, dissolves, and wipes (top-of-the-line AVID Media Composers offer fifty different varieties of this effect). With a few clicks of a mouse you

"Effect mode" images cued up on monitor of AVID's Media Composer system. Photo copyright 1993, Avid Technology, Inc.

can add audio effects and music saved on twenty-four tracks, and produce an EDL (Edit Decision List) to conform your film original to the results. On the high-definition monitors that can switch from RGB to NTSC you can run back your latest cut in digital images, then check the quality of the image directly from your source videotape (¾", Betacam SP) derived from your film original, to make sure that you haven't missed a microphone in the shot or made other disturbing mistakes.

To successfully edit your film in digital and return to film with a frame-accurate numerical list for conforming 16-mm or 35-mm for printing, you must have made a video copy of your film footage with both time code and key code that relates to the numbers on your film original. If you have transferred your film footage to Betacam SP, you'll also want to dub from that to ¾" for use with the AVID, saving the Betacam SP original for a top-quality finished video edit if needed. As you edit your footage digitally, you'll see both the time code numbers and the key code numbers running under the picture, keeping your results locked at all times to your original camera rolls. The AVID will help you build an organized filing system for your logged-in footage, which can be called up with either numbers or code names for shots. With a collection of portable hard-drive units, the AVID user can build up a storage capacity of anywhere from two and a half hours of visual and audio footage (three and a half Gigabites) to ten hours and more. If you can only afford a couple of hours of storage, you will still be able to edit your feature by working a reel at a time, then dumping that storage and adding new footage from your ¾" video transfers. At a final state of fine cut you can then run the completed feature on your monitor, fine-tune, and off-load to either a finished video copy or edit list for film. And with the digital audio capabilities of an AVID you will even be able to perform your own sound mix, which can be off-loaded to DAT or D-2, and finally to mag for answer print.

Can a no-budget feature filmmaker afford all this digital editing magic? Perhaps in small doses. Editors like Pat Barber of Seattle ([206] 340-5967), who has become an expert AVID operator in the three years since he purchased a Media Composer, offers his services for either $95 per hour or $2,000 a week, which is an incredible deal since just the AVID itself rents for that weekly price. It is not unusual for Barber to be editing a film for a producer in Boston, communicating by FAX and sending VHS copies of the current cut for inspection (for bigger budgets a producer could afford to see each day's cut transmitted by fiber optics as Steven Spielberg did for *Jurassic Park*, viewing a cut done in Los Angeles while he shot *Schindler's List* in Prague). If the low-budget feature filmmaker can somehow budget an extra $10,000, then he or she can make great headway toward a fine cut within a five-week work-a-thon, getting the film work done in time for the IFFM (Independent Feature Film Market, New York) and the Sundance Film Festival. Some AVID experts, like Greg Pecknold of Flying Spot in Seattle ([206] 464-0744) and Pat Barber, are willing to negotiate their fees even lower if they read a script that they love and feel support for a particular project, so don't be shy about approaching them or local editors in your city. If your film idea is

Ken Kortge, nonlinear editing manager at American Production Services (Seattle), cues up an edit point on the D-VISION digital system. Photo courtesy of American Production Services.

burning with passion and new insights, you may find an editor willing to collaborate on bringing your vision to the screen.

D-VISION

Another viable option for editing your film by computer is the lesser known D-VISION system produced by the Touchvision company in Chicago ([312] 989-2160). Not as high-profile as AVID, and sporting less fancy effects (only twelve wipes available), D-VISION delivers the goods as far as easy-access digital editing of picture and sound, and producing an edit decision list (EDL) that can be used to do final conforming to film. Editor Barbara Kaplan, who completed the initial fine cut of *The Fire This Time* (directed by Randy Holland) in five weeks, on its way to the Sundance Documentary Competition in 1994, swears by her five D-VISION systems which she rents out when not using them for clients. Based in Los Angeles ([213] 934-8336), Kaplan offers a D-VISION system along with her editing skills for only $1,000 per week, and has been known to defer a portion of her salary for projects that win her heart.

The most important feature of the D-VISION system is the clearheaded way in which its functions have been designed and presented on-screen, making it the most user-friendly editing system I've found. Within just a few hours of being introduced to the system at American Production Services of Seattle ([206] 282-1776) I was able to achieve enough mastery over the D-VISION software to edit a sample film fluidly, selecting shots from a bin, adding them to my assembly, changing order, deleting scenes, and adding fades and dissolves. The system is that easy to understand! And American Production Services passes that benefit along to their clients by offering their in-house D-VISION rental suite with operator ($75 per hour) and without operator ($50 per hour), the added bonus being that once you can operate the workstation yourself you're welcome to keep editing twenty-four hours a day.

SONY'S DES-500 DESTINY

A new player in the field of nonlinear editing systems is Sony's DES-500 DESTINY Editing Workstation, designed to integrate the video switcher, digital effects system, audio mixer, and editor all into one cohesive unit featuring a single point-and-click computer interface. Their system is brand-new and hasn't been personally tested by this filmmaker, but it promises to be another excellent Sony product. One of their selling points is that the overall size of the workstation is much smaller than that of other systems since the editing is performed on only one monitor instead of the usual two. Because you "scroll" across the monitor to an active screen that exists out of sight on both right and left side, the actual work space is wider on one monitor than on the usual two. The log offers a "file card" for each movie clip—containing an image, time code, scene number, take number, and notes—that gives the operator a clear idea of the available material. Although Sony offers only a "linear" editing with videotape recorders with its current DESTINY system, their publicity material indicates that a nonlinear editing system will soon be forthcoming.

On the set of *Mail Bonding*, world's first all-digital live-action movie by Robert Miller, Sony's DVW 700 wide-screen digital camera (only prototype in existence) exports images and audio to AVID's MC 800 for editing and final scan to 35-mm film. The future is here!

YOUR DIGITAL FILMMAKING FUTURE

As a low- or no-budget feature filmmaker you may still be asking yourself what all this new technology has to do with the current problem of getting a film shot and completed. Well, as with anything mechanical, or electronic, digital hardware and software are just tools to use if and when they are needed. The research I've done to write this chapter has added to my personal arsenal of filmmaking methods, to the point where I now plan to use the D-VISION system at American Production Services in Seattle to sort out different options of assembly for the partially cut 1993 Feature Workshop film *Blues for the Avatar*. Since the seventy-eight-minute rough cut is on Betacam SP in sync sound, I can transfer the video information to the D-VISION storage (this "capture" will cost me $75 per hour for operator, along with $30 per hour for the video deck = $105 × 1.5 hours = approximately $160 to enter my film onto hard disk) and try different cuts late into the night. For a few hundred dollars I can rearrange my footage and view the results in a way that would have taken me days on a flatbed editing machine. After I discover the best cut I'll simply rearrange my film work print and sync mag into the new order. So digital technology will help me improve our rough cut in midstream.

No person should go through life without at least attempting to fulfill his or her dream, whether it be spending two years hitch-hiking through Europe or making feature films. And if the art and craft of feature filmmaking is your calling, then you can't really expect to make a masterpiece the first time out. By the end of your first production you will probably know exactly what you will do differently next time. Only by repeated attempts at the feature-length form will you eventually be able to arrive at that special conglomerate of ideas, images, words, and sounds that is your own original style. It is my hope that this book has opened up your life to that possibility of future work.

APPENDICES

APPENDIX A:

COLLABORATION AGREEMENT

I, Michael Church, on this _____ day of _____ 1984, do agree to sell to Richard R. Schmidt the option to my writing THE MONOPOLE VERIFICATION EXPERIMENTS for production into a motion picture film. Schmidt agrees to pay $100 per year for this option and $1000 after principal photography is completed as a salary for the scripting. After the $1000 payment the option payments of $100 per year will terminate. If the final budget for the film is above $25,000 then Schmidt agrees to pay Michael Church one twenty-fifth ($\frac{1}{25}$) of the total budget up to a total of $10,000 for his writing and scripting.

Michael Church agrees that the final script for the film will be a collaboration between himself and Richard R. Schmidt and that the title appearing in the film will read SCRIPT BY MICHAEL CHURCH AND RICHARD R. SCHMIDT. It is also agreed that a separate title in the film will read ORIGINAL STORY BY MICHAEL CHURCH.

Schmidt with his signature below also agrees to pay Michael Church 10% of the profits above expenses for his writing and scripting of the film (if Schmidt is Producer) and $100 for the option in four $25 payments due the ninth of each month, January, February, March, April 1984. It is understood that with the signatures below Schmidt has purchased the right to Direct, Film, Edit, and Produce without restriction the film tentatively entitled THE MONOPOLE VERIFICATION EXPERIMENT.

_____   _____
Michael Church   Richard R. Schmidt

_____   _____
Date/Location   Date/Location

APPENDIX B:

SAMPLE CONTRACT FOR DEFERRED PAYMENT AND PROFIT SHARING

Description of and Assignments of Interest of Profits in "Emerald Cities," A Feature-Length Motion Picture Film

DESCRIPTION:

RICHARD R. SCHMIDT ("Schmidt"), doing business as LIVING LEGEND PRODUCTIONS (L. L. Productions/"LLP") for the production and distribution of a feature length 16 millimeter color motion picture tentatively entitled "EMERALD CITIES" ("the film"), shall be its producer, director, cameraman, and editor. The leading actors in the film will be Carolyn Zaremba ("Z"), Ed Nylund ("Ed"), Willie-boy Walker ("Willie"), Lowell Darling ("Lowell"), Lawrence Falconi ("Ted"), Dick Richardson ("Dick"), and Kelly Brock Boen ("Kelly"). The crew will consist of Nick Bertoni (sound), Neelon Crawford (sound), Bill Kimberlin (assistant camera), with Julie Schachter (stills, continuity).

The tentative budget for the production of the film, exclusive of distribution costs, is $27,500.00, and Schmidt agrees to contribute $5,000.00 of that amount. Schmidt, as Producer of the film, anticipates that at least $22,500.00 as capital will be required to complete the production of the film, and an additional amount as capital will be required to arrange for and/or distribute the film. These amounts and Schmidt's $5,000.00 contribution will be the investment of the investors for the production and distribution of the film.

The shooting schedule for the film is for a five (5) day uninterrupted period beginning on or about December 15, 1979, in and about the Upper Mojave Desert region/Death Valley, California. This five-day shooting period will be one third (⅓) of the total on-location filming necessary to complete the film. The other two thirds (⅔) of the shooting is expected to take place in the San Francisco/Oakland area during a ten-day period on or before March 1, 1980, and the editing period thereafter is expected to be approximately five (5) months (August 1980).

INTERESTS

All amounts specified below as salaries for work completed on the film tentatively entitled "EMERALD CITIES" will refer to only the first one third (⅓) of the total film production unless so indicated.

Bill Kimberlin (assistant camera) has received $300.00 out of a total of $750.00, the remaining $450.00 will be paid on or before February 15, 1980, for rental of Eclair NPR camera, Nagra and accessories, and salary.

Nick Bertoni (sound) will receive a total of $300.00 for sound recording on location salary.

Carolyn Zaremba (actress) has received $100.00 out of a total of $200.00 for salary on five-day shoot, with a guarantee of $50.00 per day for remaining acting on the film, up to but not exceeding a guarantee of $1000.00 total salary for completing her lead role in the film.

Ed Nylund and *Willie Boy Walker* will each receive $500.00 total for acting in the film, including the second period of the filming.

Lowell Darling, Lawrence Falconi, and *Kelly Brock Boen* will each receive $200.00 total for acting in the film, including the second period of filming.

Julie Schachter will receive $200.00 for stills and continuity for the film, including the second period of the filming.

Kathleen Beeler, William Farley, and *George Manupelli* will each receive $200 for second period of filming, as will Elizabeth Sher. *Flipper* and *The Mutants* will each receive $500 for music/performance.

Dick Richardson, and *Richard R. Schmidt* (writers), will each receive $500.00 total for their scripting of the film, including the second period of filming.

The first moneys received by LLP for the film will be first applied to payment of all outstanding accounts payable for the production and distribution of the film until paid in full, next to the repayment to the investors of the entire amounts of their contributions actually expended for the production and distribution of the film, and thereafter, all moneys received by LLP for the film will be paid by LLP as follows:

1. Director, producer, cameraman, editor of the film (Schmidt) — 20%
2. Investor — 7%
3. Leading actor for the film (Carolyn Zaremba) — 10%
4. Supporting actor for the film (Ed Nylund) — 8%
5. Supporting actor for the film (Willie Boy Walker) — 8%
6. Writer for the film, actor (Dick Richardson) — 10%
7. Writer for the film (Schmidt) — 5%
8. Video production (Joe Rees-Target) — 5%
9. Additional cast for the film (Lowell Darling) — 2%
10. Writer for the film, actor (Ted Falconi) — 5%
11. Music/performance (FLIPPER) — 2%
12. Additional cast for the film (Kelly Boen) — 2%
13. Camera assistant for the film (Bill Kimberlin) — 2%
14. Sound recording for the film (Nick Bertoni) — 2%
15. Stills, continuity for the film (Julie Schachter) — 2%
16. Music/performance (THE MUTANTS) — 2%
17. Camera assistant for the film (Kathleen Beeler) — 2%
18. Conceptual adviser for the film (William Farley) — 2%
19. Additional video (Liz Sher) — 2%
20. Additional filming (Jon Jost) — 2%

The listed percentages (page 3) will be payable to each of the persons set forth in parenthesis after each of the positions only in the event each of these persons actually performs the customary services for his/her position through the completion of the production of the film. Any person not providing such services will receive no percentage, unless otherwise agreed to by the producer. Any person after earning his percentage may assign all or any part of the same by written notification thereof to LLP.

By signing this agreement the parties hereto agreed to all terms and conditions set forth herein on this _____ day of December, 1979.

Date and Place of Execution	Signatures
1. _____	_____ Richard R. Schmidt
2. _____	_____ Investor
3. _____	_____ Carolyn Zaremba
4. _____	_____ Ed Nylund
5. _____	_____ Willie Boy Walker
6. _____	_____ Richard A. Richardson
7. _____	_____ Richard R. Schmidt
8. _____	_____ Joe Rees
9. _____	_____ Lowell Darling
10. _____	_____ Ted Falconi

11. _____

FLIPPER
_____

12. _____

Kelly Brock Boen
_____

13. _____

Bill Kimberlin
_____

14. _____

Nick Bertoni
_____

15. _____

Julie Schachter
_____

16. _____

THE MUTANTS
_____

17. _____

Kathleen Beeler
_____

18 _____

William Farley
_____

19. _____

Liz Sher
_____

20. _____

Jon Jost

APPENDIX C:

DEAL MEMORANDUM

Please keep one copy and sign and return the other to us.

From: Richard R. Schmidt

To: _____

Re: Motion Picture currently entitled "MORGAN'S CAKE"

This Deal Memorandum describes how deferred payments, if any, resulting from the exploitation of the motion picture currently entitled "MORGAN'S CAKE" (hereinafter referred to as the "Film") will be paid. "Deferred compensation" will be payable from all gross receipts received by Morgan's Cake, a California Limited Partnership (the "Partnership") from the exploitation of the Film after repayment of all production costs, including financing costs, and payment of all distribution costs. Richard R. Schmidt (hereinafter referred to as the "Producer") is the General Partner of the Parnership and the producer of the Film. The Producer reserves the right to distribute the Film himself, in which event his distribution fee will be at market rates. Deferrred compensation will be paid among all persons who provide services in the production of the Film who have not been paid in full. Payments will be made *pari passu,* with each person's share determined by the amount of money agreed to be paid to that person minus any money already paid to that person. The Producer will be in this equation in the same manner as all other persons. The amount set forth opposite your name below is the total amount of compensation for services to be rendered by you, as indicated above, on the Film. In the event you do not provide your full services during the production of the Film, you will receive either reduced compensation, based upon the ratio of the total amount of time provided by you in the production of the Film bears to the total amount of time agreed to be provided by you for the production of the Film; or, if you provide no such services, you will receive no compensation.

The Producer retains full copyright to the Film and reserves the right to make all marketing, financial and artistic decisions for the Film regardless of payment of any compensation to you.

If you approve of this arrangement, please sign on the line provided below for your signature and return one copy to us in the enclosed envelope.

MORGAN'S CAKE, a California Limited Partnership

By _____   _____ $_____
    Richard R. Schmidt,   Your Signature   Amount
    General Partner

APPENDIX D:

SAMPLE INVESTMENT AGREEMENT

Agreement

RICHARD R. SCHMIDT ("Schmidt") doing business as L.L. PRO-DUCTIONS, intends to produce and exploit a 16 millimeter motion picture film tentatively entitled *THE ROOMMATE* ("the picture").

The following persons named below will participate in the writing, directing, filming, and editing of the motion picture, and upon completion of such services therein will each receive ten percent (10%) interest in the gross profits derived by Schmidt from the picture and its ancillary rights. All monies invested in the making of the feature length film (including tuition) will be paid back to each investor with 10% per year interest, this payment made before percentage interests will be paid. CCAC film department will receive 5% of the net profits as a fund for feature filmmaking.

This agreement may be executed in several counterparts, each of which shall be deemed an original and such counterparts shall together constitute one and the same agreement, binding all the parties hereto notwithstanding all of the parties are not signatory to the original on the same counterpart. Signers below will equally share all profits not assigned on page 2.

Date and Place of   Signatures
Execution

_____   _____

_____   _____

_____   _____

_____   _____

_____   _____

_____   _____

_____   _____

_____   _____

APPENDIX E:

RELEASE

Release

FOR VALUABLE CONSIDERATION, including the agreement to produce the motion picture currently entitled "MORGAN'S CAKE," I hereby irrevocably grant to Morgan's Cake, a California Limited Partnership (the "Partnership"), its licensees, agents, successors and assigns, the right (but not the obligation), in perpetuity throughout the world, in all media, now or hereafter known, to use (in any manner it deems appropriate, and without limitation) in and in connection with the motion picture, by whatever means exhibited, advertised or exploited: my appearance in the motion picture, still photographs of me, recordings of my voice taken or made of me by it, any music sung or played by me, and my actual or fictitious name.

On my own behalf, and on behalf of my heirs, next of kin, executors, administrators, successors and assigns, I hereby release the Partnership, its agents, licensees, successors and assigns, from any and all claims, liabilities and damages arising out of the rights granted hereunder, or the exercise thereof.

_____   _____
Date   Signature

_____   _____
Street Address   City, State, Zip Code

_____   _____
Telephone Number   Social Security Number

I am the parent or legal guardian of _____. I hereby irrevocably consent to the foregoing grant and agreement. I agree to indemnify the Partnership, its licensees, agents, successors and assigns, and hold each of the foregoing harmless from any and all damages, losses and expenses resulting from any actual or purported disaffirmance or rescission of the above agreement by the signatory thereto.

_____   _____
Date   Signature of Parent or Guardian

APPENDIX F:

LOCATION AGREEMENT

Location Agreement

Gentlemen:

I (we) hereby grant to you, your successors, assigns and licensees, the right to photograph, reproduce and use (either accurately or with such liberties as they may deem necessary) the exteriors and interiors of the premises located at _____, and to bring personnel and equipment onto the premises and remove same.

You may have possession of the premises on or about _____, 19__, and may continue in possession thereof until the completion of your proposed scenes and work, estimated to require about _____ days of occupancy over a period of about _____ days.

However, in the event of illness of actors, director, or other essential artists and crew, or weather conditions, or any other occurrence beyond your control, preventing you from starting work on the date designated above, or in the event of damaged or imperfect film or equipment, you shall have the right to use the premises at a later date to be mutually agreed upon.

This is in connection with the motion picture photoplay tentatively entitled _____, and includes the right to re-use the photography in connection with other motion picture photoplays as you, your successors, assigns and licensees shall elect, and, in connection with the exhibition, advertising and exploitation thereof, in any manner whatsoever and at any time in any part of the world.

You agree to hold me (us) free from any claims for damage or injury arising during your occupany of the premises and arising out of your negligence thereon, and to leave the premises in as good order and condition as when received by you, reasonable wear, tear, force majeure, and use herein permitted excepted.

I (we) acknowledge that, in photographing the premises, you are not in any way depicting or portraying me (us) in the motion picture photoplay, either directly or indirectly. I (we) will not assert or maintain against you any claim of any kind or nature whatsoever, including, without limitation, those based upon invasion of privacy or other civil rights, defamation, libel or slander, in connection with the exercise of the permission herein granted.

I (we) represent that I (we) are the owner(s) and/or authorized representative of the premises, and that I (we) have the authority to grant you the permission and rights herein granted, and that no one else's permission is required.

Dated: _____   _____
                          Signature of Owner or Authorized Agent

                          _____
                          Signature of Owner or Authorized Agent

                          _____
                          Print Name(s)

APPENDIX G:

MUSIC RIGHTS AGREEMENT

Licensor: _____

Address: _____

_____

City/State: _____

This Synchronization License Agreement ("License") is made and entered into this _____ day of _____, 1993, by and between _____ ("Licensor") and ___Rick Schmidt___.

1. In full and final consideration of the sum of _____ receipt of which is hereby acknowledged, Licensor grants to Rick Schmidt the non-exclusive, irrevocable right, license, privilege and authority to record on film or videotape and use the musical compositions and recordings entitled _____ in synchronization or timed relation with the film production currently entitled _____.

2. Licensor authorizes Rick Schmidt to use or cause to be used the aforesaid musical compositions and recordings in conjunction with the aforesaid film production in any manner he deems fit including, but not limited to, the purpose of advertising and ex-

ploiting said film production and the right to license and distribute the aforesaid musical compositions in conjunction with said film production throughout the world on any medium or forum, whether now known or hereinafter created.

3. The musical compositions and recordings licensed pursuant to this agreement shall not be distributed or exploited separately or independently of said film production.

4. Licensor hereby represents and warrants that he/she has the full legal right, power and authority to grant this license and that the performance rights to the aforesaid musical compositions and recordings are available for license through ASCAP, BMI, or SESAC.

5. Licensor warrants, represents and agrees that Licensor will obtain in writing all requisite consents and permissions of labor organizations, the copyright owners, and the Artist (if applicable) whose performances are embodied in the compositions and recordings and that Licensor will pay all re-use payments, fees, royalties and other sums required to be paid for such consents and permission, in connection with Schmidt's use of the compositions and recordings. If Schmidt so requires, Licensor will obtain such persons and deliver to him any documents that he requires to confirm that they will not look to Schmidt for any payments in connection with the compositions and recordings in the film production. Licensor will indemnify and hold FEATURE WORK-SHOPS and its officers and directors harmless from any and all claims, liabilities, losses, damages and expenses including, without limitation, attorneys' fees and legal expenses arising from any breach of Licensor's warrenties, representations or covenants under this license, or in any way resulting from or connected with Schmidt's use of the compositions and recordings.

6. The term of this license is for the worldwide period of all copyrights in and to the musical compositions and recordings and any and all renewals or extensions thereof that Licensor may now or hereafter own or control.

7. The rights granted herein shall inure to the benefit of FEATURE WORKSHOPS, its licensees, successors and assigns.

_____

Date

By _____   By _____

APPENDIX H:

CALIFORNIA
LIMITED PARTNERSHIP AGREEMENT

Limited Partnership Agreement of
Morgan's Cake, A California Limited Partnership

TABLE OF CONTENTS

ARTICLE I
FORMATION OF THE PARTNERSHIP; NAME AND
PRINCIPAL OFFICE; PURPOSES; TERM; AND FILINGS   p.1

1.1	Formation of the Partnership	2
1.2	Name and Principal Office	2
1.3	Purposes and Powers	2
1.4	Term	3
1.5	Filings	3
1.6	Commencement of Operations	3

ARTICLE II
CAPITAL CONTRIBUTIONS; FINANCING   2

2.1	Capital Contribution of the General Partner	3
2.2	Capital Contributions of the Limited Partners	3
2.3	Capital Accounts	4
2.4	Borrowings	4

2.5   Funding   5
2.6   Nonassessability.   5

ARTICLE III
INTEREST OF PARTNERS IN INCOME,
LOSSES AND CASH DISTRIBUTIONS   5
3.1   Determination of Income and Loss   5
3.2   Allocation of Revenues and Costs Among the
      Partners   5
3.3   Allocations Among the Limited Partners   6
3.4   Distributions to the Partners   6

ARTICLE IV
INCOME TAX MATTERS   7
4.1   Allocations   7
4.2   Tax Elections   8
4.3   Administrative Matters   9

ARTICLE V
RIGHTS, FEES AND DUTIES OF THE GENERAL PARTNER   9
5.1   Duties, Fees and Expenses of the General Partner 9
5.2   Management Power   10
5.3   Action by the General Partner; Authority   12
5.4   Nonexclusivity   12
5.5   Obligations of the General Partner   13
5.6   Certain Specific Authorization   13
5.7   Indemnification   13
5.8   Power of Attorney   14

ARTICLE VI
RIGHTS AND OBLIGATIONS OF THE LIMITED PARTNERS   16
6.1   Limited Liability   16
6.2   Limited Partners' Right to Participate in
      Management   17
6.3   Consents, Meetings and Submissions to the
      Limited Partners   18

ARTICLE VII

ADDITIONAL PARTNERS; WITHDRAWAL OF PARTNERS;
TRANSFER OF PARTNERSHIP INTERESTS AND UNITS;
SUBSTITUTED LIMITED PARTNERS; AND ASSIGNMENT   19
7.1   Additional Partners   19
7.2   Withdrawal of Partners   19
7.3   Transfer of the Partnership Interest of the
       General Partner   19
7.4   Transfer of Any Units by a Limited Partner   20
7.5   Death, Retirement, Withdrawal, Removal,
       Incompetency or Bankruptcy of the General
       Partner   21
7.6   Death, Retirement, Withdrawal, Incompetency,
       Dissolution or Bankruptcy of a Limited Partner 21
7.7   Substituted Limited Partners   22
7.8   Assignment of Right to Distributions of the
       Partnership by a Limited Partner   22

ARTICLE VIII

RECORDS AND BOOKS OF ACCOUNT; FISCAL YEAR;
BANKING; AND REPORTS TO THE LIMITED PARTNERS   23
8.1   Documents to be Maintained   23
8.2   Books of Account   23
8.3   Inspection by and Delivery to a Limited Partner 23
8.4   Fiscal Year   24
8.5   Banking   24
8.6   Reports to the Limited Partners   24

ARTICLE IX

DISSOLUTION; LIQUIDATION; AND TERMINATION   25
9.1   Dissolution   25
9.2   Right to Continue the Business of the Partnership 25
9.3   Liquidation   26
9.4   Termination   28

ARTICLE X

GENERAL   28
10.1   Arbitration   28
10.2   Notices   29

10.3	Entire Agreement	30
10.4	Waivers	30
10.5	Headings, Gender and Number	30
10.6	Counterparts	30
10.7	Benefit	31
10.8	Recipient of Distributions and Payments	31
10.9	Further Actions	31
10.10	Prohibition Against Partition	31
10.11	Governing Law	31
10.12	Amendments	31

ARTICLE XI

CERTAIN DEFINED TERMS		32
SCHEDULE I	Limited Partners	36
SCHEDULE II	Capital Contributions	37

LIMITED PARTNERSHIP AGREEMENT OF MORGAN'S CAKE, A CALIFORNIA LIMITED PARTNERSHIP

AMENDED AND RESTATED AGREEMENT OF LIMITED PART-
NERSHIP (the "Agreement") made as of the _____ day
of _____, 1987, by and among RICHARD R. SCHMIDT,
residing at _____ (the "General Partner"), and
those Persons whose names and addresses appear on SCHEDULE
I (the "Limited Partners" and, together with the General Partner,
the "Partners").

RECITALS

Morgan's Cake, a California Limited Partnership (the "Partnership"), is formed on the date of this Agreement as a California
limited partnership, consisting of the General Partner and the Limited Partners, all upon the terms and subject to the conditions
hereinafter set forth.

AGREEMENT

Accordingly, in consideration of the foregoing and of the mutual covenants and conditions contained herein, the sufficiency of which is acknowledged by each party hereto, the parties agree that this Agreement shall read in its entirety as follows (it being agreed that capitalized terms used herein, unless defined elsewhere herein, shall have the respective meanings assigned to them in Article XI):

ARTICLE I
FORMATION OF THE PARTNERSHIP; NAME AND PRINCIPAL OFFICE; PURPOSES; TERM; AND FILINGS

1.1 <u>Formation of the Partnership.</u> The General Partner and the Limited Partners hereby form and enter into the Partnership, all upon the terms and subject to the conditions herein contained and the applicable laws of the State of California.

1.2 <u>Name and Principal Office.</u> The Partnership shall conduct its business and promote its purposes under the firm name and style "Morgan's Cake, a California Limited Partnership," or such other name or names as the General Partners hereafter may select. The principal place of business of the Partnership shall be at _____, or such other place or places as the General Partner hereafter may designate by a Notice to the Limited Partners. The Partnership may maintain such other additional offices as the General Partner shall, in his sole discretion, deem advisable.

1.3 <u>Purposes and Powers.</u> The purpose of the Partnership shall be to produce, own and exploit a feature-length motion picture currently entitled "MORGAN'S CAKE" (the "Motion Picture"), based upon a screenplay of the same title by the General Partner. In furtherance of the purposes of the Partnership, the Partnership shall have such powers as may be required or appropriate to carry out its purposes including, without limitation, the powers (i) to borrow money, (ii) to pledge, mortgage or otherwise encumber all or any part of the properties or assets of the Partnership, including, without limitation, its interests in the Motion Picture, and the

[2]

Units of all the Limited Partners as security for its obligations, and (iii) to sell, assign, license, exchange or otherwise dispose of all or any part of its properties or assets for cash, stock, securities, evidences of indebtedness or other assets or any combination thereof, all upon such terms and conditions as the General Partner shall, in his sole discretion, deem appropriate.

1.4 Term. The term of the Partnership commenced on the date hereof, and shall continue through November 30, 2038, or such earlier date as the Partnership shall be dissolved and terminated in accordance with the provisions of applicable law or Article IX.

1.5 Filings. On the date hereof, the General Partner shall file the Certificate of Limited Partnership of the Partnership (the "Certificate") in the office of the California Secretary of State. From time to time thereafter, the General Partner shall do or cause to be done all such filings, recordings, publishings and other acts, as may be necessary or appropriate to comply with all requirements for the operation of a limited partnership pursuant to the laws of the State of California and of all other jurisdictions wherein the Partnership shall conduct its business.

1.6 Commencement of Operations. Upon the admission of Limited Partners to the Partnership, their subscriptions shall be transferred to a bank account which shall be maintained in the name and for the benefit of the Partnership. Partnership operations shall commence at such time as all Persons whose subscriptions have been accepted by the General Partner shall have been admitted to the Partnership as Limited Partners.

ARTICLE II
CAPITAL CONTRIBUTIONS; FINANCING

2.1 Capital Contribution of the General Partner. On the date hereof, the General Partner shall contribute to Partnership Capital the amount and consideration set forth opposite his name in SCHEDULE II. Except as provided in Section 9.3, the General Partner shall not be required to contribute any Capital to the Partnership other than the amount specified in SCHEDULE II.

[3]

2.2 <u>Capital Contributions of the Limited Partners.</u> On the date hereof, each Limited Partner shall contribute to Partnership Capital the amount and consideration set forth opposite his name in SCHEDULE II. Except as provided in Section 9.3, no Limited Partner shall be required to contribute any Partnership Capital other than the amount specified in SCHEDULE II.

2.3 <u>Capital Accounts.</u> A Capital Account shall be established and maintained for each Partner in accordance with Proposed Treasury Regulation Sections 1.704-1(B)(2)(iv)(a) and 1.704-1(b)(20(iv)(c), and initially shall reflect the amount of his Capital Contribution and shall from time to time be (i) increased by the amount of (a) any additional Capital Contributions, (b) any income, gain or profit allocated to him, (c) his share of indebtedness of the Partnership, and (d) his distributive share of profits of the Partnership (whether actual or constructive; and (ii) decreased by the amount of (a) any loss or other deduction allocated to him, and (b) all distributions made or deemed to be made to him (including the reduction of his share of indebtedness of the Partnership). Except as otherwise expressly provided in this Agreement, no Partner shall be permitted to make any withdrawals from or in respect of his Capital Account.

2.4 <u>Borrowings.</u> If the General Partner determines that the Partnership requires the temporary use of additional funds which cannot, in the opinion of the General Partner, be obtained on terms more advantageous to the Partnership by borrowing the funds from third parties, the General Partner and/or his Affiliates, may, loan such funds from time to time to the Partnership in such amounts as they shall determine. No such loan shall be deemed to constitute an increase in the Capital Account or contribution of the General Partner nor shall the making of any such loan entitle the General Partner to any increase in his share of the profits of the Partnership or subject the General Partner to any greater share of losses of the Partnership. Rather, the amount of each loan shall be deemed to constitute a debt due the General Partner or his Affiliates from the Partnership, which debt shall be due on demand of the General Partner or his Affiliates and shall bear interest at the higher of the then loan reference rate of the Wells

[4]

Fargo Bank, in San Francisco, California, or the rate of interest paid by the General Partner or his Affiliates to obtain such funds; *provided, however*, that in no event shall any such loan bear interest at a rate exceeding the maximum rate of interest then permissible under the laws of the State of California.

2.5 <u>Funding.</u> The Capital Contributions required to be made by the Partners pursuant to Sections 2.1 and 2.2 shall be used by the Partnership to produce the Motion Picture.

2.6 <u>Assessability.</u> Except as otherwise provided herein, the Partnership Interests of the Limited Partners are not assessable.

ARTICLE III
INTEREST OF PARTNERS IN INCOME, LOSSES AND CASH DISTRIBUTIONS

3.1 <u>Determination of Income and Loss.</u> At the end of each fiscal year of the Partnership, or at such other time as the General Partner shall deem necessary or appropriate, each item of income, expense, gain, loss and deduction of the Partnership shall be determined for the period then ending and shall be allocated to the Capital Account of each Partner in accordance with the provisions of this Agreement. In the event a Limited Partner sells, assigns, transfers or otherwise disposes of all of his Units, the determination and allocation shall be made as of the last day of the calendar month preceding the sale, assignment, transfer or other disposition. Thereafter, all such allocations shall be made to the account of the transferee of his Units.

3.2 <u>Allocation of Costs and Revenues Among the Partners.</u>
   (a) All items of income, gains, losses, deductions, credits and distributions of the Partnership shall be allocated 99% to the Limited Partners and one percent to the General Partner until Payout, and 50% to the Limited Partners and 50% to the General Partner thereafter.
   (b) Notwithstanding anything herein to the contrary with the exception of Section 3.2(c), the General Partner may reduce his revenue interest and correspondingly increase the revenue interest of the Limited Partners if required by law in order for the General

Partner to participate in transactions with the Partnership or the Limited Partners or for the Partnership to participate in transactions with Affiliates of the General Partner.

(c) Notwithstanding anything herein to the contrary, and solely for the purpose of qualifying allocations under this Agreement as having substantial economic effect under Section 704(b)(1), allocations under this Agreement are to be determined under the "alternate test" for economic effect set forth in Treas. Reg. §1.704-1(b)(2)(ii)(d), and, therefore, this Agreement shall be governed by the "qualified income offset" provisions of Treas. Reg. §1.704-1(b). A Partner who unexpectedly receives an adjustment, allocation or distribution described in Treas. Reg. §1.704-1(b) (ii)(d)(4), (5) or (6) shall be allocated items of income and gain in an amount and manner sufficient to eliminate the deficit balance described in Treas. Reg. §1.704-1(b)(ii)(d) as quickly as possible. Allocations which lack economic effect under the "alternate test" shall be made in accordance with the Partners' Partnership Interests as provided in Treas. Reg. §1.704-1(b)(3). If, pursuant to this Section 3.2(c), only a portion of an allocation made to a Partner with respect to a Partnership tax year has economic effect, both the portion that has economic effect and the portion that is reallocated shall consist of a proportionate share of all items that made up the allocation to the Partner for the year.

3.3 <u>Allocations Among the Limited Partners.</u> Each Limited Partner shall be allocated a portion of any amount allocated under this Agreement to the Limited Partners as a group, determined by multiplying the amount of his Pro Rata Share.

3.4 <u>Distributions to the Partners.</u> The Partnership shall distribute to the Limited Partners and the General Partner in the same proportions that revenues and costs have been allocated to the Partners any available cash of the Partnership. Within 45 days following the end of each calendar quarter, the General Partner shall determine the amount of cash available for distribution to the Partners, including, without limitation, borrowed funds and unexpended Capital Contributions. In making that determination, the General Partner shall estimate the amount of the Partnership Revenues to be received during the current quarter and the ensuing

quarter and the cash requirements of the Partnership for such period. In determining the cash requirements of the Partnership the
General Partner shall take into account all prospective costs and
expenses of the Partnership and all indebtedness of the Partnership incurred during such period and establish adequate reserves
for the payment of indebtedness maturing thereafter and any costs
and expenses of the Partnership expected to be incurred in suc-
ceeding periods. The determination of the General Partner of the
cash available for distributions to the Partners shall be conclusive
and binding upon the Partners.

ARTICLE IV
INCOME TAX MATTERS

4.1 Tax Accounting and Allocations.
   (a) With respect to the allocations set forth in Article III, to the
extent permitted by law and except as provided below, (i) all income and gains shall be allocated to the Partners to whom the
revenues resulting in the realization of the income and gains are
allocated, (ii) all losses shall be allocated to the Partners in the
same proportion as the losses are actually borne by the Partners,
(iii) all deductions and credits shall be allocated to the Partners
charged with the expenditure giving rise to the deductions or credits, and (iv) all items of tax preference for federal income tax
purposes shall be allocated to the Partners credited with the revenues resulting in the realization of the income, gains or losses
giving rise to the items of tax preference or charged with the expenditure giving rise to the deductions or credits to which the
items of tax preference are attributable. To the extent permitted
by law, each Partner shall be entitled to his distributive share of
Partnership income, gain, loss, deduction or credit, or items of tax
preference, in computing his taxable income or tax liability, to the
exclusion of any other Partner.
   (b) In the event of a sale or assignment of Units (other than by
reason of a Partner's death), except to the extent that pursuant to
a valid Treasury Department Regulation, a different method is required, the income, gains, losses, deductions and credits of the
Partnership for the fiscal year in which such sale or assignment is

[7]

recognized as provided in Section 7.7 shall be allocated pro-rata between the assignor and assignee of the Units based on the periods of time during the fiscal year that the Units were owned by each, without regard to the periods during the fiscal year in which the income, losses, deductions and credits of the Partnership were actually realized; provided, however, that with respect to certain "cash basis items," including for this purpose Partnership items of interest, taxes, payments for services, payments for the use of property, and any other items designed as "cash basis items" under Section 706 and the regulations promulgated thereunder, such items shall be assigned to the appropriate period to which they are attributable by allocating the assigned portion based upon the Units owned by a Limited Partner during each such period.

(c) The allocations set forth in this Agreement are intended to have substantial economic effect under Treas. Reg. §1.704-1(b). The allocations may thus be changed to comply with the "qualified income offset" provisions set forth in greater detail in Section 3.2(c).

(d) Notwithstanding the previous provisions of this Article IV, in no event (i) shall the aggregate deductions allocated to (and which may be claimed by) the Partners as their distributive share of Partnership losses during the first two years of the operation of the Partnership exceed the amount of the Capital Contributions made by the Partners, or (ii) shall the General Partner's allocable share of each item of Partnership income, gain, loss, deduction or credit (including the allocable share attributable to any Units owned by him) be less than one percent thereof.

4.2 Tax Elections.

(a) No election shall be made by any Partner to be excluded from the application of the provisions of Subchapter K of Chapter I of the Code, or from any similar provisions of foreign, state or local tax laws, and no such elections shall be made by the Partnership.

(b) In the event of a transfer of Units by a Limited Partner, or the distribution of any property of the Partnership to the Partners, the General Partner on behalf of the Partnership may, in his sole discretion, upon timely request by the transferee(s) or distribu-

[8]

tee(s), make an election under Section 754, in accordance with the applicable Treasury Department regulations, to cause the basis of the properties of the Partnership to be adjusted for federal income tax purposes as provided in Sections 734 and 743. At the option of the General Partner, the Partnership also may elect to adjust the basis of the properties of the Partnership pursuant to similar provisions of foreign, state and local tax laws.

4.3 Administrative Matters.

(a) Federal, state and local income (and other) tax returns shall be prepared and filed by the General Partner covering operations reportable by the Partnership. The General Partners shall use his best efforts in the preparation and filing of the tax returns, in the manner that the General Partner believes shall be most advantageous to individual taxpayers who are not "dealers" in motion pictures for federal income tax purposes. The General Partner shall also cause to be prepared and distributed to all the Limited Partners a Schedule K-1.

(b) The General Partner shall be appointed the Tax Matters Partner of the Partnership and shall be empowered to resolve the appropriate tax treatment of Partnership items of income, deduction or credit and to serve as the primary liaison between the Service and the Partnership and its members.

(c) In the event the Partnership is required to register as a "tax shelter" under Section 6111, the General Partner shall complete and file the appropriate registration documents with the Service. In addition, the General Partner shall maintain a list of investors in accordance with Section 6112 and the regulations promulgated thereunder, and shall be the person designated by the Limited Partners to maintain a master list, including the identity of Limited Partner-transferees, as reported to the General Partner by Limited Partner-transferors.

ARTICLE V

RIGHTS, FEES AND DUTIES OF THE GENERAL PARTNER

5.1 Duties, Fees and Expenses of the General Partner.

(a) The General Partner shall be responsible for the management of the business and properties of the Partnership. Subject to the provisions of Section 5.4, the General Partner shall render all services required in connection with the management of the business and properties of the Partnership.

(b) The Partnership shall pay the General Partner: (i) for the services that the General Partner shall render for the Partnership in the production of the Motion Picture, deferred compensation in the total amount of $25,000, payable *pari passu* with all other compensation from the first Partnership net proceeds following Payout until paid in full.

(c) The Partnership shall directly pay or reimburse the General Partner and his Affiliates for the costs of goods and materials used for or by the Partnership, excluding any indirect expenses incurred in performing their services for the Partnership, such as salaries or similar compensation. However, the Partnership shall pay or reimburse the General Partner and his Affiliates for services such as legal, accounting and other services which could be performed directly for the Partnership by independent parties. The costs of the Partnership for such services shall be based upon the compensation of the parties involved plus an appropriate share of overhead allocable to each such party (such as rent, secretarial and utilities). The amounts charged to the Partnership shall not exceed those which the Partnership would be required to pay independent parties for comparable services.

5.2 <u>Management Power</u>. Except as otherwise expressly provided in this Agreement, the General Partner shall have the power and authority to make all decisions relating to the management and control of the business and properties of the Partnership, and shall have complete discretion with respect to such decisions, including, without limitation, the right to:

(a) expend the capital and profits of the Partnership in futherance of its business;

(b) manage its operations and the production and exploitation of the Motion Picture;

(c) enter into agreements with Persons who shall render services for the production and/or exploitation of the Motion Picture pursuant to which the Partnership pays cash and/or deferred compensation, provided that the total sum of deferred compensation shall not exceed $55,000 nor be payable at all prior to Payout;

(d) reimburse the General Partner and his Affiliates for any sums paid or advanced by the General Partner or his Affiliates for the production and exploitation of the Motion Picture or the offering and sale of the Units;

(e) sell, pledge, hypothecate, dispose of, trade, exchange, quitclaim, surrender or release properties of the Partnership or interests therein;

(f) give receipts, releases and discharges;

(g) loan money to the Partnership and charge the Partnership interest at the rate referred to in Section 2.4 and borrow money from third persons for, in the name of and on behalf of the Partnership;

(h) to the extent that any funds of the Partnership are, in the judgment of the General Partner, not then required for the conduct of the business of the Partnership, invest those funds in government securities, certificates of deposit, bank repurchase agreements, bankers acceptances and highest rated commercial paper for the account of the Partnership, which have maturities of less than one year from the date of investment;

(i) adjust, compromise, settle or refer to arbitration any claim in favor of or against the Partnership, and institute, prosecute and defend any legal action or proceeding or any arbitration proceeding;

(j) enter into, make, execute, acknowledge, file and perform any and all contracts, assignments, and other agreements in connection with the business and purposes of the Partnership, including, without limitation, any contract, assignment, or other agreement with any Person, including the sale or other disposition of its interests in the Motion Picture;

(k) obtain financing for the purposes of the Partnership, and issue, accept, endorse and execute promissory notes, bonds or other evidences of indebtedness and, as security therefor, mortgage, pledge, grant security interests in or otherwise encumber its assets including, without limitation, the Units, and execute any collateral assignments, security agreements, financing statements or similar agreements in connection therewith, and prepay, in whole or in part, refinance, recast, increase, modify, consolidate or extend any obligation affecting the Partnership or any security therefor;

(l) acquire and enter into any contract of insurance necessary or proper for the protection of the Partnership, the conservation of its business and/or properties, to protect the Partnership and/ or the General Partner against liability to third parties arising out of the activities of the Partnership and for any other purpose proper and beneficial to the Partnership;

(m) enter into any agreements with other partnerships, including those for which the General Partner also acts as a general partner;

(n) retain or employ and coordinate the services of all employees, producers, directors, screenwriters, actors, distributors, accountants, attorneys, consultants and other Persons necessary or appropriate to carry out the business and purposes of the Partnership;

(o) perform other obligations provided elsewhere in this Agreement to be performed by the General Partner; and

(p) execute, acknowledge and deliver any and all documents and instruments necessary or desirable to effectuate the foregoing.

5.3 Action by the General Partner; Authority. The General Partner shall have the power to execute, deliver, perform and accept on behalf of the Partnership any document, instrument or agreement incident to the business of the Partnership and in furtherance of its purposes, and any such document, instrument or agreement shall be deemed executed, delivered, performed and accepted, as the case may be, by the Partnership. No Person shall, however, be required to determine the General Partner's authority to engage in any act or undertaking on behalf of the Partnership; and third parties dealing with the Partnership may rely conclusively upon the power and authority of the General Partner to act as set forth herein and shall not be required to inquire into or ascertain the authority of the General partner to so act.

5.4 Nonexclusivity. The General Partner shall devote to the affairs of the Partnership so much time as he, in his sole discretion,

[12]

deems necessary or advisable to properly carry on the business of the Partnership and to perform his duties as the General partner under this Agreement; *provided, however,* that the General Partner shall not be required to devote his full time and attention to the Partnership or to its business. Any Partner (including the General Partner) may, independently or with others, engage in or possess an interest in any business venture involved in the acquistion, development, ownership, production, operation, leasing, licensing, management, financing, promotion, distribution, exploitation or syndication, of any motion picture rights and/or properties and interests therein; and neither the Partnership nor any Partner shall have the right, by virtue of this Agreement or the relationship created hereby, to participate in any such venture or in the income, profits or losses derived therefrom.

5.5 <u>Obligations of the General Partner.</u> Throughout the term of the Partnership, the General Partner shall:

(a) cause the Partnership or others to maintain worker's compensation, employer's liability, public liability and property damage insurance in amounts believed by the General partner to be adequate, and

(b) maintain a Capital Account for each Partner; *provided, however,* that the General Partner shall not be obligated to fund any deficiency or make any contribution with respect to that Capital Account.

5.6 <u>Certain Specific Authorization.</u> The Limited Partners hereby expressly authorize the General Partner to execute, deliver and perform, in the name and on behalf of the Partnership, such documents, instruments and agreements as the General Partner shall deem advisable in connection therewith or otherwise to advance the purposes of the Partnership.

5.7 <u>Indemnification.</u> The General Partner and his Affiliates shall be indemnified by the Partnership under the following circumstances and in the manner and to the extent indicated:

(a) The General Partner and his Affiliates shall have no liability to the Partnership or to any Limited Partner for any loss suffered by the Partnership which arises out of any action or inaction of

[13]

the General Partner or his Affiliates if the General Partner or his Affiliates, in good faith, determined that such course of conduct was in the best interest of the Partnership and the course of conduct did not constitute gross negligence or gross or willful misconduct of the General Partner or his Affiliates.

(b) The General Partner and his Affiliates shall be indemnified by the Partnership against any losses, judgments, liabilities, expenses and amounts paid in settlement of any claims sustained by them in connection with the Partnership provided that the same were not the result of gross negligence or gross or willful misconduct on the part of the General Partner or his Affiliates.

(c) Notwithstanding the above, the General Partner and his Affiliates shall not be indemnified for any losses, liabilities or expenses arising from or out of an alleged violation of federal or state securities laws unless (i) there has been a successful adjudication on the merits of each count involving alleged securities law violations as to the particular indemnitee, (ii) such claims have been dismissed with prejudice on the merits by a court of competent jurisdiction as to the particular indemnitee, or (iii) a court of competent jurisdiction approves a settlement of the claims against a particular indemnitee.

(d) The indemnification set forth in this Section 5.7 shall in no event cause the Limited Partners to incur any liability beyond their total Capital Contributions plus their share of any undistributed profits of the Partnership, nor shall it result in any liability of the Limited Partners to any third party.

5.8 <u>Power of Attorney.</u> Each Limited Partner hereby constitutes and appoints the General Partner (and his duly authorized agents) his true and lawful agent and attorney-in-fact (with full power to substitute another attorney in his place and to revoke thet substitution) to receive and reinvest for the Limited Partner all funds distributed by the Partnership if the Limited Partner is eligible and elects to reinvest Partnership distributions, and to make, execute, swear to and acknowledge, amend, file, record, deliver and publish in his name, place and stead in any way which he could do if personally present to the extent permitted by law:

(a) any Certificate of Limited Partnership or amended Certificate of Limited Partnership required or permitted to be filed on behalf of the Partnership pursuant to the California Act or required or permitted to be filed or recorded under the statutes relating to limited partnerships under the laws of any jurisdiction in which the Partnership shall engage in business;

(b) a counterpart of the Agreement executed by the Limited Partner for the purposes of (i) adding a Limited Partner or Partners or a general partner or substituting as a Limited Partner an assignee or assignees of a Limited Partner pursuant to Article VII, and (ii) recording the Agreement in the State of Louisiana to establish a partnership in commendam pursuant to the laws thereof; and any such amended Agreement or amendments to the Agreement when such shall be appropriate in such state;

(c) all certificates and other instruments necessary to qualify or continue the Partnership as a limited partnership (or partnership wherein the Limited Partners have limited liability) in the jurisdictions where the Partnership may be doing business, including, without limitation, any fictitious or assumed name certificate required or permitted to be filed on behalf of the Partnership;

(d) any other instrument which is now or may hereafter he required by law to be filed for or on behalf of the Partnership;

(e) all assignments, conveyances and other certificates or instruments evidencing the dissolution, termination or liquidation of the Partnership, when such shall be appropriate, in each jurisdiction in which the Partnership shall do business;

(f) all documents for and agreements with the Service to keep open the statute of limitations with respect to any Partnership items under examination by the Service and to take any and all other action necessary or desirable to establish the Limited Partner's liability for tax or withholding of tax, or entitlement to a credit or refund of tax; and

(g) all instruments which the General Partner deems appropriate to reflect any amendment to this Agreement or modification of the Partnership made in accordance with the terms of this Agreement or to carry out the purposes and business of the Partnership.

The existence of this Power of Attorney shall not preclude execution of any such instrument by the Limited Partner individually

[15]

on any such matter. This is a limited Power of Attorney which may not be revoked and shall survive the assignment or transfer by the Limited Partner of all or part of his Partnership Interest and, being coupled with an interest, shall survive the death, dissolution, bankruptcy, incompetency or legal disability of the Limited Partner to the extent that he may legally contract for such survival. This power may be exercised by a facsimile signature of the General Partner or any successors thereto or by listing the Limited Partner and all other Limited Partners for whom action is being taken pursuant to like Powers of Attorney next to the single signature of the General Partner. Any person dealing with the Partnership may conclusively presume and rely upon the fact that any such instrument executed by such agent and attorney-in-fact is authorized, regular and binding without further inquiry and the Limited Partner hereby agrees to be bound by any representations made by the General Partner acting in good faith pursuant to this Power of Attorney, and each Limited Partner hereby waives any and all defenses which may be available to contest, negate or disaffirm any action of the General Partner taken in good faith under this Power of Attorney. The Limited Partner shall execute and deliver to the General Partner or any substitute general partner of the Partnership, within five days after the receipt of a request therefor by the General Partner or any such substitute general partner, such further designations, powers of attorney and other instruments as the General Partner or any such substituted general partner shall reasonably deem necessary.

ARTICLE VI
RIGHTS AND OBLIGATIONS OF THE LIMITED PARTNERS

6.1 <u>Limited Liability.</u> No Limited Partner shall have any liability whatsoever for any debts, liabilities or other obligations of the Partnership, beyond the aggregate amount of (i) his agreed Capital Contribution pursuant to the provisions contained in Section 9.3, (ii) all Distributions received by him in reduction of his Capital Contribution, plus interest thereon, and (iii) his share of the undistributed net income of the Partnership.

[16]

6.2 <u>Limited Partners' Right to Participate in Management.</u>

(a) Except as otherwise expressly provided in this Agreement, the Limited Partners shall have no right to, nor shall they, bind the Partnership or take any part in or interfere with the conduct, control or management of the business of the Partnership. The Limited Partners shall have the right to vote on (i) the removal of the General Partner, provided, however, that the provisions of this clause (i) shall be ineffective until a favorable ruling shall have been received by the Partnership from the Service to the effect that the action shall not adversely affect the tax status of the Partnership or any of the Limited Partners, in form and substance satisfactory to a majority in Interest of the Limited Partners or counsel for the Limited Partners (which shall be other than counsel for the General Partner and which counsel shall be acceptable to a majority in Interest of the Limited Partners) shall have delivered to the Partnership an opinion to the same effect; (ii) the election of a successor general partner or general partners and the continuation of the Partnership; (iii) the termination of the Partnership; (iv) the amendment of this Agreement, except as otherwise expressly prohibited herein; (v) approval or disapproval of the sale, assignment, transfer, lease, exchange, lease, sublease or other disposition of all or substantially all of the assets of the Partnership in a single transaction within a 12-month period. Each of these matters shall require the vote of a majority in Interest of the Limited Partners, except clause (i), which shall require the vote of 75% of the Limited Partners.

(b) If any approval of action by vote of a majority in Interest of the Limited Partners would violate the California Act or adversely affect the Limited Partners' limited liability or the Partnership's tax status but, in the opinion of the aforementioned counsel, the same approval upon unanimous consent would not, the action may be taken upon receipt of unanimous approval.

(c) The General Partner hereby agrees to concur in any vote of the Limited Partners taken under this Section 6.2 and shall execute an amendment to the Certificate of Limited Partnership and any other documents required to give effect to such action unless the effect of the action would be to increase the liability or obligations of the General Partner or affect his rights and interests in profits, losses and capital of the Partnership or alter federal income tax allocations under this Agreement.

6.3 Consents, Meetings and Submissions to the Limited Partners.

(a) Any consent required by this Agreement may be given (i) by a written consent of the consenting Partner prior to, at the time of, or after the doing of the act or thing for which the consent is solicited, or (ii) by the affirmative vote by the consenting Partner to the doing of the act or thing for which the consent is solicited at any meeting called and held pursuant to Section 6.3(b) to consider the doing of the act or thing.

(b) Meetings of the Partners and meetings of the Limited Partners to vote upon any matters on which the Limited Partners are authorized to take action under this Agreement may be called at any time by the General Partner or one or more Limited Partners holding not less than 10% of the Units. A list of the names and addresses of all Limited Partners shall be maintained as part of the books and records of the Partnership and shall be made available by any Limited Partners or his authorized representative for inspection, at his cost, during normal business hours upon reasonable advance Notice to the General Partner. Upon written request to the General Partner by any Person(s) entitled to call a meeting, the General Partner shall, cause a Notice to be given to the Limited Partners, at a time requested by the Person(s) calling the meeting, that a meeting shall be held not less than 15 nor more than 60 days following receipt of the request. Notice of the meeting shall be given either personally by first class mail not less than 10 nor more than 60 days before the date of the meeting to the Limited Partners. Included with the Notice shall be a detailed statement of the action proposed, including a verbatim statement of the wording of any resolution proposed for adoption by the Limited Partners and of any proposed amendment to this Agreement. The Partnership shall provide for proxies or written consents which specify a choice between approval and disapproval of each matter to be decided upon at the meeting. A majority of the Units entitled to vote, represented in Person or by proxy, shall constitute a quorum at a meeting of the Limited Partners.

[18]

ARTICLE VII
ADDITIONAL PARTNERS; WITHDRAWAL OF PARTNERS;
TRANSFER TO PARTNERSHIP INTERESTS AND UNITS;
SUBSTITUTED LIMITED PARTNERS; AND ASSIGNMENT

7.1 <u>Additional Partners.</u> Except as otherwise expressly provided herein, no Person shall be admitted to the Partnership as a limited partner without the prior written consent of the General Partners; and no Person shall be admitted to the Partnership as a general partner without the prior written consent of a majority in Interest of the Limited Partners.

7.2 <u>Withdrawal of Partners.</u> Except as otherwise expressly provided herein, no Partner may voluntarily retire or withdraw from the Partnership without the prior written consent of the General Partner and a majority in Interest of the Limited Partners.

7.3 <u>Transfer of the Partnership Interest of the General Partner.</u> Except as otherwise expressly provided herein, the General Partner shall not voluntarily sell, assign, transfer, pledge, hypothecate, grant a security interest in, encumber or in any other manner dispose of all or any part of his Partnership Interest without the prior consent of a majority in Interest of the Limited Partners.

The General Partner may assign all or any portion of his right to Distributions without the consent of the Limited Partners. An assignee shall be entitled to receive Distributions attributable to any assignment from and after the effective date of the assignment.

If the General Partner is terminated as the General Partner for any reason, the Partnership shall pay all amounts then accrued and owing to the General Partner concurrently with the Notice of termination, purchase his Partnership Interest by payment of an amount equal to its then fair market value as of the end of the quarter prior to the Notice of the termination as determined by the agreement of the General Partner and the Partnership; or, if they cannot agree, by arbitration in San Francisco, California, by the American Arbitration Association in accordance with its commercial rules then in force and effect. The expense of arbitration shall be borne equally by the General Partner and the Partnership.

[19]

The fair market value of Partnership Interest of the General Partner shall be the amount the General Partner would receive upon dissolution and termination of the Partnership assuming that the dissolution or termination occurred on the date of the terminating event and the assets of the Partnership were sold for their then fair market value without any compulsion on the part of the Partnership to sell the assets.

The method of payment to the terminated General Partner must be fair, and must protect the solvency and liquidity of the Partnership. Where the termination is voluntary, the method of payment shall be by a non-interest bearing unsecured promissory note with principal payable, if at all, from distributions of the Partnership which the terminated General Partner would have received under this Agreement had the General Partner not terminated. Where the termination is involuntary, the method of payment shall be by recourse promissory note bearing interest at the then prime rate of Wells Fargo Bank, in San Francisco, California, payable in 10 equal annual installments of principal and interest, the first commencing 30 days following the determination of the then fair market value of the Partnership Interest of the terminated General Partner.

7.4 Transfer of Any Units by a Limited Partner

(a) Except as otherwise expressly provided herein, a Limited Partner shall not sell, assign, transfer, pledge, hypothecate, grant a security interest in, encumber or in any other manner dispose of all or any portion of his Units without the prior consent of the General Partner. The General Partner may, in his sole discretion, withhold his consent to the assignment or transfer of all or a portion of his Units. If, in the opinion of counsel to the Partnership, any such transfer would cause a termination of the Partnership for federal income tax purposes or would violate, or cause the Partnership to violate, any applicable federal, state or local securities or other laws, the General Partner shall not consent to the transfer. Any such transfer to which the General Partner shall consent shall be effective as of the first day of the month in which the transfer was made. Notwithstanding the foregoing, the disposing Limited Partner shall remain responsible for his obligations to the Partnership unless and until the transferee or assignee of that Limited Partner is admitted to the Partnership as a substituted Limited Partner as provided in Section 7.7.

(b) If a Limited Partner at any time attempts to sell, assign, transfer, pledge, hypothecate, grant a security interest in, encumber or otherwise dispose of his Units in violation of the provisions of this Section 7.4, no purchaser, assignee, transferee, pledgee, lender or holder of the mortgage or encumbrance with respect thereto shall be deemed a substituted Limited Partner, and the Partnership, the other Partners, or any of them, shall, in addition to all other rights and remedies which they may have at law, in equity or under the provisions of this Agreement, be entitled to a decree or order restraining and enjoining such attempted sale, assignment, transfer, pledge, hypothecation, grant of security interest, encumbrance or other disposition, and the transferor shall not be entitled to plead in defense thereto that there would be an adequate remedy at law, it being recognized and agreed that the injury and damage resulting from such breach would be impossible to measure monetarily.

7.5 <u>Death, Retirement, Withdrawal, Removal, Incompetency or Bankruptcy of the General Partner.</u> Except as otherwise expressly provided in Section 9.2, the death, retirement, withdrawal, removal, incompetency or Bankruptcy of the General Partner shall cause a dissolution of the Partnership and shall require a liquidation of the assets of the Partnership.

7.6 <u>Death, Retirement, Withdrawal, Incompetency, Dissolution, or Bankruptcy, of a Limited Partner.</u> Except as otherwise expressly provided in this Agreement, the death, retirement, withdrawal, incompetency, dissolution or Bankruptcy of a Limited Partner shall not cause a dissolution of the Partnership, nor shall the Partnership be required to take cognizance of, or take any action with respect to, such death, retirement, withdrawal, incompetency, dissolution or Bankruptcy. The Partnership Interest of a deceased, retired, withdrawn, incompetent, dissolved or Bankrupt Limited Partner shall pass to his representative or successor-in-interest, who shall be deemed and treated for all purposes as an assignee of his economic interest.

7.7 <u>Substituted Limited Partners.</u> Anything herein to the contrary notwithstanding, no successor-in-interest of a Limited Partner and no assignee or transferee of all or any portion of his Units shall be admitted to the Partnership as a Substituted Limited Partner except upon: (i) submitting to the General Partner a duly executed and acknowledged counterpart of the instrument or instruments effecting or evidencing the transfer; (ii) submitting to the General Partner a counterpart of this Agreement (as amended through the date of transfer) signed by the transferee and appropriately signifying the agreement of the transferee to be bound by all the provisions of this Agreement (as amended through the date of transfer); (iii) the transferee's obtaining the written consent of the General Partner thereto; and (iv) the transferee's paying all costs and expenses, including, without limitation, attorneys' fees of the Partnership incurred in effecting the substitution.

An assignee who does not, for any reason, become a substituted Limited Partner shall be entitled as a result of the assignment only to receive the share of the Distributions attributable to the Units to which his assignor otherwise would be entitled, and the assignee shall not have any right to demand or to receive any account of the business of the Partnership or to inspect the books and records of the Partnership or any other rights as a Limited Partner, unless and until he is admitted to the Partnership as a substituted Limited Partner.

7.8 <u>Assignment of Right to Distributions of the Partnership by a Limited Partner.</u> A Limited Partner may assign all or a portion of his right to Distributions upon (i) submitting to the General Partner a duly executed and acknowledged counterpart of the instrument or instruments effecting or evidencing the assignment and (ii) the assignee's paying all costs and expenses, including, without limitation, attorneys' fees of the Partnership incurred in effecting the assignment.

An assignee shall be entitled to receive Distribution attributable to any assignment from and after the effective date of the assignment. As assigning Limited Partner shall remain responsible for his obligations, if any, to the Partnership, unless and until the General Partner agrees that his assignee may become a substituted Limited Partner.

ARTICLE VIII
RECORDS AND BOOKS OF ACCOUNT; FISCAL YEAR;
BANKING; AND REPORTS TO THE LIMITED PARTNERS

8.1 <u>Documents to be Maintained.</u> The General Partner shall maintain (or cause to be maintain) at the principal office of the Partnership the following documents of the Partnership:

(a) A current list of the full name and last known business or residential address of each Partner, together with his Capital Contribution and his Pro Rata Share in the profits and losses of the Partnership.

(b) A copy of the Certificate of Limited Partnership and all amendments thereto, and an executed copy of any powers of attorney pursuant to which any certificate has been executed.

(c) Copies of federal, state and local income tax or information returns and reports of the Partnership, if any, for the six most recent taxable years.

(d) Copies of this Agreement and all amendments to this Agreement.

(e) Financial statements of the Partnership for the six most recent fiscal years.

(f) The books and records of the Partnership for at least the current and past three fiscal years.

8.2 <u>Books of Account.</u> The books of account of the Partnership, which shall be maintained on the cash receipts and disbursements method of accounting or such other method of accounting as may be determined by the General Partner to be in the best interest of the Partnership.

8.3 <u>Inspection by and Delivery to a Limited Partner.</u>
(a) Upon the request of a Limited Partner, the General Partner shall promptly deliver to him, at the expense of the Partnership,

a copy of the documents set forth in Sections 8.1(a), 8.1(b), 8.1(c), 8.1(d) and 8.1(e).

(b) Each Limited Partner has the right upon reasonable request to the General Partner, (i) to inspect and copy at his own expense and during normal business hours, any of the documents set forth in Section 8.1, and (ii) to obtain from the General Partner promptly after becoming available, a copy of the federal, state and local income tax or information returns of the Partnership for each year.

8.4 <u>Fiscal Year.</u> The fiscal year of the Partnership shall be the calendar year.

8.5 <u>Banking.</u> An account or accounts in the name of the Partnership shall be maintained at such bank or banks as the General Partner may select. All uninvested funds of the Partnership shall be deposited in one or more bank accounts of the Partnership. All funds so credited to the Partnership in any such account shall be subject to withdrawal by checks made in the name of the Partnership and signed in such manner as may be determined from time to time by the General Partner. To the extent that any funds of the Partnership are, in the judgment of the General Partner, not then required for the conduct of the business of the Partnership, such funds may be temporarily invested by the General Partner in accordance with the provisions of Section 5.2(h).

8.6 <u>Reports to the Limited Partners.</u> For as long as economically reasonable, the General Partner shall deliver to each Limited Partner (i) no later than 90 days after the close of each fiscal year of the Partnership, a balance sheet of the Partnership as of the end of, and an income statement for, that year, each of which shall have been unaudited and reviewed by a firm of independent public accountants, which may be the independent public accountants of any Partner, (ii) no later than 75 days after the close of each taxable year of the Partnership, a statement setting forth his allocable share of all items of income, gains, losses, deductions, credits and tax preferences of the Partnership for the taxable year which are to be included by him on his federal income tax return for the taxable year, and (iii) no later than 60 days after the end of each of the first three quarters in each fiscal year of the Partnership, a

[24]

report on the operations of the Partnership for the quarter, containing a summary of Partnership income and expenditures for the quarter and such other information, if any, as the General Partner deems necessary to keep him advised with respect to the operations of the Partnership. Each of the financial statements and documents referred to above shall be conclusive and binding upon him unless a written objection thereto is received by the General Partner within one year after the statement has been delivered to him.

ARTICLE IX

DISSOLUTION; LIQUIDATION; AND TERMINATION

9.1 <u>Dissolution.</u> Subject to the laws of the State of California, the Partnership shall be dissolved and its assets liquidated upon the first to occur of:

(a) the expiration of the term provided for in Section 1.4;

(b) the death, retirement, withdrawal, removal, insanity or Bankruptcy of the General Partner, unless the business of the Partnership is continued pursuant to Section 9.2;

(c) the sale, assignment, transfer, license or other disposition of all or substantially all of the assets of the Partnership and the collection and distribution of the proceeds thereof; or

(d) the election of the General Partner or a majority in Interest of the Limited Partners to dissolve the Partnership; *provided* that such election shall be effective 60 days following a Notice thereof to all of the Partners.

9.2 <u>Right to Continue the Partnership's Business.</u> Upon the death, retirement, withdrawal, removal, incompetency (or, if permitted by applicable law, the Bankruptcy) of the General Partner, the remaining Partners (if they have the right to do so under applicable law) shall have the right, but not the obligation, exercisable by the vote of a majority in Interest of the remaining Partners, within 60 days from such death, retirement, withdrawal, removal, incompetency (or, if applicable, Bankruptcy), to elect to continue the business of the Partnership, in a reconstituted form as provided in this Agreement. Each Partner hereby agrees to such continuation in the event the election is made. In that event, the assets of the

[25]

Partnership shall not be liquidated, the business of the Partnership shall continue in a reconstituted form. If, upon the death, retirement, withdrawal, removal, incompetency (or, if applicable, Bankruptcy) of the General Partner, the remaining Partners shall have the right under applicable law to elect to continue the business of the Partnership, and if they so elect as provided in this Section 9.2, the remaining Partners shall, by the vote of a majority in Interest of the remaining Partners, designate one or more Persons to be the new general partner or general partners, which Person(s) shall become the general partner or general partners of the Partnership upon delivering to all the Partners an instrument pursuant to which such Person(s) agree to be bound by all the obligations of the General Partner under this Agreement.

9.3 Liquidation.

   (a) Except as otherwise set forth in Section 9.2, upon dissolution of the Partnership, the General Partners shall take (or cause to be taken) a full accounting of the assets and liabilities of the Partnership as of the date of such dissolution, subject to the right of the General Partner or his successor(s) to continue the business of the Partnership for the purpose of winding up its affairs. The General Partner shall proceed with reasonable promptness to liquidate the assets of the Partnership (including, without limitation, by way of the sale, assignment, transfer, exchange, license or other disposition of any or all the properties and other assets of the Partnership) and to terminate its business; *provided, however*, that the assets of the Partnership which are, in the opinion of the General Partner, suitable for distribution in kind, may, in the sole discretion of the General Partner, be distributed in kind to the extent that the liquidation thereof is not necessary to satisfy the requirements of clause (i) below. The cash proceeds from the liquidation shall be applied in the following order:

   (i) First, to the payment of all taxes, debts and other obligations and liabilities of the Partnership (excluding therefrom the principal and accrued interest on all then outstanding loans made by the Partners to the Partnership) and to the necessary expenses of liquidation thereof; *provided, however*, that all debts, obligations and other liabilities of the Partnership as to

[26]

which personal liability exists with respect to any Partner shall, to the extent permitted by applicable law, be satisfied, or a reserve established therefor, prior to the satisfaction of any debt, obligation or other liability of the Partnership as to which no such personal liability exists;

(ii) Second, to the payment and discharge of all indebtedness of the Partnership owed to the Partners, but if the amount available for such payment and discharge shall be insufficient, then the indebtedness owed to the Limited Partners shall be paid first (and as among them, pro rata in proportion to their respective amounts of such indebtedness) and indebtedness owed to the General Partner shall be paid and discharged thereafter; and

(iii) Thereafter, all remaining assets of the Partnership shall be distributed to the Partners with positive Capital Accounts (pro rata with such accounts) until such accounts are reduced to zero, and then the balance shall be distributed 99% to the Limited Partners (and among them, in accordance with their respective Pro Rata Shares) and one percent to the General Partner until Payout, and 50% to the Limited Partners (and, among them, in accordance with their respective Pro Rata Shares) and 50% to the General Partner.

(b) If, upon the dissolution of the Partnership, any Partner has a deficiency in his Capital Account as determined in accordance with generally accepted accounting principles immediately prior to the liquidating distributions to the Partners, and if the assets of the Partnership available for distribution upon dissolution are insufficient to allow distributions to the Partners of amounts equal to the then balances in their Capital Accounts as determined in accordance with generally accepted accounting principles, the Partner shall contribute in cash to Partnership Capital an amount which is equal to the lesser of (i) the deficiency in his or its Capital Account, or (ii) the amount required so that distributions may be made to the Limited Partners in an amount equal to the then balances in their Capital Accounts.

(c) The General Partner shall administer the liquidation of the Partnership and the termination of its business but shall receive no compensation therefor except for fees and compensation spe-

cifically referred to herein. The General Partner shall be allowed
a reasonable time for the orderly liquidation of the assets of the
Partnership and the discharge of its liabilities to creditors so as to
minimize losses resulting from the liquidation of the assets of the
Partnership.

(d) Anything herein to the contrary notwithstanding, no Limited
Partner shall have any right to demand or receive property other
than cash in connection with any distribution, and the General
Partner shall not be personally liable for the return of all or any
part of his Capital Contribution. Any such return shall be made
solely from the assets of the Partnership, if at all.

(e) Except as otherwise expressly provided herein, no dissolution or termination of the Partnership shall relieve, release or discharge any Partner, or any of his successors, assigns, heirs or legal
representatives, from any previous breach or default of, or any
obligation theretofore incurred or accrued under, any provision of
this Agreement, and any and all such liabilities, claims, demands
or causes of action arising from any such breaches, defaults and
obligations shall survive the dissolution and termination.

9.4 Termination. Upon compliance with the foregoing plan of liquidation and distribution, the General Partner shall file or cause a
Certificate of Cancellation of the Certificate of Limited Partnership
for the Partnership to be filed in the appropriate offices in the State
of California and all other jurisdictions where the Partnership is
then conducting business, and the Partnership thereupon shall be
terminated.

ARTICLE X
GENERAL

10.1 Arbitration. Except to the extent that the disputants agree in
writing to any other method of resolution of a given dispute and
except to the extent the resolution of any question is final, binding
and conclusive upon the Partners under the terms of this Agreement, any dispute arising among the Partners, or any of them, or
their successors-in-interest, or the estate of a deceased Partner,
concerning the meaning or interpretation of this Agreement, or the
rights, duties, or obligations of the Partners, including their suc-

cessors-in-interest and the estate of a deceased Partner, shall, with reasonable promptness, be submitted to and determined by arbitration in San Francisco, California, by the American Arbitration Association in accordance with its commercial rules then in force and effect, and judgment upon any award rendered may be entered in any court having jurisdiction thereof, and any such party may, if he so elects, institute proceedings in any court having jurisdiction for the specific performance by any party of any such award. In any such arbitration all disputes with respect to accounting matters, including, without limitation, (i) the financial condition of the Partnership at any date, (ii) its operating results for any period, (iii) the accuracy of any computation, and (iv) the proper accounting treatment under this Agreement for any asset, liability or other item or for any transaction, shall be referred to and conclusively determined by the then independent public accountants of the Partnership, or if such accountants are unable or unwilling to act, by a firm of independent public accountants of recognized standing designated by the arbitrator(s). Except for failure to make a Capital Contribution pursuant to Article II, no party shall be considered in default during the pendency of an arbitration proceeding by virtue of a default with respect to matters which are the subject of such arbitration and which occurs during the pendency of such arbitration.

10.2 Notices. Unless otherwise provided herein, any offer, acceptance, election, approval, consent, certification, request, waiver, notice or other communication required or permitted to be given under this Agreement (hereinafter collectively referred to as a "Notice"), shall be deemed given only if in writing and delivered personally (with receipt acknowledged) or mailed first class, certified or registered mail, return receipt requested, postage prepaid (i) if to the General Partner, to him at his address set forth in the opening paragraph of this Agreement, and (ii) if to any Limited Partner, to him at the address designated for him in SCHEDULE I. A Partner may designate another address by delivery or mailing a Notice thereof to the other Partners in accordance with the provisions of this Section 10.2.

[29]

10.3 <u>Entire Agreement</u>. This Agreement, including the SCHED-ULES attached hereto and incorporated by this reference herein, contains the entire agreement of the parties hereto with respect to the subject matter hereof and supersedes all prior agreements and understandings, whether written, oral or otherwise, among the parties hereto with respect to such subject matter.

10.4 <u>Waivers.</u> Except as otherwise expressly provided herein, no purported waiver by any party of any breach by another party of any of his obligations, agreements or covenants under this Agreement, or any part thereof, shall be effective unless made in a writing subscribed by the party or parties sought to be bound thereby, and no failure to pursue or elect any remedy with respect to any default under or breach of any provision of this Agreement, or any part hereof, shall be deemed to be a waiver of any other, subsequent, similar or different default or breach, or any election of remedies available in connection therewith, nor shall the acceptance or receipt by any party of any money or other consideration due him under this Agreement, with or without knowledge of any breach under this Agreement constitute a waiver of any provision of this Agreement with respect to such or any other breach.

10.5 <u>Headings, Gender and Number</u>. The section headings herein contained have been inserted only as a matter of convenience of reference and in no way define, limit or describe the scope or intent of any provisions of this Agreement nor in any way affect any such provisions. Where appropriate as used herein, the masculine gender shall be deemed to include the feminine, the feminine gender shall be deemed to include the masculine, the singular number shall be deemed to include the plural and the plural number shall be deemed to include the singular.

10.6 <u>Counterparts.</u> This Agreement may be executed in two or more counterparts and each of those counterparts, for all purposes, shall be deemed to be an original, but all of those counterparts together shall constitute but one and the same instrument, binding upon all of the parties, notwithstanding that all those parties may not have executed the same counterpart.

[30]

10.7 <u>Benefit.</u> This agreement shall be binding upon and inure to the benefit of the parties hereto and their respective executors, administrators and successors, but shall not be deemed for the benefit of creditors or any other Persons, nor shall it be deemed to permit any assignment by a Partner of any of his rights or obligations under this Agreement except as expressly provided herein.

10.8 <u>Recipient of Distributions and Payments.</u> All distributions and payments of cash or property to be made pursuant to the provisions of this Agreement shall be made directly to the parties who are entitled thereto at their respective addresses hereinbefore stated or at such other addresses as have been set forth in Notices sent in accordance with Section 10.2.

10.9 <u>Further Actions.</u> Each partner hereby agrees that he shall hereafter execute and deliver such further instruments and do such further acts and things as, in the opinion of the General Partner, may be required or useful to carry out the intent and purpose of this Agreement and as are not inconsistent with the terms hereof.

10.10 <u>Prohibition Against Partition.</u> Each Partner does hereby permanently waive and relinquish any and all rights he may have to cause any property of the Partnership to be partitioned, it being the intention of the Partners to prohibit any Partner from bringing a suit for partition against the other Partners, or any of them.

10.11 <u>Governing Law.</u> This Agreement and all matters pertaining thereto shall be governed by the laws of the State of California.

10.12 <u>Amendments.</u> Except as otherwise expressly provided herein or as otherwise required by law, this Agreement may only be amended upon the written consent of a majority in Interest of the Limited Partners; *provided, however*, that (i) any amendment which shall reduce the Units or enlarge the obligations of any Limited Partner shall require his consent; (ii) no amendment shall be made to Sections 6.2 or 7.1 without the unanimous written consent of the Limited Partners; and (iii) the General Partner may, without the consent of any Limited Partner, amend any provisions of this Agreement to reflect any:

(a) change in the name or location of the principal place of business of the Partnership;

(b) admission of substituted or additional Limited Partners in accordance with this Agreement;

(c) reduction in, return of, or withdrawal of, all or a portion of the capital contribution of any Limited Partner as permitted under this Agreement; and

(d) change which is necessary to qualify the Partnership as a limited partnership under the laws of any state or other jurisdiction, or which is necessary or advisable in the opinion of the General Partner to ensure that the Partnership will not be treated as an association taxable as a corporation for federal income tax purposes.

ARTICLE XI
CERTAIN DEFINED TERMS

Affiliate. An "Affiliate" of a Person means (i) any Person directly or indirectly controlling, controlled by or under common control with such Person; (ii) a Person owning or controlling 10% or more of the outstanding voting securities or beneficial interests of such Person; (iii) any officer, director, general partner, general trustee or anyone acting in a substantially similar capacity as to such Person; and (iv) any Person who is an officer, director, general partner, trustee, or holder of 10% or more of the outstanding voting securities or beneficial interests of any of the foregoing.

Bankruptcy. "Bankruptcy" shall be deemed to have occurred whenever a petition (whether voluntary or involuntary) in bankruptcy shall have been filed with respect to a Person and shall remain in effect, without being dismissed or stayed, for a period of not less than 60 days.

California Act. California Revised Uniform Limited Partnership Act.

Capital Contributions or Partnership Capital. The total amount of the capital contributions to the Partnership by the General Partners and the Limited Partners.

Capital Contribution of the General Partner. On the Closing Date, the General Partner shall contribute $152 to Partnership Capital.

Capital Contribution of a Limited Partner. On or before the Closing Date, each Limited Partner shall contribute for each Unit $5,000 in cash.

Cash Flow. Partnership Revenues minus cash disbursements (including, without limitation, debt service payments of principal and interest), computed in accordance with generally accepted accounting principles applicable to cash basis taxpayers, except that the following rules will apply:

(i) Depreciation or amortization of any kind will not be a deduction from gross receipts;

(ii) Expenditures from other than funds previously reserved, pursuant to paragraph (iii) below, to replace or repair capital assets will be deemed a cash operating expense; and

(iii) Any reserves that the General Partners may reasonably establish (or increase) will be deemed a cash operating expense when funded into the reserve.

Code. The Internal Revenue Code of 1954, as amended.

Distributions. A distribution of the Partnership to the Partners of all or a portion of the Cash Flow or Capital Contributions.

Interest. With respect to any Partner or transferee thereof, his entire interest in and to the capital, profits, losses, cash flow and properties of the Partnership.

Partnership Agreement. The Agreement of Limited Partnership of the Partnership in the form of EXHIBIT A.

Partnership Revenues. The total gross receipts of the Partnership derived from all sources whatsoever, including, without limitation, interest, and the license, sale or other disposition of its interest in the Motion Picture.

Payout. When the total amount of cash distributions made by the Partnership to the Partners equals the total amount of their Capital Contributions plus 10% per annum, noncompounded.

Person. A natural person or corporation, partnership, trust, company, association or other entity.

Pro Rata Share. With respect to any Limited Partner, the quotient obtained by dividing his Capital Contribution by the amount of the aggregate Capital Contributions of all the Limited Partners.

Section. Unless otherwise indicated, all section references are to the Code.

Unit. A Capital Contribution of $5,000 by a Limited Partner. The total number of Units is three.

IN WITNESS WHEREOF, the parties have hereunto set their hands as of the day and year first above written.

GENERAL PARTNER:

_____

Richard R. Schmidt

LIMITED PARTNERS:

By _____

Richard R. Schmidt, the
General Partner of the
Partnership and the attorney-in-
fact for each of the Limited
Partners listed in SCHEDULE I

STATE OF CALIFORNIA   )
) ss.
COUNTY OF SAN FRANCISCO   )

On the _____ day of _____, 1987, before me, the undersigned, a Notary Public in and for the City and County of San Francisco, State of California, personally appeared Richard R. Schmidt,

___ personally known to me
___ proved to me on the basis of satisfactory evidence

to be the person whose name is subscribed to this instrument, and acknowledged that he executed it as a general partner of Morgan's Cake, a California Limited Partnership.

    WITNESS my hand and official seal.

                                    _____
                                    NOTARY PUBLIC

STATE OF CALIFORNIA   )
) ss.
COUNTY OF SAN FRANCISCO   )

On the _____ day of _____, 1987, before me, the undersigned, a Notary Public in and for the County of San Francisco, State of California, personally appeared Richard R. Schmidt,

___ personally known to me
___ proved to me on the basis of satisfactory evidence

to be the person whose name is subscribed to this instrument, as the attorney-in-fact of those Persons listed in SCHEDULE I, the limited partners of Morgan's Cake, a California Limited Partnership, and acknowledged to me that he subscribed their names as principals and his own name as attorney-in-fact.

    WITNESS my hand and official seal.

                                    _____
                                    NOTARY PUBLIC

[35]

SCHEDULE I
LIMITED PARTNERS

Names	*Addresses*

SCHEDULE II
CAPITAL CONTRIBUTIONS

Name   *Contribution*

GENERAL PARTNER
Richard R. Schmidt

LIMITED PARTNERS

APPENDIX I:

PURCHASE OFFER (LIMITED PARTNERSHIP)

Morgan's Cake,
A California Limited Partnership

PURCHASE OFFER

By executing this Purchase Offer, the undersigned, a prospective Limited Partner of Morgan's Cake, a California Limited Partnership (the "Partnership"), agrees to be bound by the terms of the Amended and Restated Agreement of Limited Partnership of the Partnership (the "Partnership Agreement"), grants a power of attorney to the general partner of the Partnership, agrees to purchase limited partnership interest(s) in the Partnership (the "Units") and makes certain representations and warranties as follows:

1. Agreement to be Bound by Partnership Agreement and Grant of a Power of Attorney to the General Partner of the Partnership. He acknowledges that by executing this Purchase Offer, he agrees that upon becoming a limited partner in the Partnership, he will be bound by each and every provision of the Partnership Agreement. He hereby constitutes and appoints Richard R. Schmidt (the

[1]

"General Partner"), the general partner of the Partnership (and his duly authorized agents), his true and lawful agent and attorney-in-fact (with full power to substitute another attorney in his place and to revoke the substitution) to receive and reinvest for him all funds distributed by the Partnership if he is eligible and elects to reinvest Partnership distributions, and to make, execute, swear to and acknowledge, amend, file, record, deliver and publish in his name, place and stead in any way which he could do if personally present to the extent permitted by law:

(a) any Certificate of Limited Partnership or amended Certificate of Limited Partnership required or permitted to be filed on behalf of the Partnership pursuant to the California Act or required or permitted to be filed or recorded under the statutes relating to limited partnerships under the laws of any jurisdiction in which the Partnership shall engage in business;

(b) a counterpart of the Partnership Agreement executed by him for the purposes of (i) adding a Limited Partner or Partners or a general partner or substituting as a Limited Partner an assignee or assignees of a Limited Partner pursuant to Article VII of the Partnership Agreement, and (ii) recording the Agreement in the State of Louisiana to establish a partnership in commendam pursuant to the laws thereof; and any such amended Agreement or amendments to the Partnership Agreement when such shall be appropriate in such state;

(c) all certificates and other instruments necessary to qualify or continue the Partnership as a limited partnership (or partnership wherein he has limited liability) in the jurisdictions where the Partnership may be doing business, including, without limitation, any fictitious or assumed name certificate required or permitted to be filed on behalf of the Partnership;

(d) any other instrument which is now or may hereafter be required by law to be filed for or on behalf of the Partnership;

(e) all assignments, conveyances and other certificates or instruments evidencing the dissolution, termination or liquidation of the Partnership, when such shall be appropriate, in each jurisdiction in which the Partnership shall do business;

(f) all documents for and agreements with the Service to keep open the statute of limitations with respect to any Partnership

[2]

items under examination by the Service and to take any and all other action necessary or desirable to establish the undersigned's liability for tax or withholding of tax, or entitlement to a credit or refund of tax; and

(g) all instruments which the General Partner deems appropriate to reflect any amendment to the Partnership Agreement or modification of the Partnership made in accordance with the terms of the Partnership Agreement or to carry out the purposes and business of the Partnership.

The existence of this Power of Attorney shall not preclude execution of any such instrument by him individually on any such matter. This is a limited Power of Attorney which may not be revoked and shall survive the assignment or transfer by him of all or part of his Partnership Interest and, being coupled with an interest, shall survive his death, dissolution, bankruptcy, incompetency or legal disability to the extent that he may legally contract for such survival. This power may be exercised by a facsimile signature of the General Partner or any successors thereto or by him and all other Limited Partners for whom action is being taken pursuant to like Powers of Attorney next to the single signature of the General Partner. Any person dealing with the Partnership may conclusively presume and rely upon the fact that any such instrument executed by such agent and attorney-in-fact is authorized, regular and binding without further inquiry and he hereby agrees to be bound by any representations made by the General Partner acting in good faith pursuant to this Power of Attorney, and he hereby waives any and all defenses which may be available to contest, negate or disaffirm any action of the General Partner taken in good faith under this Power of Attorney. He shall execute and deliver to the General Partner or any substitute general partner of the Partnership, within five days after the receipt of a request therefor by the General Partner or any such substitute general partner, such further designations, powers of attorney and other instruments as the General Partner or any such substituted general partner shall reasonably deem necessary.

2. Limited Partnership Unit Purchase Offer. In consideration of others similarly agreeing and in consideration of the activities of

the Partnership, he agrees to purchase the number of Units set forth above his signature, for each Unit for $5,000 in cash and tenders payment for each Unit by check payable to the Partnership in the amount of $5,000.

3. <u>Representations and Warranties.</u> He hereby represents and warrants that:

a. He has carefully read and understands the contents of the Partnership Agreement, this Purchase Offer.

b. He has relied solely upon the Partnership Agreement and investigations made by him in making his decision to purchase Units.

c. No representations or warranties have been made to him with regard to the purchase of Units other than those contained in the Partnership Agreement.

d. He is aware that an investment in the Partnership is speculative and involves a high degree of risk.

e. He is (or his spouse and he are) an adult under the laws of the jurisdiction of his residence, and acknowledges the Units he is offering to purchase will be purchased solely for his own account, for investment purposes only, and not with a view to, or for the resale in connection with, any distribution thereof.

f. He has such knowledge or experience in financial and business matters that he is capable of evaluating the merits and risks of an investment in the Partnership as a limited partner.

g. He has either (i) a net worth (exclusive of home, furnishings and automobiles) of no less than (i) $75,000, or (ii) a net worth (exclusive of home, furnishings and automobiles) of not less than $50,000 and had during his last tax year or estimates that he will have during his current tax year, gross income of not less than $30,000, without regard to an investment in the Partnership, or that he is purchasing Units in a fiduciary capacity for a Person who meets such conditions.

h. He is able to bear the economic risk of investment in the Partnership, which could result in a total loss of his investment.

i. Prior to the sale of Units, the General Partner afforded him full and complete access to all the information with respect to the Partnership, the General Partner, the Motion Picture, and the pro-

[4]

posed operations of the Partnership that deemed necessary to evaluate the merits and risks of an investment in the Partnership, to the extent that the General Partner possesses such information or could acquire it without unreasonable effort or expense.

j. He is aware that the General Partner reserves the right to reject this Purchase Offer in its entirety or to allocate to him a smaller number of Units than he has offered to purchase. In the former event, the General Partner will return to him his subscription funds and, in the latter event, he may either withdraw his Purchase Offer or complete, sign and return to the General Partner, a new Purchase Offer and provide the General Partner with a new subscription check.

k. He understands that as a limited partner he will have no right to participate in the management of the business of the Partnership or in the decisions of the General Partner.

l. He understands that the Partnership is not a "tax shelter."

m. He is aware that there is no public market for the Units, that the transfer of Units is subject to certain restrictions including obtaining the approval of the General Partner, and either registration under the Securities Act of 1933, as amended, applicable State securities laws or an opinion of counsel satisfactory to the General Partner that such registrations are not required, and that, as a consequence, it is not likely for him to liquidate his Units in the event of any emergency.

n. He is aware that each Certificate of Limited Partnership Interest will bear a legend setting forth the following restrictions on transfer of Units:

"IT IS UNLAWFUL TO CONSUMMATE A SALE OR TRANSFER OF THIS SECURITY, OR ANY INTEREST THEREIN, OR TO RECEIVE ANY CON- SIDERATION THEREFOR WITHOUT THE PRIOR WRITTEN CONSENT OF THE COMMISSIONER OF CORPORATIONS OF THE STATE OF CALI- FORNIA, EXCEPT AS PERMITTED IN THE COMMISSIONER'S RULES."

o. He acknowledges and understands that the Partnership will pay the General Partner for the services that the General Partner will render for the Partnership in the production of the Motion Picture, deferred compensation in the total amount of $25,000, payable *pari passu* with all other deferred compensation from the first Partnership net proceeds following Payout until paid in full.

[5]

p. He further acknowledges and understands that the General Partner will make a contribution of $152 to Partnership Capital and will be allocated one percent of all items of income, gains, losses, deductions, credits and distributions of the Partnership until Payout, and 50% of those items thereafter.

q. He understands that all documents, records and books pertaining to an investment in the Partnership have been made available to him and that such documents, records and books of the Partnership will be available upon reasonable notice, for inspection by him at the offices of the Partnership.

If he is purchasing the Units in a fiduciary capacity, the above representations and warranties will be deemed to have been made on behalf of the Person(s) for whom he is so purchasing the Units.

If he is a corporation, he is authorized and otherwise duly qualified to hold interests in the Partnership.

Notwithstanding any of the representations, warranties and acknowledgments contained herein, he does not hereby or in any manner waive any rights granted to him under any securities laws.

This subscription was offered in the State of _____ and purchased in the State of _____.

He agrees to notify the General Partner immediately if any of the statements made herein become untrue.

PURCHASE OFFER FOR
INDIVIDUAL SUBSCRIBER

To be fully completed by subscriber, who by executing this Purchase Offer, offers to become a limited partner in Morgan's Cake, a California Limited Partnership (the "Partnership"), on the terms provided in the Partnership Agreement, grants a power of attorney to the General Partner of the Partnership as provided in Section 1 of this Purchase Offer, agrees to purchase the number of Units listed below, makes the representations and warranties set forth in Section 3 of this Purchase Offer, and declares that the statements and matters set forth in this Purchase Offer are true and correct.

Number of Units Offered to be Purchased: _____

Subscription Amount: $_____

Signature(s): _____

_____

ADDITIONAL INFORMATION TO BE
FURNISHED BY INDIVIDUAL SUBSCRIBERS
(PLEASE PRINT OR TYPE)

Subscriber: *Full legal name(s) in which the Units should be
registered. (See Note Below.)

Mr.   Mrs.   Ms.   Dr.   (1) _____

Mr.   Mrs.   Ms.   Dr.   (1) _____

(Check One)
Individual ownership   _____
Joint tenants with right
  of survivorship   _____ Both must sign.
Tenants in common   _____ Both must sign.
Community Property   _____ Both must sign.

Soc. Sec. No.   (1) __ __ __ - __ __ - __ __ __ __

Soc. Sec. No.   (1) __ __ __ - __ __ - __ __ __ __

[7]

State of Residence   _____

Mailing Address   _____

City, State and Zip Code   _____

If the Subscriber(s) is a resident of a community property state
(i.e., Arizona, California, Idaho, Louisiana, Nevada, New Mexico,
Texas or Washington), the registration should indicate whether the
Units will be owned as separate or community property. If the
Units are not to be owned as community property, and the Units
are to be registered jointly in the name of more than one person,
the nature of joint ownership should be indicated (i.e., tenants-in-
common, joint tenants with right of survivorship, tenants by the
entirety, or other designation as may be permitted by law in the
State of residence of the Investor).

PURCHASE OFFER FOR CORPORATION, PARTNERSHIP OR TRUST

To be fully completed by subscriber, who by executing this Purchase Offer, offers to become a limited partner in Morgan's Cake, a California Limited Partnership (the "Partnership") on the terms provided in the Partnership Agreement, grants a power of attorney to the General Partner of this Partnership as provided in Section 1 of this Purchase Offer, agrees to purchase the number of Units listed below, makes the representations and warranties set forth ini Section 3 of this Purchase Offer, and declares that the statements and matters set forth in this Purchase Offer are true and correct.

Attached hereto is an opinion of counsel or other document establishing the subscriber's authority to subscribe for and purchase Units and to execute this Purchase Offer, including, without limitation, a copy of the Articles of Incorporation, Bylaws and authorization by the Board of Directors to make this offer, or a copy of the partnership agreement or trust document, if applicable.

Number of Units Offered to be Purchased: _____

Subscription Amount: $_____

Name of Partnership, Corporation   _____
   or Trust:

                         By: _____

                         Title: _____

ADDITIONAL INFORMATION TO BE FURNISHED BY
CORPORATE, PARTNERSHIP OR TRUST SUBSCRIBERS
(PLEASE PRINT OR TYPE)

(Check One)
Corporation   _____
Partnership   _____
Trust   _____
Other   _____

[9]

If Corporation: _____ Indicate office of signer.
If Partnership: _____ Indicate title of signer.
If Trust: _____ Indicate name of Trustee.
                _____ Indicate date of Trust.

Federal I.D. No.   __ __ - __ __ __ __ __ __ __ __

State of Residence   _____
Mailing Address   _____
City, State and Zip Code _____

If the Units are to be registered in the name(s) of the trustee(s),
the date of the trust agreement must be furnished.

ACCEPTANCE BY THE GENERAL PARTNER

The General Partner of Morgan's Cake, a California Limited Partnership, has the right to accept or reject this Purchase Offer in whole or in part.

Accepted: _____

Richard R. Schmidt, the General Partner

Date: _____ __, 1987

APPENDIX J:
COLLABORATIVE FEATURE AGREEMENT

Agreement

RICK SCHMIDT ("Schmidt") doing business as FEATURE WORK-SHOPS, intends to produce and exploit a 16 millimeter motion picture film tentatively entitled _____ ("the picture").

The following people named below will participate in the creation of the 16MM film and upon completion of their services therein as producers, will each receive an equal share of the gross profits derived by Schmidt from the picture and its ancillary rights, in the amount indicated after their name. In exchange for necessary completion costs for the film ($15,000 for conforming, sound mix, answer and release prints) 10% of the gross profits will be reserved for an INVESTOR. FEATURE WORKSHOPS will receive 5% of the gross profits to cover overhead during distribution and sales.

On my own behalf, and on behalf of my heirs, next of kin, executors, administrators, successors and assigns, I hearby release FEATURE WORKSHOPS and RICK SCHMIDT, his agents, licensees, successors and assigns, from any and all claims, liabilities and damages arising out of my participation with the production of this motion picture. This agreement may be executed in several counterparts, each of which shall be deemed an original and such counterparts shall together constitute one and the same agreement, binding all the parties hereto notwithstanding all of the parties are not signatory to the original on the same counterpart. Profits unclaimed, or not assigned on page 3, will be shared equally among "the Producers" of the film.

Signatures   Date and Place
                                              of Execution

_____   _____
Investor (10%)

_____   _____

_____   _____

_____   _____

_____   _____

_____   _____

_____   _____

_____   _____

_____   _____

On my own behalf, and on behalf of my heirs, next of kin, executors, administrators, successors and assigns, I hearby release
FEATURE WORKSHOPS and RICK SCHMIDT, his agents, licensees, successors and assigns, from any and all claims, liabilities and
damages arising out of my participation with the production of
this picture. Upon completion of my services as defined below, I
will receive one half percent (½%) of the net profits as derived by
Schmidt from the picture and its ancillary rights.

Signatures   Date and Place
                                        of Execution

_____   _____

_____   _____

_____   _____

_____   _____

_____   _____

_____   _____

_____   _____

_____   _____

Authorized by Rich Schmidt _____

INDEX

Page numbers in *italics* refer to illustrations.

AB rolls, 51, 165, 168–70, *171, 172*, 246
  cue sheet for printing, 182–84, *183*
  from original, 174–78, 182
  from work print, 175–78, *179, 180, 181*, 182
Academy Awards, 240
actors, 60, 63, 95, 97, 98, 134
  casting of, 64, 66–67, 68–71, 93, 94
  continuity and, 121
  directing of, *see* directing
  emotions and, 101, 138
  food for, *see* food
  lighting and, 103, 107, 108
  locations as sources for, 71
  paying of, 9, 41, 42–44, 46, 48, 49, 57, 64, 69; *see also* payments
  placement of, for first shot, 105–6
  release form for, 11, 71, 93, 94, 280–281
  replacing, 138
  screenings for, 136–37, 189–90
  self-direction by, 69
  shooting schedule for, 93, 95
  in stills and videos, 125–26
  storyboarding and, 74
  trained, 68–69
  transportation for, *see* transportation
  untrained, 70–71, 117
  see also characters; dialogue; scenes
advertising, 125

for alternative distribution, 215–16
  see also promotion
AFD Photogard, 185
AFI/LA Fest, 200
agents, 212–13
agreements, *see* contracts and forms
airline credit cards, 205
AIVF, *see* Association of Independent Video and Filmmakers
Albertson, Jim, 135
Allen, Woody, 229
Alpha Cine Lab, 252, 260
American Film Institute, xxxv, xxxvi, 62
American Orpheus, xxix, xli, *102*, 219, 253, 257
  directing in, 118, 119
  food costs and, 120
  musical score for, 253–54
American Production Services, *263*, 264, 265
Angel City, 23
Ann Arbor Film Festival, xxxiii, xxxv, xxxvi, 82
answer print (projection print), 51, 57, 58, 132, 185–86, 246, 257, 258
  on Estar stock, 185, 188
  protective coating for, 185
  screening of, 186–88
ARD, 207
Arizona, University of, 98–99

Arriflex camera, 76, *79*
Association of Independent Video and
    Filmmakers (AIVF), 56, 67, 199,
    204, 249
    Independent Film and Video Monthly
    magazine of, 34, 56, 62, 197
At Close Range, 7
Atomic Cafe, 209
Attraction, The, 34–35
auteur theory, 233–34
AVID Media Composer, 260–63, *261,
    265*

Baker, Paul, 253–54
Bals, Hubert, xxxix
Barber, Pat, 262
barney, 91, 123
Barrish, Jerry, 212–13
batteries, 75, 80–81
battery belt, 90, 100
Bean, Henry, 27, 66
Beeler, Kathleen, 84, 85, 86
Benning, James, 9
Bergersen, Kyle, *227*
Bergman, Ingmar, 111
Berlin Film Festival, 200
Berlinger, Joe, 214
Bertolucci, Bernardo, 111
Bertoni, Nick, 43
Betacam SP, 193, 194, 239, 240, 241–43,
    244, 246, 248, 261
BHP Modular Printer, 257–58
Blank, Harrod, *210*
Bleecker Street Cinema, xxxiv–xxxvi,
    xxxix, 202
Blues for the Avatar, 224, *227*, 252,
    265–66
boom pole with shock mount, 80
Boza, Peter, 71, 148
Brother's Keeper, 110, 214
budget, 44, 47, 56, 61, 94–95
    for collaboration, 226–29
    contract and, 46–47
    editing costs in, 44, 48, 50–58
    emergency funds and, 57, 63, 95
    filming costs in, 47–50, 57–58
    filmstock costs in, 40, 47, 48, 49, 56,
        57, 89–90
    food costs in, 41, 47, 48, 49, 57, 75,
        95, 120
    grants and, 61, 62, 63
    location and, 5–6, 9–10, 40–41, 43,
        44
    money-raising and, 44, 58–61, 64
    production limitations and, 40–41
    story concept and, 5–6, 9–10

transportation costs in, 41, 47, 48, 57
    for video feature, 241–46, 247–48
    see also payments
"bullet screen" effect, 195, *198*
Bully, The, 7, 9, 12–13
    characterization of "Ned" in, 20–23
    treatments for, 13–17, 20–23

Cabinet of Dr. Caligari, The, 111
calendar, preproduction, 93
California College of Arts and Crafts
    (CCAC), xxix, xxx–xxxii, 5, 13, 44–
    45, 47, 58, 65, 111
California limited partnership agree-
    ment, 61, 287–326
    purchase offer, 327–37
camera, 58, 64, 76–78, *79*, 80, 98, 99,
    101, 134, 223
    Arriflex, 76, *79*
    CP-16, 76, *79*, *81*, *98*
    Eclair, 104, 239
    film scratches and, 133
    focusing eyepiece on, 104
    in "freeze" method of shooting for
        cuts, 113
    lenses for, *see* lenses
    loading of, 101–4
    maintenance of, 91, 105
    placement of, 74, 105–6, 109–10, 113;
        see also framing; scenes
    rental of, 40, 48, 57, 76–77, 103–4,
        105, 239
    scripted instructions for, 27, 37–38
    support equipment for, 90, 91, 116
camera assistant, 41, 48, 49, 57, 67, 105
Canby, Vincent, 209
Canestro, Art, 110
Cannes Film Festival, 197–99, 213
Canyon Cinema, 204, 214
Capra, Frank, 8
Carney, Ray, xv-xxviii
Carver, Jasmine, 119
Cassavetes, John, 38
cast, *see* actors
CCAC (California College of Arts and
    Crafts), xxix, xxx–xxxii, 5, 13, 44–
    45, 47, 58, 65, 111
certified public accountants, 61
Chang, George, xxxii
changing bag, 90, 103
Chan Is Missing, 42, 173, 209
    editing of, 148, 157, 161
Channel Four, xxxix, 59, 207
characters:
    budget and, 5, 9, 10
    development of, 17–23, 29

scriptwriting and, 27, 29, 32, 37
  see also dialogue
Charles, Scot, 252
Cherkerzian, Diane, xv–xxviii
Chicago Art Institute, 203
Chicago Filmmakers, 203
Chinatown, 111
Church, Mike, 34–35
Cinema Arts Centre, 203, 205
Cinema 5, xxxiv
Cineprobe, 201
Cinequest, 201
Citizen Kane, 32, 38
clap board (slate board), 41, 67, 91,
  123–24, 140, 146, *147*, 151–52
Clerks, 124, 212, 240
collaboration, 5, 6, 45, 58, 221–38
  agreement contract, 34–35, 223, 224,
    269–70, 338–40
  auteur theory and, 233–34
  budget for, 226–29
  choosing people for, 33–34
  communication and, 231–32
  competitiveness and, 233
  directing and, 232–33
  editing and, 234–36
  Feature Workshops, 222–24
  film completion and, 235–37
  paying collaborators in, 33, 35, 237–
    238; *see also* payments
  promotion and, 237–38
  quality control in, 226, 230–32
  script in, 32, 33–35, 226, 229–30
  shooting order and, 232–33
  stories vs. segments in, 226, 229–30
color balance, 184–85, 187, 193
commercial films, 36, 109
  equipment for special shots in, 116
  framing and, 110
communication, 13
  collaboration and, 231–32
computers, *see* digital technology
concept, *see* story concept
conforming original for printing, 51, 56,
  57, 58, 165, 174–78, 261
  see also AB rolls
Conformist, The, 111
Conner, Bruce, 9
continuity, 121
contracts and forms, 44–45, 46–47, 60,
  68, 94, 97, 269–340
  actor release, 11, 71, 93, 94, 280–81
  checklist for, 45–47
  collaboration agreement, 34–35, 223,
    224, 269–70, 338–40
  deal memorandum, 42–43, 276–77

deferred payment, 42–43, 271–75,
  276–77
distributors and, 210–11
as first step in filmmaking, 44–45, 46
as incentives, 44
investment agreement, 278–79
limited partnership, 61, 287–326,
  327–37
location release, 73, 94, 282–83
music rights, 10, 159, 254, 284–86
profit sharing, 43, 64, 68, 71, 271–75
purchase offer, 61, 327–37
Coppola, Francis Ford, 229
copyrights, 23–24, 38, 39
costs, *see* budget
CP-16 camera, 76, *79*, *81*, *98*
crane shots, 116
Crawford, Neelon, 42, 65, 81, 104, 135–
  136, 254, 255
credit cards, 98
  airline, 205
credits, *see* titles and credits
crew, 41, 93, 95, 97
  collaborators as, 223, 227, 228, 232
  food for, *see* food
  paying of, 41, 42–44, 46, 64; *see also*
    payments
  screenings for, 136–37, 189–90
  selection of, 64, 66–68, 94
  transportation for, *see* transportation
critical response, 11, 205, 209, 215–16
Csicsery, George, 137
cue sheet for printing, 182–84, *183*, 186
Cummings, Bob, xxxiii
cutaways, 113–14
cutting, *see* editing

Dan's Motel, 212–13
DAT (digital audio tape) recorder, 255–
  256
deadlines, 32, 44, 93
deal memorandum, 42–43, 276–77
Death of a Salesman (Miller), 7
deferred payment, 42–44, 64, 68, 271–
  275, 276–77
DESTINY Editing Workstation, 264
dialogue, 70, 116, 165
  adding of, in studio, 114
  improvisation and, 118–19
  recording room tone for editing of,
    114
  scriptwriting and, 29, 36, 37
DiFrancesco, David, 260
digital audio tape (DAT) recorder, 255–
  256
digital technology, 251–66

digital technology (*cont.*)
  AVID Media Composer, 260–63, *261,*
    265
  DESTINY Editing Workstation, 264
  D-VISION editing, 260, 263–64, *263,*
    265–66
  editing, 167, 259–66
  Filmlook, 258–59
  lab printing, 256–58
  music, 159, 253–54
  sound mixing, 252–53
  sync sound on location, 255–56
directing, 13, 116–19
  collaboration and, 232–33
  of trained actors, 69
  in video, 247
  "voice command" technique in, 119
  see also production
director of photography, 103
dissolves, 166, 186, 187, 257–58
  marking of, 167, *169*
distribution, 237–38
  alternative forms of, 213–16
  theater rentals, 213–14
distributors, 192, 209–11, 212, 213–14
  contracts with, 210–11
DiVincenzo, Joe, 65, 66
dolly shots, 116
Du Art Film Laboratories, 110
D-VISION, 260, 263–64, *263*, 265–66

Ebert, Roger, 199
Eclair camera, 104, 239
edge numbers, 50, 51, 56–57, 146, 148–
  150
  log book for, 150–51, *151*
edge numbers, latent, 175–77
editing, 13, 41, 98, 112, 134, 139–58
  and amount of film to shoot, 124
  on AVID Media Composer, 260–63,
    261, 265
  beginning rough cut, 156–57
  breakthrough cut, 160
  collaboration and, 234–36
  costs of, 44, 48, 50–58
  cutaways and pauses for transitions,
    113–14
  cutting for structure, 153–55
  on DESTINY workstation, 264
  digital, 167, 259–66
  on "dirty dupe" work print, 128–29
  discarding favorite scene, 157–58
  on D-VISION system, 260, 263–64,
    263, 265–66
  edge numbering, *see* edge numbers
  "fat," 152

filing "outs," 146, 150–51, 152, 156,
  176
  film damage and, 128
  of first five minutes, 157
  of found footage, 9
  "freeze" method of shooting for, 113,
    156
  grease-pencil marks in, 167
  lighting and, 107
  long takes and, 50, 128
  of original, 128, 165, 167
  placing scenes in order of story, 152–
    153
  recording room tone for, 114
  shooting without sound, 114–16
  sound equalization and, 135
  of sound track, 48, 115–16, 255; *see
    also* sound mix
  splices in, *see* splices
  stills and, 125
  story concept and, 154–55
  syncing, *see* sync, syncing
  testing of, 155–56
  transitions in, *see* transitions
  of video feature, 239, 242–43, 245,
    247–48, 249–50
  on video vs. film work print, 129–31
  viewing footage as a "movie," 151–52
  see also postproduction; work print
editing bench, 140, 175
  homemade, 52–56, *53, 54*, 129, 175
editing machine, flatbed, 58, 128, 129,
  140, 166
  rental of, 50, 51–52, 57
editing tape, 51, 57, 58
Egar, Linda, xxxii
Eggert, Katrina, 257
8-mm film, 76
Emerald Cities, xxix, xxxix, 70, 71, 72,
  77, *118*, 187, 205, 215, 245
  contract for, 43, 44
  editing of, 148
  lighting for, 83
  location for, 74–75
  narration in, 162
  photographs in, 163
  preproduction for, 66
  profit sharing on, 49
  story concept for, 7–8
  video portions of, 241
Entertainment Weekly, 215
equalization, sound, 134–35, 170, 173
equipment and supplies, 34, 58, 64, 75–
  76, 101
  checklist for, 91–92
  collaboration and, 223, 227

digital, *see* digital technology
loading of, 100–101
protecting from theft, 99, 100
rental of, 13, 40–41, 47, 78–80, 90, 94, 99–100
support, 90–91
see also budget; *specific items*
essay formats, 9, 26
Estar-based stock, 185, 188
Esther, Jody, *102*, 119, 254
Expo Opticals, 110
exposure:
of actors' faces, 108–9
light readings and, 108–9; *see also* light meters, light readings
printing and, 109, 184–85, 186–87, 193
extension cords, 82, 88, 99, 107
eyepiece, focusing of, 104

fade-outs and fade-ins, 166, 186, 187
marking of, 167, *169*
FAF, *see* Film Arts Foundation
failure and rejection, 218–20, 238
fear of, 96–97
Farley, Bill, xxxv, 27, 66, 111
Feature Workshops, 222–24, *227*, 252, 265
see also collaboration
festivals, *see* film festivals
Field, Syd, 31, 32
film, filmstock, 13, 64, 75
amount to shoot, 40, 56, 69, 116–17, 119, 124
ASA 500, 87–88
buying of, 40, 47, 48, 49, 56, 57, 89–90, 94
checking first footage, 132–34
8-mm, 76
emergency self-funding and, 63
emulsion batch numbers on, 89, 94
found footage, 9
labeling cans of, 103
lab processing of, *see* lab; print, printing
lighting and, 82, 83–84, 86, 87–88
loading and unloading of, 90, 101–4
long takes and, 112
negative, *see* negative filmstock
reel tension and, 176
reversal, 175–76, 177, 182, 187
saving of, on sync takes, 123–24
scratches on, 128, 133, 167, 182, 185, 187
16-mm, 76, 240, 249, 250
storage of, 127

syncing with sound track, *see* sync, syncing
testing of, 88, 89
35-mm, 76, 110, 240
transfer to video, 110, 193–94, 237
video transfer to, 240–41, 244, 245–246, 249
video vs., 249–50
work print, *see* work print
Film Arts Foundation (FAF), 33–34, 52, 56, 67, 81, 129, 155, 193, 199, 204, 248, 249, 253
Release Print newsletter of, 34, 56, 62, 197
Film Comment, 215, 222
Film Craft Lab, 194, 241
film festivals, 34, 110, 166, 185, 192, 193, 195, 197–201, 205, 208, 212, 216, 218–20, 221, 237, 238
calendar of, 197
foreign, 59, 60–61
list of, 200–201
Sundance, 200, 212, 219, 262, 263
video copies for entering, 131, 194, 197, 217, 238
video features and, 248–49
Film Forum, xxxiv, 201, 207, 209
filming, *see* production; scenes
Filmlook, 258–59
Filmmaker Magazine, 197
Filmmaker's Co-op, 214
film markets, 208–9
film showcases, 59, 60, 166, 192, 195, 202–6, 207, 208, 216, 219, 237
contacting, 202
list of, 203–4
New York premieres, 201–2, 207
Film Threat, 222
filters, 91
Fire This Time, The, 263
"flow," trusting in, 119, 254
Flying Spot, 262
focus, 134, 230, 231
focusing the eyepiece, 104
food, 75
catering services and, 120
costs of, 41, 47, 48, 49, 57, 75, 95, 120
Ford, John, 8, 38
Forde Lab, 257
Four Media Company, 241
"four walling," 213–14
frame line registration marks, 187
framing, 106, 109–10
for commercial features and television, 110
lighting and, 108–9

framing (*cont.*)
    long takes and, 112
"freeze" technique, 113, 156
f-stops, 107
    light meters and, 108, 109; *see also*
        light meters, light readings

gaffer, 107
Gasser, Adolph, 104, 155, 241
gels, 91
Gilbert, Peter, 234
Gilliam, Jeff, 83
Godard, Jean-Luc, 111, 209
Go Fish, 240
Samuel Goldwyn, 209
Grainy Pictures, 212
grants, 61, 62, 63, 185, 217
Grapes of Wrath, The (Steinbeck), 8
graphics, promotional, 65, 66, 125, 194–
        196
    "bullet screen" effect, 195, *198*
    letterhead, 60, 66, 194
    posters, 33, 65, 66, 125–26, 194, 195,
        196
    pressbook, 126, 194, 195
    stills, 125, 195, 196
gross vs. net profits, 46, 210–11

Harvey, Will, 252–53
Hawk, Bob, 212
Hi8, 125, 239, 240, 244–46, 250
Hinton, Michael, 110
Hitchcock, Alfred, 74
Holland, Randy, 263
Hoop Dreams, 234
Hopper, Dennis, xxxix
Huestis, Marc, 241

ICI, see Independent Consultation for
        Independents
ideas, for film concept, 6–9, 63
    nontraditional, 8–9, 23
    see also story concept
IFFM, *see* Independent Feature Film
        Market
IFP, *see* Independent Feature
        Project
images, story supported by, 111–12
Image Transform, 241
Impavido, Tony, 215
improvisation, 98, 118–19
    lighting and, 84
Imrie, Curtis, 254
Independent Consultation for Indepen-
        dents (ICI), 212
Independent Feature Film Market

(IFFM), 208, 212, 213, 224, 237, 252,
        262
Independent Feature Project (IFP),
        208–9
Independent Film and Video Monthly,
        34, 56, 62, 197
inspiration, 38
investors, 58–61, 131, 221
    agreement form for, 278–79
invoices, 132
Israel, Bob, 255–56
It's a Wonderful Life, 8

James, Steve, 234
Jarmusch, Jim, 209
jazz, cinematic, 235
Jerk, The, 8
Jost, Jon, 23, *81*, *98*, 112
Jurassic Park, 262

Kaplan, Barbara, 263–64
Kazan, Nick, 7, 27, 66
keyboards, digital, 253–54
Kimberlin, Bill, 43
Kinder, David, 205
Kodak Film Center, 63
Kortge, Ken, *263*

lab, 89, 126–27
    answer print from, *see* answer print
    building relationship with, 127, 131–
        132
    buying filmstock from, 89, 94
    costs of, 44, 47, 48, 49, 56, 57, 60, 89,
        94, 131–32, 185
    cue sheet for, 182–84, *183*, 186
    digital printing at, 256–58
    errors made by, 186–88
    invoices from, 132
    marking film cans for, 103
    printing procedures, 184–86; *see also*
        print, printing
    processing without a work print,
        128–29
    timer at, 184–86, 187
    work print from, *see* work print
laser discs, 126
Last Chants for a Slow Dance, 112
Last Laugh, The, 111
Last Roommate, The, xxix, 71, 97, 122–
        123, 136, 148
    characterization of "Greg" in, 17–20
    credits in, 122
    "freeze" method used in, 113
    lighting for, 83–84, 85
    plot points in, 31–32

pressbook for, 195
profit sharing on, 60
scripting of, 29–32
story concept and budget for, 5–7, 9,
    11
latent edge numbers, 175–77
lawyer(s), 46–47, 61, 213
    distribution contracts and, 211
    see also contracts and forms; legal
    issues
leader, 51, 57, 123, 140, 146, 166, 176,
    177–78, 188
Lee, Spike, 209
Lee, Tinnee, 71
legal issues, 46–47, 61, 213
    registration of treatment and script,
    23–24, 38, 39
    rights, 10, 11, 159, 254, 284–86
    see also contracts and forms
Legal Operation, The, xxxii
lenses, 75, 77, 94
    choosing of, 77–78
    focusing eyepiece and, 104
    f-stops and, 107
letterhead, 60, 66, 194
letters, in promotion, 202
light meters, light readings, 41, 67, 75,
    88, 91, 107–9
    incident, 108
    reflected, 108
lights, lighting, 58, 64, 75, 82–89, 90, 91,
    112, 116, 223
    accessories needed for, 82
    actors' faces and, 107
    checking footage for, 133
    damage caused by, 107
    editing and, 107
    extension cords for, 82, 88, 99, 107
    Filmlook and, 259
    filmstock and, 82, 83–84, 86, 87–88
    framing and, 108–9
    f-stops and, 107
    Hollywood style of, 84, 85–86, 109
    improvisation in, 84
    light flares and, 106–7
    long takes and, 112
    for low budgets, 86–89
    natural, 86, 87–88, 106
    and order of shooting scenes, 84
    "painting" with, 86, 91, 106
    reflections and, 106
    rental of, 57, 82
    replacement bulbs for, 108
    in Schmidt's films, 82–84
    selection of, 84–89
    setting up, 41, 67, 103, 108

soft, 82–83, 87, 88–89, 106
tips for, 106–8
Tota kits, 82, 106, 108
for video feature, 241–42, 246–47
Light Video, 222
Lightworks, 260
limited partnership agreement, 61
    California, 61, 287–326
    purchase offer, 327–37
liquid gate, 133, 182, 187, 258
Live with This (Adrift in America),
    245
location(s):
    budget and, 5–6, 9–10, 40–41, 43, 44
    long-distance, 74–75
    miracles and, 122–23
    organization at, 101–3
    release form for, 73, 94, 282–83
    scouting and selecting, 63, 64, 65, 66,
    72–73, 74–75, 93, 94, 98
    scriptwriting and, 27, 29, 37
    shooting schedule for, 93, 95
    shooting titles at, 51, 57, 121–22, 153
    as source of actors, 71
    transportation to, 41, 47, 48, 57, 75,
    95, 100–101
London Film Festival, xxxix, 200, 217
long takes, 50, 112–13, 128

magazines, 215–16
mag cleaner, 168
mag track, 48, 50, 55, 56–57, 166
    blank ("slug"), 140, 146, 159, 168
    buying of, 90, 94
    syncing picture to, see sync, syncing
    transfer to, 48, 94, 134–36
    see also sound track
Mail Bonding, 265
Makanna, Phil, xxxi–xxxii
Maltese Falcon, The, 161
Maltin, Leonard, 8
Man, a Woman, and a Killer, A, xxix,
    xxxiv–xxxvi, xxxvii, xxxix, 32, 71,
    104, 125, 154, 160, 161, 197–99, 202
    editing of, 148
    lighting for, 82
    location for, 74, 75
    photographs in, 163
    preproduction for, 65
    profit sharing on, 49
    screening of, 189
    script for, 26–27
    sound in, 135, 136, 158, 159
    story concept and budget for, 6, 9
Man Bites Dog, 125
Mann, Hunter, 210

Manupelli, George, 82–83
Marin Film Festival, xxxiii
Martin, Steve, 8
Marx, Fred, 234
Mayer, Jim, 83
McCormick, Tasha Roth, 252
microphones, 78, 123
    directional, 78–80, *81*
    lavaliere, 80
    shotgun, 78–80
Millennium, 202
Miller, Arthur, 7
Miller, Robert, *265*
Miramax, 209, 211, 212
mistakes, 218–20
    see also failure and rejection
Mitchell, Jean, 71, 122–23
Monaco Video, 110, 193
money:
    emergency funds, 57, 63, 95
    raising of, 44, 58–61, 64
    see also budget; payments
montages, 125
mood, 27, 84, 247
Morgan's Cake, xxix, xli, 43, 61, 118,
    219, 245
    video portions of, 241, *244*
Morris, Freuda, 70
Movie Maker Magazine, 215
Moviescope, 52, *54*, 55, 128, 129, 140
Murelius, Marie, xxxi
Murnau, F. W., 111
Museum of Fine Arts, 203
Museum of Modern Art, New Directors/
    New Films Showcase at, xxxiv,
    201, 204, 209, 212
museums, 59, 219, 249
    New York premieres, 201–2, 207
music, 38, 158–59, 161
    digital, 159, 253–54
    rights to, 10, 159, 254, 284–86
Music Annex, 252
My Dinner with Andre, 235

Nagra recorder, 48, 57, 58, 78, 80–81,
    80, 82, 89, 134, 223, 255, 256
    cushioning of, 99–100, 101
Nagra T recorder, 78, 256
narration, 9, 114, 125, 154, 161–62
    budget and, 10
narrative, 5
    long takes and, 112
    traditional, alternatives to, 8–9
    see also structure
National Endowment for the Arts
    (NEA), xxxix, 62

National Film Preserve, 199–200
negative filmstock, 128, 182, 187, 188,
    240, 241, 258
    AB rolling of, 175, 176–77, 178
Neighborhood Film Project, 203
net vs. gross profits, 46, 210–11
New Directors/New Films Showcase,
    xxxiv, 201, 204, 209, 212
New Line Cinema, xxxiv, 209, 211
Newman, Jim, xxxviii
New York *Daily News*, xxxvi, 202
New Yorker Films, xxxiv, 209, 213
New York Film Festival, 209
New York premieres, 201–2, 207
New York Stories, 229
New York Times, xxxvi, 201, 202, 207,
    209
Nilsson, Rob, 241
911 Media Arts Center, 34, 56, 62, 129,
    203, 249
1944, xxxiii
1988—The Remake (Showboat 1988),
    xxix, xxxv, xxxvi–xxxix, 27, 42, 62,
    73, 209, 211, 217
    editing of, 148
    lighting for, 83
    Los Angeles premiere of, *199*
    photographs in, 163
    preproduction for, 65–66
    profit sharing on, 49
    promotional graphics for, 196, *198*
    script for, *28*
    on television, xxxix, 207
    title change of, xxxix
Nylund, Ed, xxxv, 66, 70, 71, 125, 158,
    163

Of Men and Angels, 111
originality, 8–9, 10, 11, 98
Oster, Jerry, xxxvi
O'Toole, Anne, 193

Pacific Film Archive, xxxiv, 203
Palmer, Bill, 241
W. A. Palmer Films, 163, 173, 241, 245
Parry, Bruce, xxxiii, 18
partnership, limited, 61
    California, 61, 287–326
    purchase offer, 327–37
payments, 43, 44, 46, 47, 49, 67, 97
    to actors, 9, 41, 42–44, 46, 48, 49, 57,
        64, 69
    to collaborators, 33, 35, 237–38
    to crew, 41, 42–44, 46, 64
    deferred, 42–44, 64, 68, 271–75, 276–
        277

per diem salaries, 69, 95
profit sharing, *see* profit sharing
  see also budget
Pecknold, Greg, 262
photographs, *see* still photographs
picture tape, 51, 57, 58
Pierson, John, 212
Pittsburgh Filmmakers, 204
PIXAR, 260
places, *see* location
plot, *see* scriptwriting; story concept
plot points, 31–32
Polanski, Roman, 111–12
Popdefect, 244–45
posters, 65, 66, 194, 195, 196
  collaborators and, 33
  stills for, 125–26
postproduction, 139–90
  AB rolling, 51, 165, 168–70, *171, 172,*
    174–78, *179, 180, 181,* 182, 246
  adding elements, 158–59, 160–64
  beginning rough cut, 156–57
  breakthrough cut, 160
  conforming original for printing, 51,
    56, 57, 58, 165, 174–78, 261
  cue sheet for printing, 182–84, *183*
  cutting for structure, 153–55
  digital printing, 256–58
  discarding favorite scene, 157–58
  edge numbering, 50, 51, 56–57, 146,
    148–51, *151*
  exposure balance, 109, 184–85, 186–
    187, 193
  filing "outs," 146, 150–51, 152, 156,
    176
  finalizing structure, 166–67
  final tightening and pacing, 164–65
  lab procedures for printing, 184–86
  music in, 158–59, 161, 253–54
  narrations in, 10, 114, 161–62
  placing scenes in order of story, 152–
    153
  preparing sound rolls for the mix,
    168–70, *171, 172*
  print assembly, 188–89
  screening answer print, 186–88
  screening finished film, 189–90
  screening sound mix, 173–74
  shooting additional footage, 163–64
  sound effects in, 10, 114–15, 158–59,
    256
  sound mix in, *see* sound mix
  splices in, *see* splices
  still photographs added in, 163
  syncing picture with sound track, *see*
    sync, syncing

testing edits, 155–56
video vs. film work print in, 129–31
viewing footage as a "movie," 151–52
  see also editing; lab
power cables, 75, 99
preproduction, 64–95
  camera equipment and, 64, 76–78,
    79, 80
  casting of actors in, 64, 66–67, 68–
    71, 93, 94
  checklist for, 94–95
  crew selection in, 64, 66–68, 94
  equipment checklist, 91–92
  items needed in, 75–76; *see also*
    equipment and supplies
  lighting in, 64, 82–89; *see also* lights,
    lighting
  location selection in, 63, 64, 65, 66,
    72–73, 74–75, 93, 94, 98
  long-distance locations in, 74–75
  paperwork, errands, and lists in, 93–
    94
  saving money on filmstock and sound
    track, 89–90
  setting time limit for, 64–65
  sound gear and, 64, 78–82, *81,* 90–91
  storyboarding in, 74
  support equipment in, 90–91
presentation package, 60
pressbook, 194, 195
  electronic, 126
press release, 66
print, printing, 166
  answer, *see* answer print
  assembling of, 188–89
  conforming original for, 51, 56, 57, 58,
    165, 174–78, 261; *see also* AB
    rolls
  costs of, 44, 89, 94
  cue sheet for, 182–84, *183,* 186
  digital, 256–58
  exposures and, 109, 184–85, 186–87,
    193
  lab procedures for, 184–86; *see also*
    lab
  work, *see* work print
processing, *see* lab; print, printing
production, 39, 96–138
  budget limitations on, 40–41, 97–98;
    see also budget
  camera maintenance, 105
  checking first footage, 132–34
  checking sync sound, 134–36
  completing filming, 137–38
  continuity and, 121
  costs in, 47–50, 57–58

production (*cont.*)
  cutaways and pauses for transitions,
    113–14
  deadlines and, 32, 44
  developing and work printing with
    the lab, 126–27; *see also* lab; print,
    printing
  directing actors, *see* directing
  equipment loading, 100–101
  fear of failure and, 96–97
  "flow" and, 119, 254
  focusing the eyepiece, 104
  food in, *see* food
  "freeze" method of shooting for cuts,
    113, 156
  lab costs in, 131–32
  lighting tips, 106–8; *see also* lights,
    lighting
  light readings in, 107–9
  loading the camera, 101–4
  location miracles in, 122–23
  long takes, 50, 112–13, 128
  organization on location, 101–3
  picking up actors and crew, 100–101
  picking up rental equipment, 99–100
  placing camera for the first shot,
    105–6
  processing without a work print,
    128–29
  rules for, 97–99
  saving film on sync takes, 123–24
  schedule for, 124
  screening footage for cast and crew,
    136–37
  shooting titles on location, 51, 57,
    121–22, 153
  shooting without sound, 114–16
  special-effect apparatus in, 116
  stills and videos of, 125–26, 195
  supporting story with images, 111–12
  video vs. film work print, 129–31
  what and how to shoot, 109–11
production assistant, 67, 68, 101
production company, 44
production crew, *see* crew
production manager, 67, 72–73, 75–76
profit sharing, 9, 11, 33, 35, 41, 42, 43,
    44, 49, 60, 67, 69, 71
  contract for, 43, 64, 68, 71, 271–75
  deferred payments combined with,
    43, 271–75
  gross vs. net profits in, 46, 210–11
projection print, *see* answer print
promotion, 190, 191–217
  advertising for alternative distribu-
    tion, 215–16

agents and, 212–13
of collaborative film, 237–38
controversy and, 205
distribution, 213–16, 237–38
distributors in, 192, 209–11, 212,
    213–14
film festivals, *see* film festivals
film markets, 208–9
film showcases, *see* film showcases
graphics in, 65, 66, 125, 194–96, *198*
"in-person" tours, 202–6
letterhead, 60, 66, 194
by letters and phone, 202
New York premieres, 201–2, 207
posters, 33, 65, 66, 125–26, 194, 195,
    196
pressbook in, 126, 194, 195
price-setting in, 216
promotional package in, 192–96
reviews, 11, 205, 209, 215–16
stills in, 125, 195, 196
television, *see* television
typesetting, 60, 195
video copies for, 61, 125–26, 192–94,
    197, 206–7, 213, 217, 237, 238
of video feature, 248–49
props, 64, 75, 93
publicity, *see* promotion
Public Theatre, 202
purchase offer, 61, 327–37

Quality Photos, 125

reaction shots, 114
reality checks, 40, 218–20
recorders, *see* sound recorders
recording sound, *see* sound track
reels, 128, 129, 140
Rees, Joe, 249
registration, legal, 23–24, 38, 39
Reichl, Ruth, 73
rejection, *see* failure and rejection
Release Print, 34, 56, 62, 197
releases:
  actor, 11, 71, 93, 94, 280–81
  location, 73, 94, 282–83
  for newspaper stories, 11
reversal filmstock, 182, 187
  AB rolling of, 175–76, 177
reviews, 11, 205, 209, 215–16
rewinds, *54*, 55, 129, 140
Richardson, Dick, xxxiii, 6, 65, 70, 71,
    125
rights, legal, 11
  to music, 10, 159, 254, 284–86
Rocky films, 7

Rome/Florence Film Festival, 200, 245
Room, The, 257
room tone, recording of, 114
Rotterdam Film Festival, xxxix, 200
Round of Justice, The, 13, 14–15
Roxie Cinema, 204, 213
rushes, 136–37

salaries, *see* payments
sandbags, 90
scenes, 27
    continuity in, 121
    cutaways and pauses for transitions,
        113–14
    equipment for special shots, 116
    favorite, discarding of, 157–58
    film shooting ratio and, 40, 69
    first, camera placement for, 105–6
    framing of, *see* framing
    "freeze" method of shooting for cuts,
        113, 156
    improvisation and, 98, 118–19
    long takes, 50, 112–13, 128
    order of shooting, 84
    placing in order of story, in editing,
        152–53
    plot points, 31–32
    reaction shots, 114
    reshooting of, 40, 69, 116–17
    saving film on sync takes, 123–24
    scripted, expanding cards into, 29–32
    shooting ratio and, 116–17, 119
    shooting schedule for, 93, 95
    in simple script, 25–26
    stills and videos of, 125–26
    storyboarding of, 74
    supporting story with images, 111–12
    syncing up, 41
    treatment as inspiration for, 29
    what and how to shoot, 109–11
    writing on cards, 27–29
    see also production
schedule, 93, 95, 124
Schindler's List, 262
Schmidt-Feng, Morgan, *244*
schools:
    access to equipment in, 58
    editing costs and, 52
    film screenings and, 155
    finding actors at, 68
    finding crew members at, 67, 105
    sound mixing and, 56, 173
Scorsese, Martin, 229
screenings, 34, 166
    of answer print, 186–88
    of finished film, 189–90
    of footage, 136–37
    of sound mix, 173–74
    testing edits with, 155–56
Screenplay (Field), 31, 32
script(s), 39, 40, 60, 64, 93, 95, 98
    complex form of, 26–27
    improvisation and, 118–19
    location miracles and, 122–23
    as recipe, 25, 27
    registration of, 38, 39
    simple form of, 25–26
    standard form of, 27
scriptwriting, 13, 25–38, 63, 97
    by collaboration, 32, 33–35, 226,
        229–30
    deadlines and, 32
    expanding cards into scripted scenes,
        29–32
    finalizing the script, 35–37
    first draft in, 29, 35
    identifying problems with, 32
    love for, 36–37
    professional, 36
    shooting instructions in, 27, 37–38
    story concept and, 13, 23–24; *see also*
        story concept
    using tape recorder in, 27
    writing scenes on index cards, 27–29
Seattle International, 200
Serie, Lee, 65, 136
Sex Is, 241
S. F. Cinematheque, 203
Sheldon Film Theater, 203
Sher, Liz, 163
She's Gotta Have It, 209
shooting, *see* production; scenes
"Shooting 16-mm or Super 16-mm for
    Blowup to 35-mm," 110
Show Boat, xxxv, xxxix
Showboat 1988, see 1988—The Remake
showcases, *see* film showcases
Shuttlecock, 213
Signal 7, 241
Simonds, Charlie, xxxi, xxxii
Sinofsky, Bruce, 214
16-mm film, 76, 240, 249, 250
Skolnick, Vic, 205
Slacker, 240
Slak, Franci, 240
slate board, *see* clap board
Smith, Kevin, 124, 212
Smith, Lela, xxxix
Sony, 209, 211
Sony DESTINY Editing Workstation,
    264
Sony TCD-5 recorder, 81–82

Sony Walkman Professional recorder, 81, 89, 134, 162
sound effects, 114–15, 158–59
    budget and, 10
    DAT recording of, 255–56
    in shooting script, 37–38
sound equipment, 41, 64, 78–82, *81,* 90–91
    microphones, 78–80, *81,* 123
    rental of, 78–81, 82
    see also sound recorders
sound levels, 123
sound mix, 50–51, 56, 58, 89, 132, 166, 168–70, *171, 172,* 173
    digital, 252–53
    screening of, 173–74
    see also sound track
soundperson, 41, 42, 43, 48, 49, 57, 63, 67, 68, 78, 81, 94, 115–16, 123, 135–36, 223
    for video features, 243
sound reader, 52, *54,* 55, 129, 140
sound recorders, 75, *81*
    DAT, 255–56
    Nagra, 48, 57, 58, 78, 80–81, *80,* 82, 89, 99–100, 101, 134, 223, 255, 256
    Nagra T, 78, 256
    in scriptwriting, 27
    Sony TCD-5, 81–82
    Sony Walkman Professional, 81, 89
sound speaker, *54,* 55
sound tape, 51, 57, 58, 75, 94, 123
sound track, 25, 48, 97, 115–16, 230, 231, 255
    checking, 134–36
    cue sheet for mixing of, 168
    digital mixing of, 252–53
    equalization of, 134–35, 170
    "great location sound" and, 135–36
    mixing of, 50–51, 56, 58, 89, 132, 166, 168–70, *171, 172,* 173–74, 252–53
    music in, 10, 38, 158–59, 161, 253–254, 284–86
    narration in, 9, 10, 114, 125, 154, 161–162
    "pops" on, 168, 174, 188
    preparing AB rolls for mixing, 168–170, *171, 172*
    recording room tone for editing of, 114
    reprinting of, 188
    saving film on sync takes, 123–24
    saving money on, 89–90
    screening of, 173–74
    shooting without, 114–16

sound effects in, 10, 114–15, 158–59, 255–56
syncing picture to, *see* sync, syncing
    transfer to mag track, 48, 94, 134–36; *see also* mag track
    for video features, 243
    "wild" sounds in, 114, 115, 255
Spielberg, Steven, 262
splicers, 58, 175
    for negative film, 177
    operation of, 140, *141–45*
splices, 50, 146, 165, 174, 177–78, *179, 180, 181,* 187
    faulty, 170
    mag track, *143–45*
    in print assembly, 188–89
split reels, 128, 140
Stagecoach, 38
Steinbeck, John, 8
still photographs, 125–26
    for promotion, 125, 195, 196
    as transitions, 161, 163
storyboard, 74, 105, 114
    location miracles and, 122–23
story concept, 5–24, 27, 32, 36, 37, 40
    budget and, 5–6, 9–10
    and choice of collaborator, 33
    clarification of, 13
    editing's effects on, 154–55
    essential qualities needed in, 10–11
    expanding into one-page treatment, 13–17, 25, 29
    ideas for, 6–9
    images as support for, 111–12
    improving treatment through characterization, 17–23, 29
    legal registration of treatment, 23–24, 38, 39
    newspaper as source for, 7, 11
    originality of, 8–9, 10, 11
    selection of, 9–10
    writing in one sentence, 12–13, 25, 27–29
    see also scriptwriting
Stranger Than Paradise, 209
structure, 156, 173
    breakthrough cut and, 160
    cutting for, 153–55
    finalizing, 166–67
    final tightening and pacing, 164–65
    narration and, 161, 162
    traditional, alternatives to, 8–9
    see also editing; narrative
subtitles, 154
Sundance Film Festival, 200, 212, 219, 262, 263

superimposition, 112
supplies, *see* equipment and supplies
sync, syncing, 41, 48, 50, 81, *98*, 115,
128, 134, 135, 140–46, *147, 149,
150*, 184, 187
checking of, 134–36
clap board in, 41, 67, 91, 123–24, 140,
146, *147*, 151–52
digital, 255–56
edge numbering and, 148–50
"freeze" method of shooting for cuts,
113
saving film on takes, 123–24
see also sound track
synchronizer, 52, *54*, 55, 128, 140
sync mark, 140, *147*
sync pulse generator, 81, *81*

tape recorders, *see* sound recorders
tape splicers, *see* splicers
Target Video, 249
tax deductions, 59, 61
taxes, 58, 61
technicians, *see* crew
telephone, promotion by, 202
television, 59, 60, 112, 192, 195, 206–7,
208, 237, 240
foreign, 59, 207, 208
scene framing and, 110
Telluride Film Festival, 199–200
"ten-minute take," 112–13
theater rental, 213–14
35-mm film, 76, 110, 240
Thou Shall Not Kill, 13, 15–17
3M, 90
¾" video, 239, 240, 244–46, 248, 261
Time for Justice, A, 20–23
timer, at lab, 184–86, 187
title, legal registration of, 23–24, 38, 39
titles and credits, 59, 67, 132, 161, 186
for *Chan Is Missing*, 157
collaborators and, 33, 35
photographs in, 163
shooting of, 10, 51, 57, 121–22, 153
for video feature, 243
Touch of Evil, 106
Touchvision, 263
transitions, 134, 152
digital, 167
dissolves, 166, 167, *169*, 186, 187,
257–58
fade-outs and fade-ins, 166, 167, *169*,
186, 187
pauses for, 113–14
photographs as, 161, 163
transportation, 75, 95, 100–101

costs of, 41, 47, 48, 57
see also location
treatment:
character development in, 17–23, 29
expanding story concept into, 13–17,
25, 29
legal registration of, 23–24, 38, 39
tripod, 75, 90, 106
Troia, Dominic T., 194
Tucson, University of Arizona at, 98–99
TV Movies (Maltin), 8
typesetting, 60, 195

Vanderburg, Brad, 244–45
Variety, 8, 197
VCRs (video cassette recorders), 242,
248
Vedvick, Rich, 257
VHS, 193, 194, 239, 240, 242, 244–46,
248
video, videotapes, 78, 185
editing of, 239
film transfer to, 110, 193–94, 237
pressbooks, 126
promotion copies, 61, 125–26, 192–
194, 197, 206–7, 213, 217, 237, 238
sales and rentals, 193, 215, 216, 217
television premieres, 206–7
transfer to film, 240–41, 244, 245–46,
249
of work in progress, 125–26
work prints, 129–31
video, shooting in, 239–50
budget for, 241–46, 247–48
camera rental, 239, 244, 245
directing and, 247
editing, 239, 242–43, 245, 247–48,
249–50
Filmlook and, 258–59
film vs., 249–50
lighting for, 246–47
promotion and, 248–49
see also video formats
video cassette recorders (VCRs), 242,
248
video formats:
"amateur," 240, 244–46
Betacam SP, 193, 194, 239, 240, 241–
243, 244, 246, 248, 261
broadcast quality, 240, 241, 244, 250
Hi8, 125, 239, 240, 244–46, 250
selection of, 240–41
¾", 239, 240, 244–46, 248, 261
VHS, 193, 194, 239, 240, 242, 244–46,
248
Video Free America, 243, 248

Video Presentation, 194
video scan lines, 241
Vidor, King, xxxvi
viewfinder, focusing eyepiece on, 104
Village Voice, 201, 207
voice-overs, *see* narration

Walker, Willie Boy, xxxii, xxxiii
Walker Art Center, 203
Wang, Wayne, xxix, xxxii, xxxiii, xxxvi,
    6, 42, 65, 71, 74, 135, 148, 157, 161,
    154, 209
Warhol, Andy, 9
Waters, John, 209
Watkins, Will, 257
WDR, 207
Webster University, 203, 205
Wehrer, Anne, xxxiv
Weine, Robert, 111
Weinstein, Bobby, 73
Weiss, Marc, xxxiv
Welles, Orson, 38, 106
Wertmuller, Lina, 111
What Flirting Cost Me, xxxii–xxxiii
When I Close My Eyes, 240
Whitney Museum, xxxiv, 201, 204, 207,
    217, 249
Wilbur, J. Cheyenne, 252

Wild Strawberries, 161
Wild Wheels, 210
Wisconsin, University of, 203
Witherspoon, Diane, 254
work print, 47–48, 50, 56–57, 61, 89,
    94, 126–27, 132
    AB rolling from, 175–78, *179, 180,
        181,* 182
    checking of, 132–34
    "dirty dupe," 128–29
    "one light," 128, 129
    saving money on, 50
    video vs. film, 129–31
    see also editing; sync, syncing
Writers Guild of America, 39
    registering script with, 38, 39
    registering treatment with, 23–24, 38,
        39
writing, *see* scriptwriting

Yellen, Mark, 71, 148
Young Filmmaker's Foundation,
    248

Zaremba, Carolyn, 6, 66, 125
ZDF-Strasse 1, 207
zoom shots, 110–11
Zsigmond, Vilmos, 85